Walk

A walk through the places that inspired the songs and marked the history of Dire Straits and Mark Knopfler

---

J.B. Aparicio and David M. Gray

© 2022 J.B. Aparicio and David M. Gray
Edited by Janet Woodward

Cover, back cover and book design: Rafael Montero

ISBN: 978-1-4709-9501-0

Maps from OpenStreetMap, with Creative Commons Attribution-ShareAlike 2.0. License.

Pictures:
David Gray: pictures in Glasgow, Newcastle and Edinburgh, except where indicated
Val and Colin Tallis: pictures in Leeds , except where indicated
Julio Bricio: pictures in London and New Forest chapters, except where indicated
Aidan Williamson: pictures in Pennan chapter, except where indicated
Jose Ignacio Corbalán: pictures in New Orleans, Nashville and Alabama chapters, except when indicated.
Roberto Sánchez: National guitar on book cover
Back cover pictures: Aidan Williamson, Glenda Bogdanovs, Carles Buyreu, Elian Poupard and Rafael Montero.

Additional pictures:
Thanks to the following people, who provided pictures with generosity to illustrate the chapters of this book. If this book looks great it is because of you.
THANK YOU!:

Christian Almstrom, David Barragués, Olaf Bauschat, Rick Bello, Jordi Benítez, Juan Pablo Bernardo, Daniel Betts, Glenda Bogdanovs, Colin Bodiam, Adrian Boot / www.urbanimage.tv, Julio Bricio, Carles Buyreu, Roisin and Mairead Carty, Michael Cook, Leslie Cooke, Jose Ignacio Corbalán, David from packetofthree.com, John Dawson, Kenneth Donaldson, Matt Duncan, Jimmy Emmerson, Alberto Fernández Burgos, Monika Focht (owner of thePennan Inn B&b), Alejandro Garcia Cervera, Jose Luis Gomez del Pozo, David Gray, Tim McGuinness, Guido Harari, Stephen Harris, L. Harwell (www.Findagrave.com), José López Talavera, Marion MacKay, David Martin, Francisco Martínez, Miquel Martínez, Francisco Javier Matas, Manuel María de Miguel, Dan Molda, Rafael Montero, Jordi Morilla, Andra Nelki, Òscar Pallarés, Javier Peláez, David Perbal, Elian Poupard, Andrea Rason, Adrian Riley, Igor Salmi, Chris Saunders, Clifford Stead, Jesús de la Torre, Ingrid Van de Maat, Aidan Williamson, Janet Woodward.

ALSO AVAILABLE IN LULU.COM:
WALK OF LIFE IN FULL COLOR

WALK OF LIFE

The places and stories behind
Dire Straits and *Mark Knopfler's* songs

J. B. Aparicio & David M. Gray

This book was written by fans, for fans. It is in no way official and its only purpose is to be informative about the places that inspired Dire Straits and Mark Knopfler songs and that were important in key moments of his career.

It's a new creation of the guide called "Dire Straits and Mark Knopfler's London", adding new chapters, expanding the information in the previous book and including a lot of new pictures. The content of this book is based on information collated from different books, articles and interviews with the people involved over the years (check the bibliography section) and, as almost all stories have many sides, some facts may not be 100% correct. Thanks to the internet, some of the people involved were contacted to gather their opinions and information directly when needed to fill gaps from the above mentioned sources.

As much as was possible, the pictures in this book were provided by fans who very kindly helped with this project. Thanks to all of you. Hopefully you like the ways they have been used to illustrate the text. Professional photographers were also approached and they kindly agreed to the use of their images, all of them credited.

This book is dedicated to our family and friends who kindly helped with material, especially those on the internet forums "A Mark In Time"and "Mark Knopfler News", as well as Facebook groups, "Mark Knopfler Fans Worldwide" and "Spanish City".

Special thanks to:

- David Knopfler, John Illsley, Colin Bodiam, Andra Nelki and Roisin Carty for their help and contributions to the text.
- David Gray, who not only co-wrote this book but also edited all the parts written by J.B.Aparicio, to make them sound like he can write in English, thanks mate!.
- Val and Colin Tallis for their invaluable help with the Leeds chapter, not only providing information and pictures, but also editing the text. Without them, the Leeds chapter wouldn't exist.
- Also special thanks to Dan Molda, for his invaluable help with the New York chapter.
- Jose Ignacio Corbalán, for his friendship and assistance specially with New Orleans and Nashville chapters.
- Alejandro García, who suggested most of the information which made this book even more interesting, and provided many rare pictures of promos, posters etc etc
- Adrian Boot / www.urbanimage.tv, Glenn Woolley of "The Lost Pubs Project" and David from packetofthree.com.
- Adrian Riley, from Electric Angel Design LLP
- Jeroen Van Tol from "On Every Bootleg" website
- Mariano Korman for opening the New Forest for us, and also to Steve Anstey for help with New Forest maps and indications.
- Mimmo Carrata for always being there when needed.
- Óscar Rosende, for his help regarding fingerpicking and national guitars
- Janet and Ian Woodward for all their kindness, generosity and helping with the proof reading.

CONTENTS

1	GLASGOW	11
2	NEWCASTLE	29
3	LEEDS	77
4	DEPTFORD & GREENWICH	103
5	ISLINGTON	135
6	CLAPHAM	147
7	CAMDEN	157
8	WEST END	165
9	NOTTING HILL & HYDE PARK	181
10	NEW YORK	207
11	PENNAN	229
12	HAMMERSMITH & SHEPHERD'S BUSH	251
13	WEMBLEY	263
14	NEW ORLEANS	269
15	EDINBURGH	277
16	SILVERTOWN	305
17	NEW FOREST	311
18	SOUTHWARK	329
19	EXTRAS: ALABAMA	339

20	Extras: Nashville	343
21	Extras: Philadelphia	353
22	Extras: Detroit	357
	Bibliography	361
	Glossary	363
	Also Available from Lulu.com	368

1 GLASGOW

The start of the journey through the places that inspired Mark Knopfler's songs and which marked their history is the city where the Knopfler brothers were both born and lived in until 1956, when they moved to their mother's hometown, Newcastle-Upon-Tyne.

Mark was born in **Glasgow** in 1949. During their time there, the Knopfler family lived in two different parts of the city, **Bearsden** and **Scotstoun**, and memories of those years stayed with Mark Knopfler and served as inspiration for songs he composed many years later, such as 'So Far From The Clyde' and 'Border Reiver'.

Now we are going to overview the places in this city that could be of particular interest relating to the history and songs of **Mark Knopfler** and **Dire Straits**.

The song 'So Far From the Clyde', released on his 2009 record 'Get Lucky', tells the story of the 'breaking' of ships, including their long journeys to the distant shores of India, their final destination. These ships he speaks of come from some of the shipyards of the **River Clyde**, the most famous of these being the **John Brown Shipyards**. Although these are now closed, the giant **Finnieston Crane** still stands by the quayside in memory of Glasgow's long and proud engineering history and a walk along the river offers good views and a reflection upon past times. These shipyards built such world-famous ships as RMS Lusitania, RMS Queen Mary, RMS Queen Elizabeth and RMS QE2.

Shipwrecks (River Clyde)

Walk by the Clyde and the Govan shipyards

Very close to that river walk are three venues in which Mark Knopfler has played during different tours: the **Hydro,** a modern venue opened in 2013 where Mark Knopfler played during his 2015 'Tracker' tour and in also his "Down The Road Wherever" tour in 2019; the **SECC** (Scottish Exhibition and Conference Centre) where Dire Straits and Mark Knopfler have played over the years; and the **Clyde Auditorium,** used by Knopfler in 2001 on the 'Sailing to Philadelphia' tour.

EXHIBITION CENTRE WALKWAY,
FROM THE TRAIN STATION TO THE COMPLEX.

SECC COMPLEX IN 2011

THE HYDRO AND THE FINNIESTON CRANE

THE CLYDE AUDITORIUM, THE SECC AND THE HYDRO

After their successful experience with his previous film 'Local Hero', Mark Knopfler was asked by writer and director **Bill Forsyth** in 1984 to write some music for his new film 'Comfort And Joy'. The film was shot in Glasgow and in some of the scenes you can see different parts of the city. Some scenes were shot by the River Clyde, in which the main character, played by **Bill Patterson**, is talking into a voice recorder. One of those scenes was used as the cover for the soundtrack featuring three new songs by Mark Knopfler. In that photo you can see the **Kingston Bridge** behind Bill Patterson. The entire area has seen much redevelopment since then and now it looks like this:

KINGSTON BRIDGE, AS PICTURED IN THE
'COMFORT AND JOY' SOUNDTRACK COVER

The boat moored up at the bank is a venue called **The Ferry**, coincidentally one played by **John Illsley** in 2017.

The mooring ties that can also be seen in the film and on the soundtrack cover with the letters 'AS' are nowadays hidden behind the fences but they are still there, as can be seen in this picture, looking across the Clyde to where the soundtrack cover photo was shot. Again, this part has changed significantly, including the **Clyde Arc**, known locally as the '**Squinty Bridge**', which opened in 2006.

Bearsden is the place where he spent his first years, the school he first attended being **Bearsden Primary**. This is in a fairly affluent area of the city. It appears from the 'Sailing to Philadelphia' press-kit that the Knopfler family lived in an estate with houses built in the 1930s, quite representative of those from that era to be found across central Scotland. The Knopfler family later moved to another area of the city and the young Mark would spend only about one year at Bearsden Primary.

BEARSDEN PRIMARY SCHOOL

SCOTSTOUN PRIMARY SCHOOL

The rest of his Scottish primary school education would be at **Scotstoun Primary**. There is video evidence of this in the 'Sailing to Philadelphia' press-kit where Mark is standing outside Scotstoun Primary. In Scotland schooling starts at age five and Mark said he went to Scotstoun from age six, so it appears that he attended school there for only one year, given the family's move to Newcastle-upon-Tyne in 1956.

Scotstoun was also the location of the former **Albion** truck manufacturing plant, subject of the song 'Border Reiver', also from the 'Get Lucky' record. There are three references to the Albion factory in the song: 'My Scotstoun lassie', referring to the location of the plant, 'She's an Albion''' referring to the truck´s marque and 'Sure as the Sunrise' which was the Albion motto. Today the plant is still operational but it makes axles under the name Albion Automotive. Offering a sense of nostalgia, the distinctive Albion sign has been retained on the building, making it worth a visit.

ALBION OFFICES

The visit to Glasgow, recorded for the aforementioned press-kit probably inspired the lyrics for the song "A Place Where We Used to Live", released on Mark's third solo record "The Ragpicker's Dream". In this song he recalls details of his childhood, his house and neighbourhood etc...

The town of **Dumbarton** was home to the **Hercules Linton shipyards** where the famous **Cutty Sark** clipper, mentioned in the Dire Straits' song 'Single-Handed Sailor', was built in 1869. Unfortunately, complications and difficulties during the building of the Cutty Sark led to bankruptcy for the shipbuilders and the shipyards are now closed and demolished. Currently occupying the site is a tall red brick building which is a former distillery. This industry has also now left the town and, at the time of writing, the building is unoccupied.

Many of the ancillary buildings have since been demolished and much of the surrounding area is wasteland. As a part of the **Scottish Maritime Museum** building, though, there is still a leftover to be found from the shipbuilding days - the Ship Model Experiment Tank. It has a dedication plaque to William Froude, the famous Victorian naval engineer and architect, on the outside.

The film 'A Shot At Glory', for which Knopfler composed the score, had some location

FORMER LINTON SHIPYARDS

MARITIME MUSEUM

shooting at the former football ground of **Dumbarton Football Club**. Their current stadium sits in a picturesque location beside **Dumbarton Castle**, upon Dumbarton Rock. The Castle has an illustrious history and many well-known figures from Scottish and British history have visited it. Although Dumbarton has clearly seen better days it is still worth a visit.

DUMBARTON CASTLE

DUMBARTON BRIDGE OVER THE RIVER LEVEN

It is interesting to note that this is where the **River Leven** meets the River Clyde. The River Leven is a stretch of water that flows from **Loch Lomond**.

'What It Is', a song inspired by the city of Edinburgh, which has its own chapter in this book, has a line/lick in it that Mark has said many times he 'borrowed' from the old Scottish song 'The Bonnie, Bonnie Banks O' Loch Lomond'. During his 2001 tour he used to play it as an introduction to 'What it Is' and nowadays he still plays some parts of it during the interlude of the song.

It is easy to visit Loch Lomond, an area of outstanding natural beauty and therefore worth seeing in its own right. There is a small shopping centre with a place to eat and lochside walks. There are many activities based around the loch area, which is a designated National Park. There are walks, cycle hire and many water activities.

Visit http://www.lochlomond-trossachs.org for information on Loch Lomond and activities there.

Loch Lomond

LOCH LOMOND

LOCH LOMOND SHOPPING AREA. PICTURE: JULIO BRICIO

GLASGOW MAPS

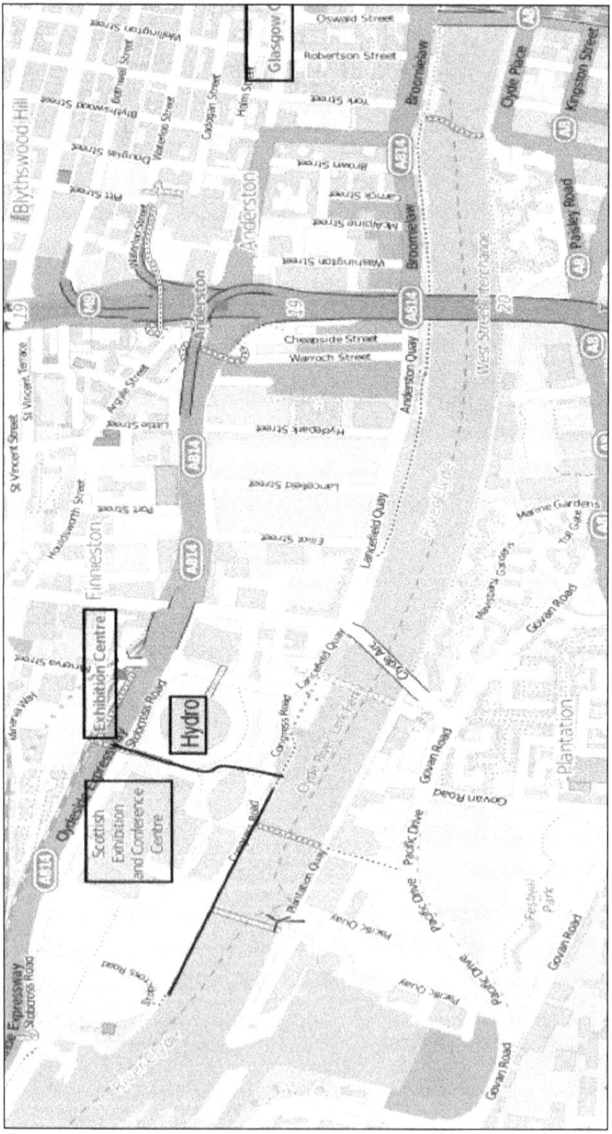

RIVER CLYDE SHIPYARDS

You can go there by local train from **Glasgow Central to Exhibition Centre** and heading toward the river, passing by the **Hydro**, the **SECC** and the **Clyde Auditorium**. Note that there is a walkway to take pedestrians across the motorway from the railway station to the SECC.

Bearsden

The fastest way to reach **Bearsden** is by train. From **Glasgow Central** take the Milngavie (pronounced "mill-guy") route and it is about an eighteen-minute journey to **Bearsden Station**. If you visited the Exhibition Centre area you can take the Milngavie train directly from there and in five stops, around thirteen minutes' travel, you will arrive in Bearsden. Leaving the station turn left and then left again onto **Drymen Road**. Continue along here to the crossroads and the primary school is on your right-hand side before **Thorn Road**. This is only a short walk from the station.

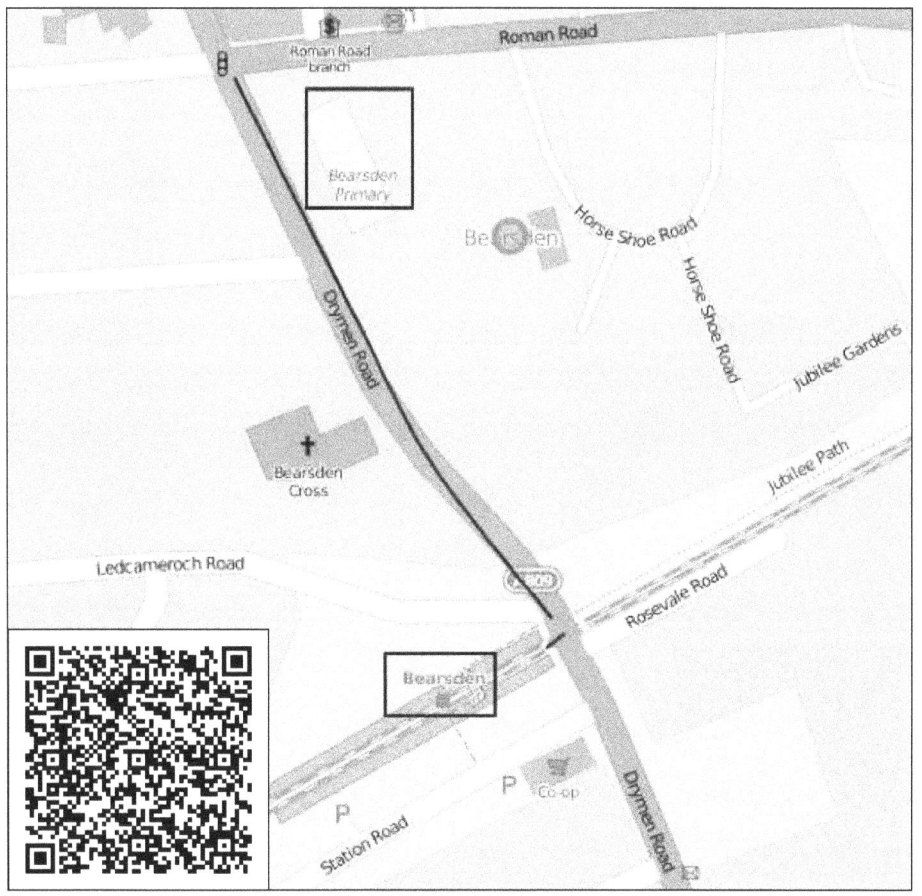

Hercules Linton Shipyards

To get to **Dumbarton**, go to **Glasgow Central** and take the **Helensburgh Central** train, alighting at **Dumbarton Central**. This journey takes about three-quarters of an hour. Come out of the station and walk along **Church Street**. Keep walking along this road, go straight ahead at the first roundabout and then you will enter the town centre, turning into **High Street** as the road turns to the right. From here you can take a walk down to the waterside. Or, from the roundabout at **Church Street**, take second left onto **Glasgow Road** and walk along for a short while and you will find the **Maritime Museum**. The area just behind this building is the former site of the shipyards.

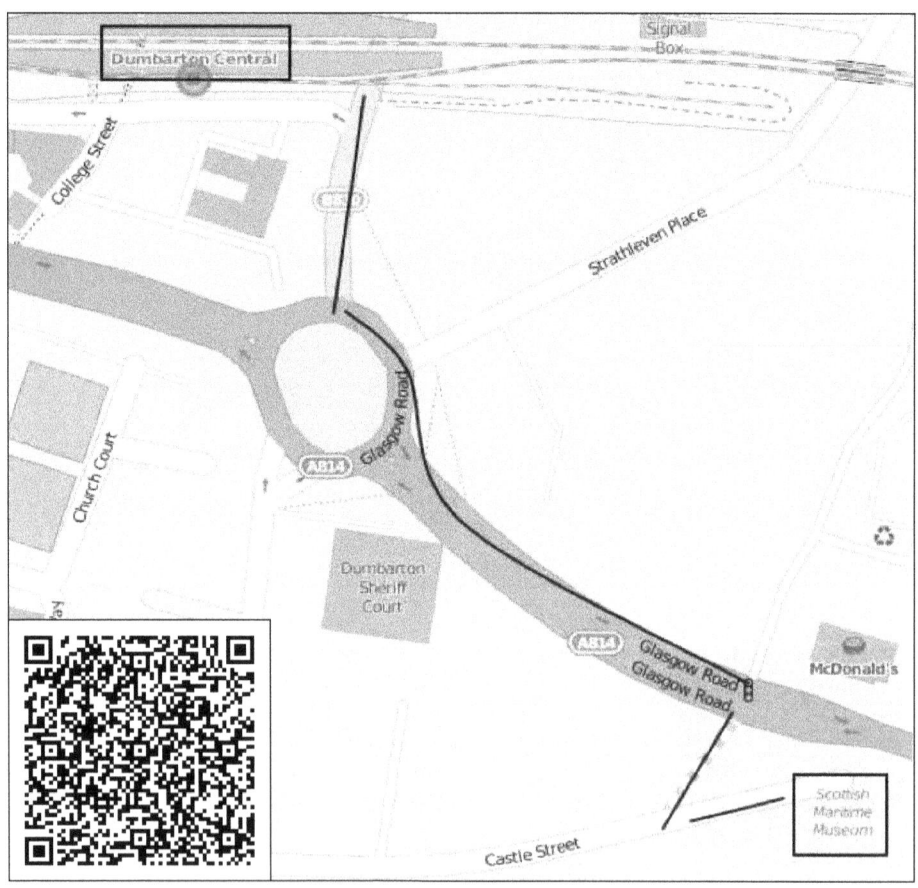

Dumbarton Football Club

From **Glasgow Road** start walking in the opposite direction from **Dumbarton Central** station until you reach **Victoria Street,** which is the third on the right after the roundabout. Go straight down **Victoria Street** to its end, then on to **Castle Road.** Follow this and the football ground is on your right, beneath the Castle. When leaving, you can join your train back to Glasgow at **Dumbarton East** if you turn right at the top of **Victoria Street**. This is the nearest station.

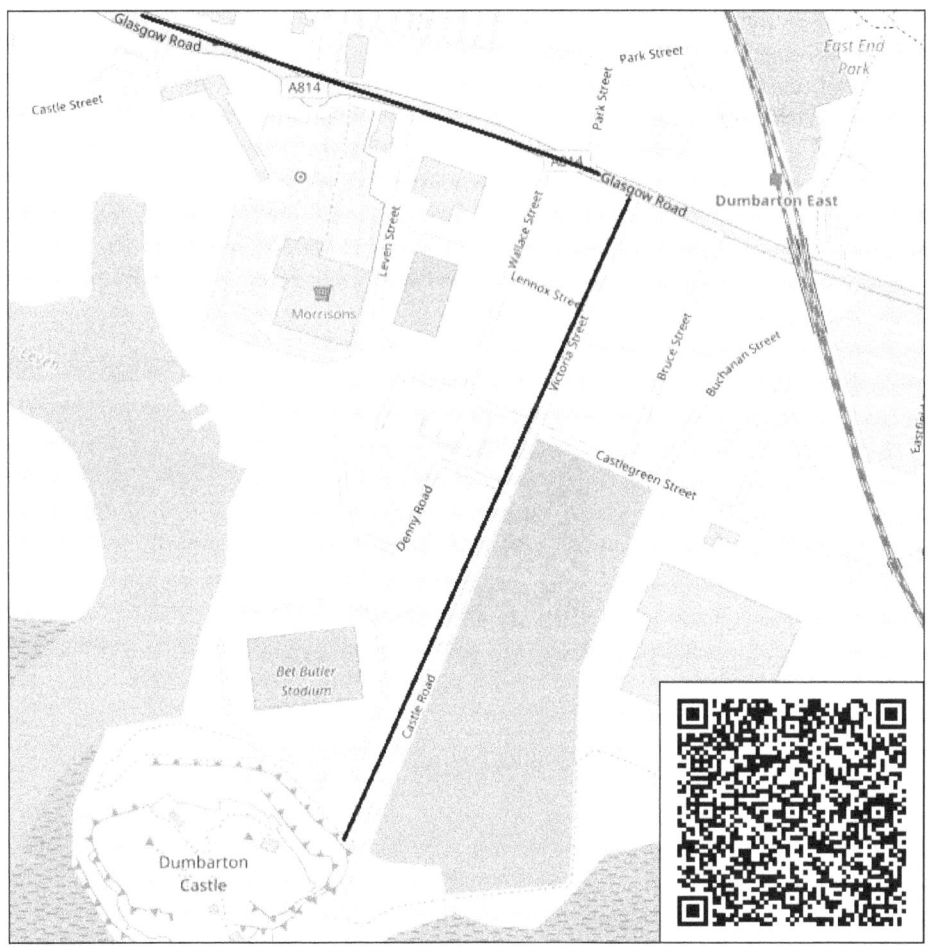

Scotstoun

If you are in Glasgow, a train is the best way to get to **Scotstoun** so go to **Glasgow Central** station and catch the **Dalmuir** train to **Scotstounhill**. This journey will take around thirteen minutes. If you are in Bearsden, you need to catch the **Motherwell** train. After three stops, about eight minutes' travel, alight at **Hyndland** and there take the **Dalmuir** train and in two stops, about five minutes' travel, you will arrive in Scotstounhill.

Since you are about to walk through a residential area the following instructions are quite complicated. Exiting the station, head south toward **Goldberry Avenue**. Turn left onto **Esselmont Avenue** to the end of this street and then right onto **Birchfield Drive**. After the sixth street on the left you will come upon **Scotstoun Primary School**.

To visit the old **Albion Plant**, look for **Ormiston Avenue** which runs along the side of the school, cross the road and walk straight down to **Dumbarton Road**. Turn right and walk along to **Balmoral Street** (second left) and walk down here. The Albion Automotive plant is on the corner of this street and South Street at the bottom of the road.

GLASGOW MAPS

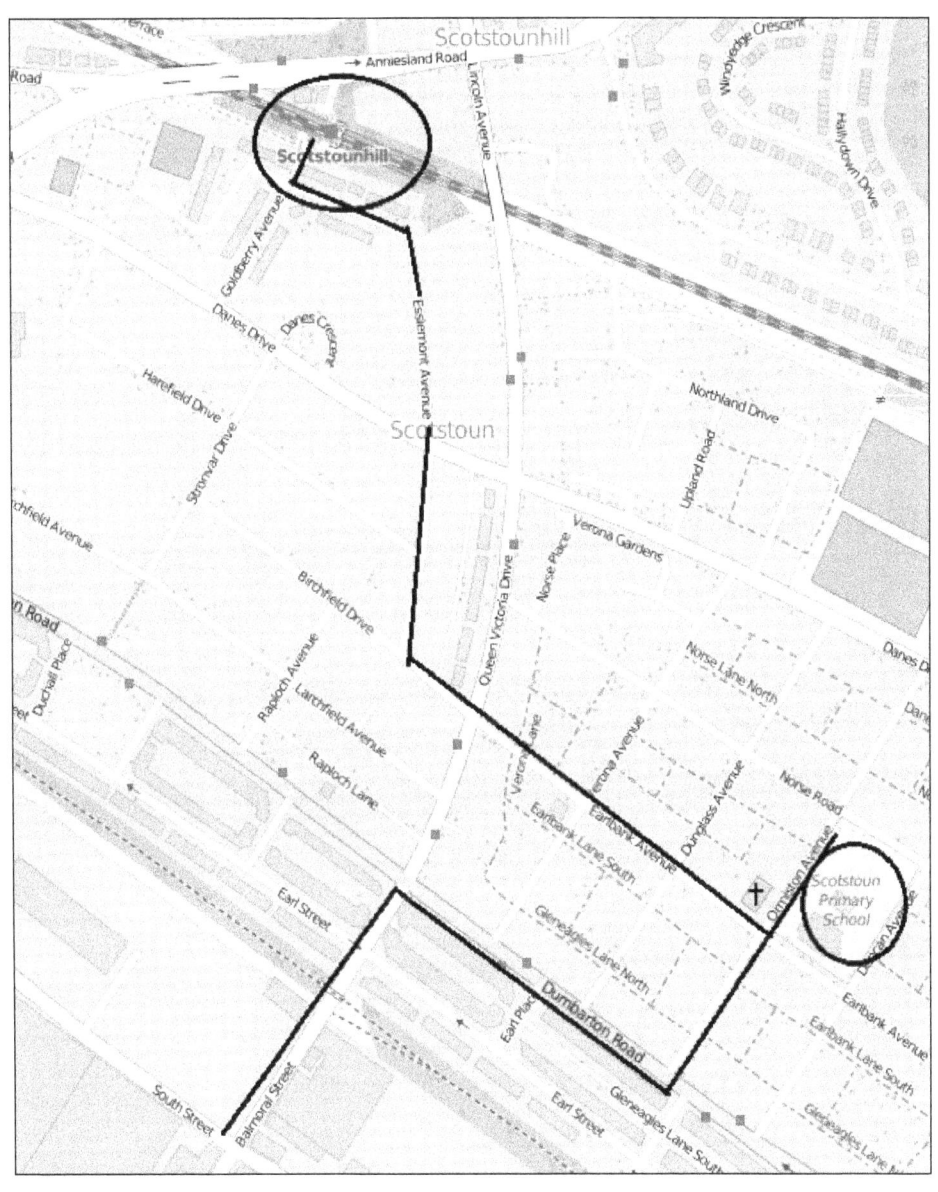

Loch Lomond

If you would like to visit **Loch Lomond**, it's possible to go there by train too. From **Glasgow Queen Street** station catch the train to **Balloch Central**, the end of the line. The journey time is about an hour. When you come out of the station, turn left and walk along **Balloch Road** until the roundabout, then turn right (third exit) along **Ben Lomond Way**. At the next roundabout turn right (second exit) and **Loch Lomond Shores** is on your left with the loch behind it. You can also catch a Loch Lomond Cruise, just turning right when coming out the station.

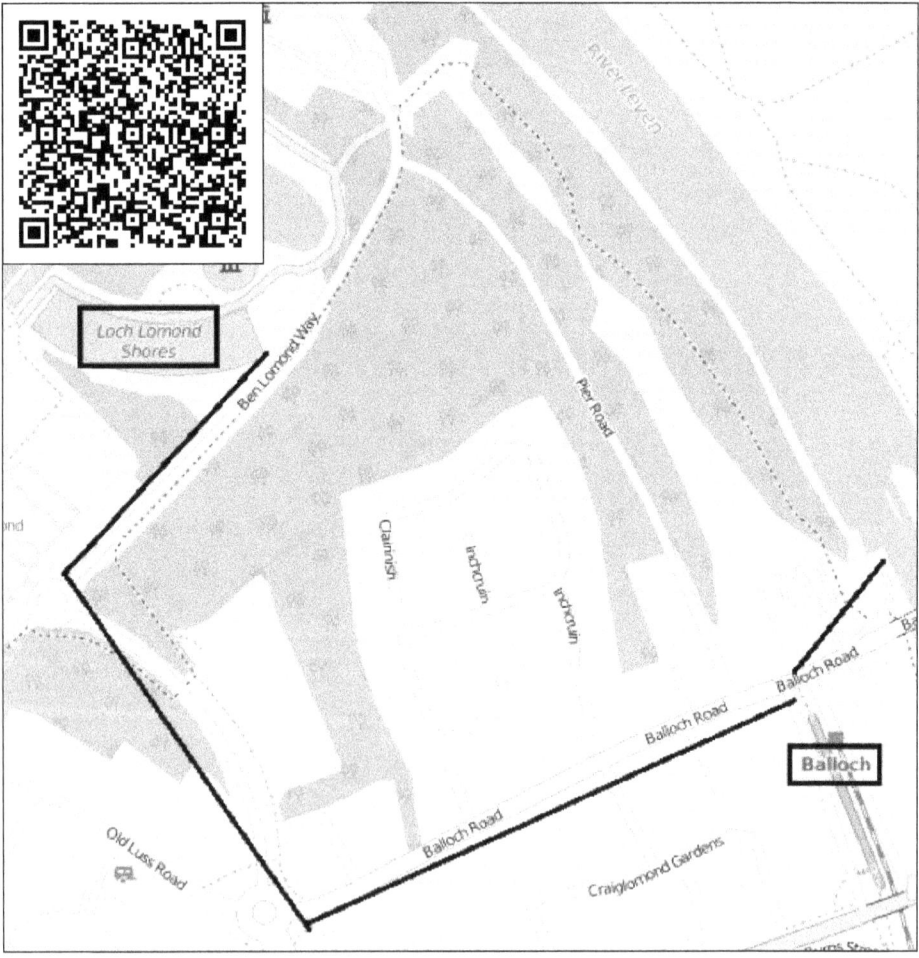

2 NEWCASTLE

PICTURE: CARLES BUYREU

It was in 1956 that the Knopfler family decided upon a move from Glasgow to **Gosforth**, an area in his mother's home town of **Newcastle-upon-Tyne**. This was a move made by many people between the two cities in an effort to find work since they had correlative industries such as shipbuilding. It was here in Newcastle that musical inspiration came to him from his Uncle Kingsley who played harmonica and boogie-woogie piano. It was this musical inspiration combined with memories from his childhood that would inspire some of Mark Knopfler's more popular songs such as 'Down to the Waterline', 'Southbound Again', 'Tunnel Of Love', '**5.15 am**' and, more recently 'Basil' and 'Just a Boy Away From Home'.

GREY'S MONUMENT. PICTURE: JULIO BRICIO

While in Newcastle the young Mark attended **Gosforth Grammar School**. Today it doesn't exist under that name: it is now **Gosforth Academy**. Although founded in 1921 the current school is formed of various buildings built between the mid-1960s and the early 2000s. While at school he performed the song 'Chilly Winds' on local television with school friend Sue Hercombe in 1966.

Mark was spending much of his spare time gazing into guitar shop windows, lusting after a red Fender Stratocaster like the one Hank Marvin used. Eventually, his Dad bought him his first guitar, a Höfner V2 Super Solid, from **Kitchen's music store** which occupied the corner unit of **Higham House** on **New Bridge Street West**. Although it was turned into a pub in 2009, the owner said he has always been a Dire Straits fan.

FORMER PLACE OF THE KITCHEN'S MUSIC STORE.
PICTURE: MICHAEL COOK

Another shop he would visit is in the **Central Arcade**. This shop was featured in the 2013 Sky Arts documentary '<u>Guitar Stories</u>' with **John Illsley**. Both Mark and John stood outside discussing old times, his visits to the shop and his younger days in Newcastle. The arcade is part of a domed building, a part of Richard Grainger's plan of the area. It was rebuilt in the early 20th century, at which time they built the arcade in an Art Nouveaux manner.

Pictures: Julio Bricio

They visited the **J.G. Windows** instruments shop, where Mark shows and plays his above mentioned first guitar for the documentary.

Picture: Carles Buyreu

After school the young Mark Knopfler spent his spare time at **Newcastle City Hall** where he attended his first rock concerts featuring artists such as **Joe Brown** and **Chuck Berry**. He would go on to perform there himself when touring with Dire Straits and also as a solo artist, at least in his first tours.

He has said he played there for personal reasons, until he changed to a venue with a larger capacity as Newcastle became one of the most in-demand shows by his fans, not only from the city, but from Europe, so he decided to move to the **Metro Radio Arena**.

CITY HALL, PICTURE: MICHAEL COOK

METRO RADIO ARENA. PICTURE: JULIO BRICIO

The Metro Radio Arena was opened in 1995 and, bearing in mind its seating capacity of 11,000 compared to only 2,000 in the City Hall, it becomes obvious as to why Mark and his management have chosen to use this venue, even although the intimacy of

Mark Knopfler and his band, performing at the Newcastle Utilita Arena, May 19th 2019. Picture: Carles Buyreu

the City Hall is lost. The arena clearly filled a hole in the market with Glasgow and Sheffield being the nearest venues of this magnitude. It was built as the Newcastle Arena and nowadays renamed '**Utilita Arena**'.

Although he was born in Glasgow, spending his more formative years in Newcastle has made locations in the latter city both more plentiful and prominent in his songs. Indeed, many familiar streets and buildings reveal themselves as you take a stroll through the city. Places such as the **Dog Leap Stairs**, **Black Gate**, **Mark Toney's** or **Grainger Street** are all within a short walking distance of each other. Significantly, Grainger Street is named after **Richard Grainger**, a local builder whose work to redevelop the centre of Newcastle in the 19th century created very much the city we see today.

At Grainger Street, at the point where it crosses with **Westgate Road,** you can find **St. John the Baptist Church** . This rather finely-proportioned 13th century church is most likely the 'black church' mentioned in the lyrics of the song '<u>Basil</u>'. 'Black' may be metaphorical as the church itself is not black but it likely refers to the 'starlings swarming a cloud' and casting a dark shadow. This is one theory, but there isn't any evidence regarding which church it may indeed be. The nearby **Cathedral Church of St. Nicholas** is another possibility.

GRAINGER STREET

ST JOHN THE BAPTIST CHURCH

CATHEDRAL CHURCH OF
ST. NICHOLAS

Along Grainger Street is **Mark Toney's Ice Cream Parlour**. It is a fine establishment and recommended for lunch or a tea and cake. Established in 1892, the café is a mainstay of the Newcastle scene and it is not surprising if Mark did indeed meet 'Vince at Mark Toney's" (as mentioned in the lyrics to the song 'Basil') especially as it is so near-at-hand to the Chronicle offices.

THIS AND NEXT PAGE: MARK TONEY'S

Now in a 1960s brutalist office block at Thomson House in the Groat Market, just off Grainger Street, the former offices of the **Chronicle** occupied a building called Kemsley House on Westgate Road. It was demolished in 1965 when the Chronicle moved out to their new premises. Mark would have worked as a copy boy at the former offices as he said in an interview he was working there aged fourteen and fifteen. However, since they vacated these premises in the May of 1965 and Mark didn't turn sixteen until the August of that year he may well have worked for a time at the new offices too. Mark had met the poet **Basil Bunting** during his time at The Chronicle and has mentioned this in promotional material for the 'Tracker' album. The Chronicle was founded in 1764, the first copy produced on a hand press in a small room in Middle Street, now long gone.

Top: Site of the former Chronicle's offices.
Bottom: Current site of the Chronicle.
Pictures: Michael Cook

Current site of the Chronicle with the 'Black Church' and the Black Gate at the back. Picture: Michael Cook

A building still standing however is **The Castle**, a medieval fortification on the site of a previous fortress that gave the city its name. The gatehouse to the Castle is called the Black Gate, mentioned in the song 'Basil'. You can walk through this without entering the Castle building itself. **The Black Gate** was added to the Castle between 1247 and 1250 and there was a drawbridge to the front and rear. Many alterations over the years have included the addition of the top two floors. The Castle was leased in 1619 and the Black Gate was turned into a house! Popularly thought to get its name from its appearance, the 'Black' Gate actually derives from Patrick Black, a London merchant who occupied the building in the 17th century.

THE BLACK GATE

The Castle

Just behind the Black Gate is the **Dog Leap Stairs**, made famous by the song 'Down to the Waterline' from Dire Straits' first album. According to folklore, in 1772 Baron Eldon, later Lord Chancellor of England, eloped with Bessie Surtees making their escape on horseback up Dog Leap Stairs. They lead from Castle Garth to Side, alongside the railway viaduct. Side was where a lot of the Georgian silversmiths worked when Newcastle still had an assay office. The buildings there today post-date that era by around a century though, but are of a bold Baroque design with curved frontage. They were built for a shipping owner and were home to many Newcastle firms with a maritime link.

Dog Leap Stairs

Down by the **quayside** (mentioned in the very first line of the song 'Down To The Waterline') there is now a plaque honouring MK. There are numerous plaques honouring other famous Geordies scattered all along so this may be a time-consuming task, but as you walk along toward the Millennium Bridge the plaques are clearly visible on the slabs.

There are some coffee shops along the quayside to cater for the offices and redevelopment and also some good photo opportunities.

MARK KNOPFLER'S PLAQUE ON GATESHEAD'S WALK.
PICTURE: CARLES BUYREU

Top: The plaque is located at Gateshead, in the right part of the picture, in concrete, close to the Baltic Art Gallery.

Bottom: The Baltic Art Gallery. The plaque is where the family are standing.

Pictures: Michael Cook

There is a view across the river to Gateshead which is mentioned in the lyrics of the song 'Basil', and there are a few interesting bridges too. Furthest to the right is certainly the highlight of these in the **High Level Bridge**, perhaps recognisable from the Mike Hodges gangster film 'Get Carter', starring Michael Caine. Opened in 1849 by Queen Victoria, it was the first bridge built with both cast and wrought iron. It has an upper railway and lower roadway. Across the other side of the River Tyne you can see the glass-roofed **Sage Gateshead**.

HIGH LEVEL BRIDGE

QUAYSIDE

THE QUAYSIDE AND THE TYNE BRUDGE BETWEEN NEWCASTLE AND GATESHEAD.
PICTURE: JULIO BRICIO

In the song 'Just A Boy Away From Home', included in his 2018 album 'Down The Road Wherever', Mark reminisces about when his father was in **Newcastle General Hospital** after a heart attack. In the official press release for the record he explains the story behind the song:

"He was in Newcastle General, which as anyone from the North-East of England will know is very close to the football ground. He was lying awake in the middle of the night feeling a bit sorry for himself, and he heard a lad walking on the deserted street outside singing 'You'll Never Walk Alone.' Of course, he was a Liverpool fan and he'd been to the match—or who knows, he might have missed it somehow. But there he was in Newcastle singing his song.

My dad found it inspiring, the spirit of it." The track includes a full, stirring reprise of the famous melody. *"It just felt good to play it on the slide,"* says Mark. *"I thought, 'I've started, so I may as well finish. And it's fun for the band to play."*

ST JAMES'S PARK STADIUM, HOME OF NEWCASTLE UNITED F.C. PICTURE: JULIO BRICIO

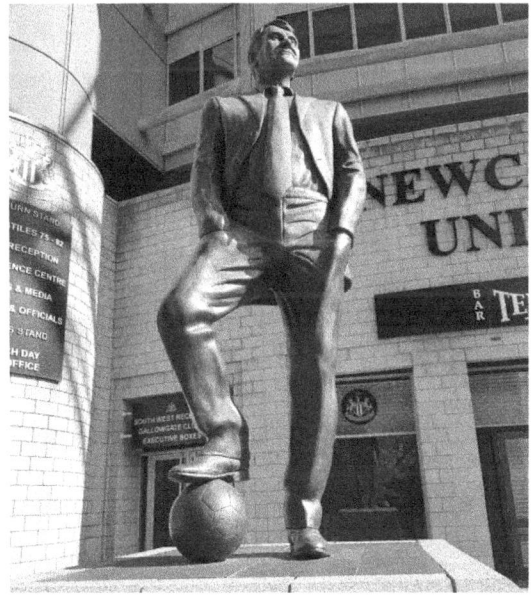

PICTURES: CARLES BUYRFEU

The song '5:15 am' from his 2004 record 'Shangri-La' recalls the murder of **Angus Sibbet** in 1967 by his business associates Stafford and Luvaglio. Both Stafford and Luvaglio were Londoners who 'came up from Cockneyland'. The case gained the nickname '*One-Armed Bandit Murder*' through the connection to the supply of fruit machines, also known colloquially as 'one-armed bandits' to clubs, hence the use of the phrase in the song 'one-armed bandit man". The case was one of the most notorious killings in the north east, and the first gangland killing, sparking fears that organised crime was gaining a foothold in the north east. This was a very high-profile case and apparently, memories of these events lingered long in the memory for Mark and the impression they made inspired him to write about it.

Sibbet's body, shot three times, was discovered in the back seat of his Jaguar at 5.15am by a passing miner. The car was under **Pesspool Bridge** in **South Hetton**. As motive for his murder, the prosecution alleged Sibbet had been skimming the takings, estimated as £1,000 a week, supported by the fact he could afford to buy a Jaguar Mark 10. The police case was that Stafford and Luvaglio left nearby Durham the night before in an E-type Jaguar, and met Sibbett, who had left **La Dolce Vita** nightclub in Newcastle.

THE PLACE WHERE THE BODY WAS FOUND (THE PESSPOOL BRIDGE WHERE MORE OR LESS THE CAR CAN BE SEEN IN THE PICTURE)
PICTURE: TIM MCGUINNESS

This is the place were "La Dolce Vita" club was located. Picture: Tim McGuiness

On the night of the murder, Stafford and Luvaglio were to meet Sibbet at The Birdcage Casino, sixteen miles away from where the body was found. The case can be related to the Newcastle-set film 'Get Carter' in its style. Indeed, it is said to have inspired the novel 'Jack's Return Home' by Ted Lewis upon which the film is based. These clubs were hugely popular in the 1960s around the time of the murder and attracted big names. **Joe Brown**, who appeared at Mark Knopfler concerts at the Royal Albert Hall as a guest with Mark in 2008, played at La Dolce Vita. It went into decline in the 1970s, finally closing in 2002.

Outwith the city is the location referred to in arguably the most famous song Mark has written about his time in the area and his younger years. The seaside town of Whitley Bay is mentioned in the lyrics of the epic 'Tunnel of Love', from Dire Straits' third album 'Making Movies'.

The lyrics mention the '**Spanish City**' which is, or rather was, a fairground with rides such as the waltzers, the ghost train, a big wheel, a carousel and one-arm bandit machines, all fronted by a white building dominated by a central dome flanked by towers. The granite stepping around this building has been etched with lyrics from the song 'Tunnel of Love' and a plaque installed in a 2014 regeneration of the area, including the Spanish City building which had fallen into disrepair. Filming of a 2019 Sky Arts documentary with Brian Johnson (AC DC singer), "*A Life On The*

Road", showed the two band leaders meeting outside here, going to the Cumberland Arms where Mark played some acoustic songs including '<u>Go, Love</u>' and also Johnson revealing the etched lyrics. Mark explains Brian that this songs talks about leaving Newcastle, and going back, again and again. The "love" in this song is not a person but the city where he grew up.

PICTURES: MATT DUNCAN

Top: Whitley Bay Station and his famous clock tower.
Bottom: Spanish City in 2019.
Pictures: Carles Buyreu

WHITLEY BAY AND THE SPANISH CITY DOME.
PICTURE: AIDAN WILLIAMSON

'GETTING CRAZY ON THE WALTZERS'
SPANISH CITY IN 1998.
PICTURE: AIDAN WILLIAMSON

SPANISH CITY IN 1998.
PICTURE: AIDAN WILLIAMSON

Incidentally, the term '**Rockaway**' used in the song refers to **Rockaways' Playland** amusement park in **New York** which is a similar place. Mark has said during concerts that it was the first time he heard rock music played loud. Spanish City used to open its doors with 'Tunnel of Love', until it closed them for the final time in 2000.

As well as Whitley Bay, where Spanish City is located, 'Tunnel of Love' also mentions the nearby seaside town of **Cullercoats**. This was originally a small fishing village founded in the 16th century. The harbour today hosts a marine laboratory, part of Newcastle University. Mark uses it the line '*from Cullercoats and Whitley Bay out to Rockaway*'.

CULLERCOATS
PICTURE: CARLES BUYREU

CULLERCOATS
PICTURE: MICHAEL COOK

There have been rumours for years that Spanish City will be refurbished; however, it still lies unused and sadly in a state of dilapidation. New proposals released in July 2016 breathe some new hope, however. Much work has been done on the rest of the promenade though, including one thing of interest to the Dire Straits fan. Some of the lyrics to 'Tunnel of Love' have been engraved and displayed on tiles. There is also a commemorative plaque thanking Mark for allowing them to be used.

PICTURES: MICHAEL COOK

Part of the 'Tunnel Of Love' lyrics in the promenade with the dome at the back.
Picture: Aidan Williamson

It was in Newcastle where Mark met the person who would turn out to be his first wife, Kathy White, his long-term girlfriend from school days. Kathy's family owned a farm in Dinnington that Mark would work on and this experience has inspired him to write some songs many years later such as 'Hill Farmer's Blues', 'Get Lucky' and 'Yon Two Crows'. Mark later started making journeys south in pursuit of a musical career.

It was these journeys south pursuing a musical career that inspired the early Dire Straits song 'Southbound Again'. In the lyrics '...*roll across the rolling River Tyne*' and also '...*moving down the line*' it is likely he is talking about crossing the Tyne by train. The woman in the song is undoubtedly Kathy White. These journeys are also the inspiration to the song "Go, love", according to what Mark Knopfler told Brian Johnson in the previously mentioned documentary.

An important building in the city is the **Central Railway Station**. It was designed in the mid-19th century by the architect John Dobson for the York, Newcastle and Berwick Railway Company. Although the portico is a later addition it is one of the finest city stations in the UK.

NEWCASTLE CENTRE RAILWAY STATION

Dobson worked with the aforementioned Richard Grainger in the design of Newcastle City Centre. The station is mentioned in the lyrics of the song 'Fare Thee Well Northumberland', featured on 'The Ragpicker's Dream' album. The song describes a young Mark Knopfler leaving home by train to fulfil his ambitions.

Another song about Geordies leaving home is 'Why Aye Man'. This is about a gang of builders leaving home and going to Germany to find work. The reason for this is the high unemployment in the North-East at the time. The song itself was used for the classic television show 'Auf Wiedersehen, Pet' when it was revived in 2002. Both guest vocalists **Jimmy Nail** and **Tim Healy** starred in the show. The comedy drama is generally regarded as one of the finest ever made in British television.

Jimmy Nail is not only an actor but also a singer, born in Newcastle. In 1995 he released a song called 'Big River' in which Mark Knopfler played some good guitar; the song reminisces about the golden days of shipbuilding and industry on the **River Tyne** and also about their decline. The song is very emotive and Knopfler's guitar adds something very special to it.

The decline of the industry around the Tyne in Newcastle was also reflected in Mark Knopfler´s music as he received in 1993 a petition to compose some music for a television documentary about the struggle of the **Swan Hunter shipyard**. He recorded three instrumental songs, one of them a cover version of the folk song of Scottish origin 'The Water Is Wide', (also known as 'O Waly, Waly'); the other two were titled 'Last Ship' and 'Song For Swans', and also a song with lyrics, 'My Claim To Fame'. In this Mark compares his success as a music star with the lack of recognition of the work of all the shipbuilders who spend their lives building ships.

The documentary was aired in 1994 and the only song from the four written for the documentary that was released was 'My Claim To Fame', as a bonus track in the cd-single for 'Darling Pretty', from Knopfler´s first solo album 'Golden Heart' in 1996.

Also in 1993 Mark reunited his "second band", **The Notting Hillbillies**, for a special charity concert to raise money to attempt to prevent the closure of the **Swan Hunter shipyard**. It was held at the City Hall on 6th July. It featured **Alan Clark**, who played in Dire Straits from 1980 to 1992 and is also from Newcastle, on keyboards instead of Guy Fletcher, who wasn´t available for that concert; Steve Phillips and Brendan Croker on guitars and vocals; Ed Bicknell on drums; Marcus Cliffe on bass and of course, Mark Knopfler on guitar and vocals, in a very special night for Mark as a proud citizen of Newcastle.

After he studied journalism at **Harlow**, they moved south to **Leeds**, where Mark found work as a cub reporter at **The Yorkshire Evening Post**, but knew that music was his ambition. Mark had separated from Kathy White by 1973 when Mark had moved to London.

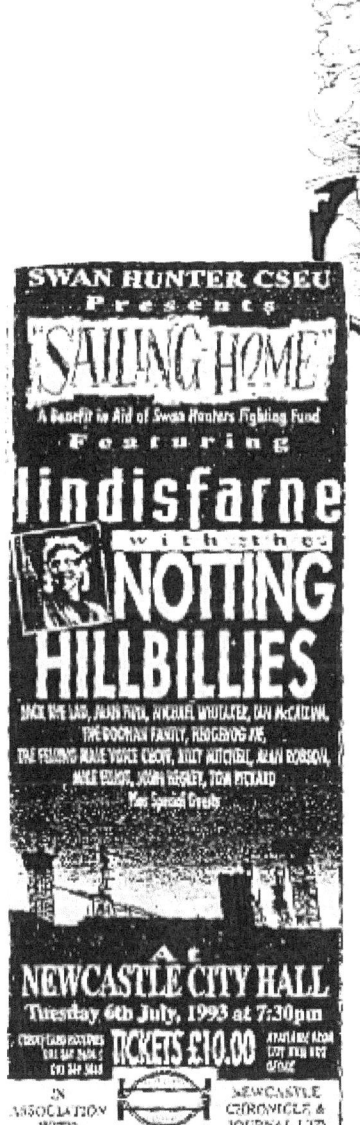

'I never thought unemployment could be this painful'

NEWCASTLE MAPS

Gosford

The nearest Metro stop is **Regents Centre**. When exiting on to **Great North Road** turn left and after a very short walk, **Gosforth Academy** will appear on your left.

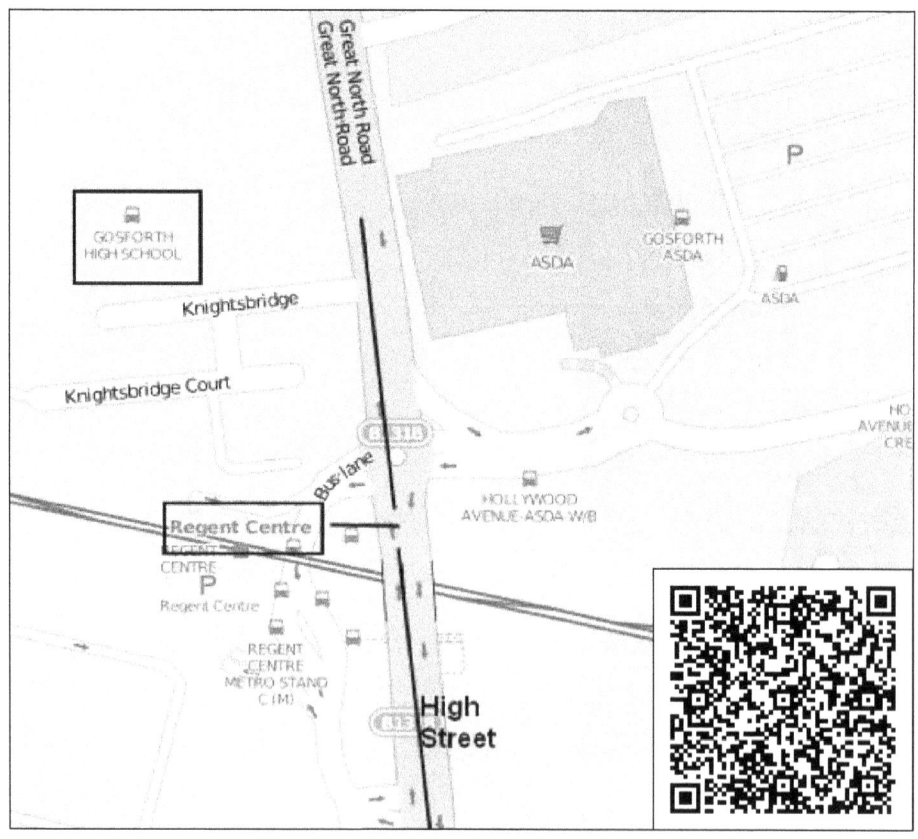

City Hall

To visit City Hall, the closest Metro stop is **Haymarket**. This is just a five-minute walk. When exiting, turn right at **Northumberland Street** and then turn down the third street on the left, **Northumberland Road** and just after the intersection with **John Dobson Street**, you are at City Hall.

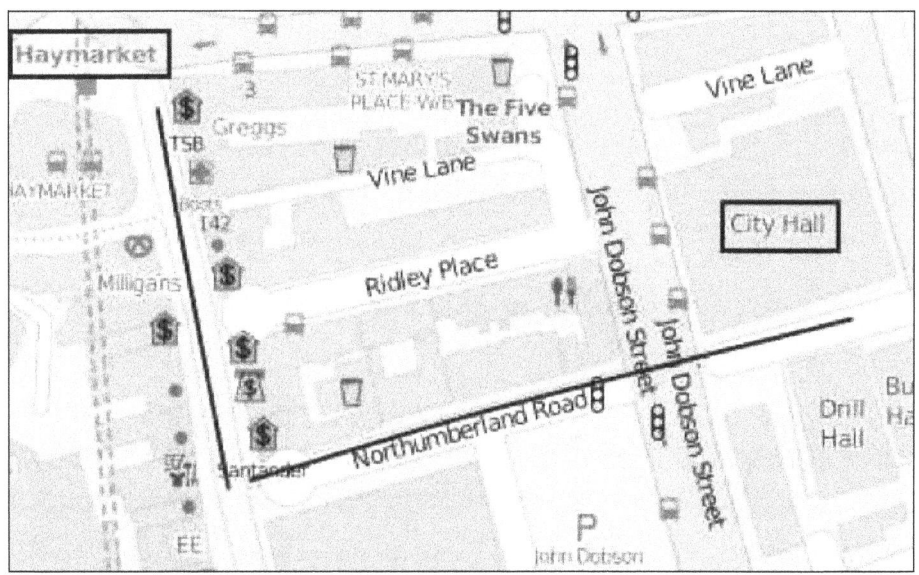

Former Kitchen's Music Store

From the **City Hall** walk along **Northumberland Road** until you reach the traffic lights then turn left onto **John Dobson Street**. Walk down until you see **New Bridge Street West** on your left, just after the **Laing Art Gallery**. The guitar shop was located in **9 Higham House**, the corner unit of a 1960s building.

Central Arcade / Evening Chronicle Offices

Walk from **Higham House**, back to **Northumberland Street** until you see on your right **Grey's Monument**, a tall column dominating the skyline with a statue of Earl Grey on its plinth. Head toward the monument along **Blackett Street** and from there go along **Grainger Street**, a street named in his song '<u>Basil</u>'. In a few metres you'll find one of the entrances on your left.

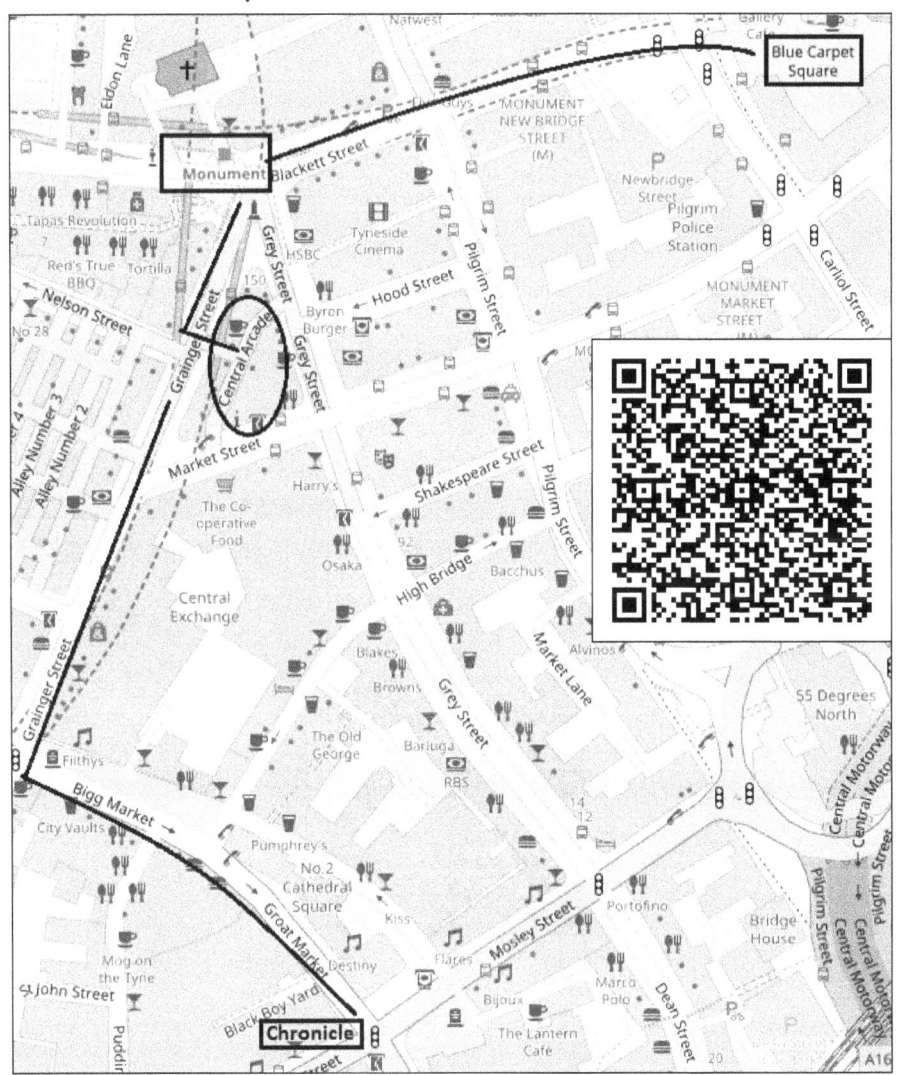

Mark Toney's

Heading back onto **Grainger Street** you will find **Mark Toney's Ice Cream Parlour**. Turn left back onto **Grainger Street** and very soon you will find Mark Toney's on the right.

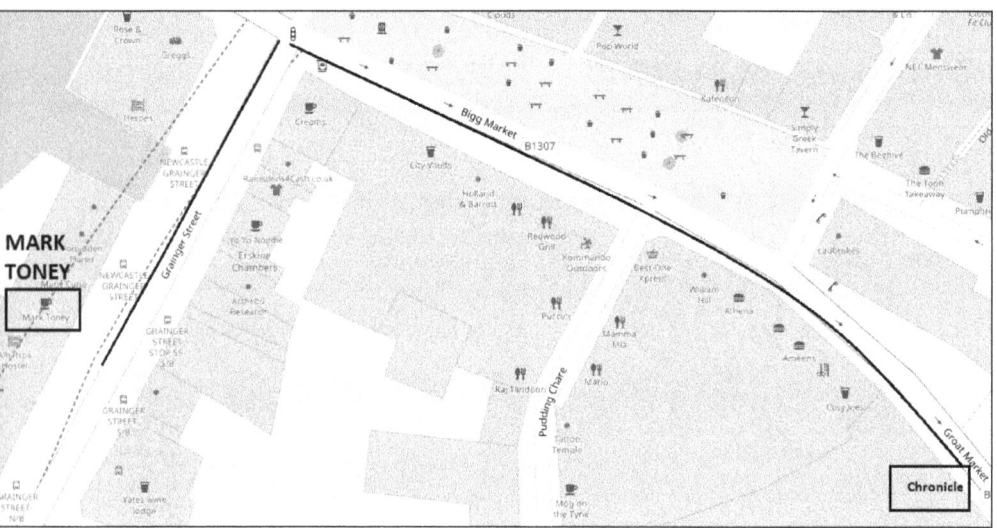

Black Church / Black Gate / Dog Leap Stairway

Walking to the very end of **Grainger Street** you will discover **St. John the Baptist Church**. Turn left and walk along **Westgate Road**, onto **Collingwood Street** you will soon come across the **Cathedral Church of St. Nicholas** which is on the right.

From the Cathedral Church of St. Nicholas walk along **St. Nicholas' Street** and you will find the **Black Gate** on the left just before the railway bridge. Walk through it and onto your next visit - **Dog Leap Stairway**.

Immediately as you pass through the Black Gate you will see a **railway bridge**. Look carefully to the left and adjacent to the bridge is the top of a flight of steps. **This is Dog Leap Stairway**. Descending these steps will help you to make our way toward the **quayside**.

QUAYSIDE

After you have made your way down **Dog Leap Stairs** start walking right, down Side until the road splits. Take the right turning, **Sandhill** and walk down to the traffic lights. Take the left turn where the road splits and you will find yourself under the **Tyne Bridge**. The **Swing Bridge** is on your right and beyond that is the spectacular **High Level Bridge**, made famous in the film 'Get Carter'. Further to your left is the **Gateshead Millennium Bridge**. Plaques have been placed along the pavement here in honour of famous Geordies and one was presented to Mark Knopfler. Why not try to find it?

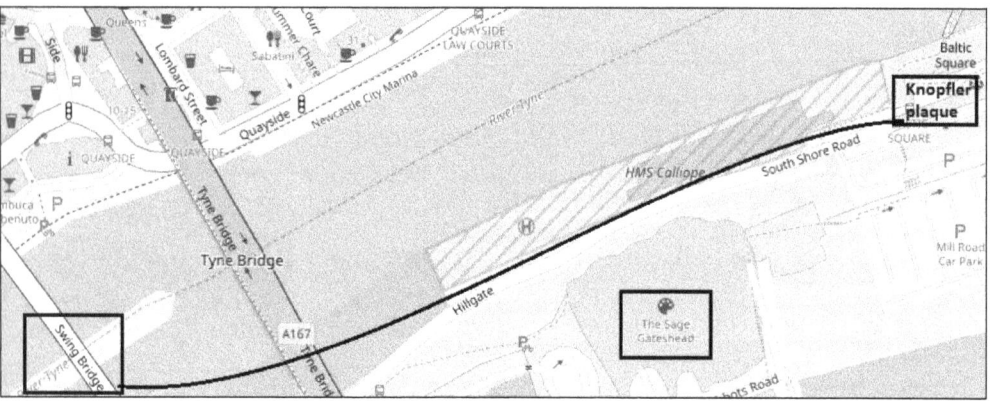

SOUTH HETTON

Next you should visit some of the locations mentioned in the song '5:15 am'. Please note that some of these are many miles away. **Pesspool Bridge** is long since gone as is one side of the street! **Fallowfield Terrace**, a part of **Front Street**, is where the Mark X Jaguar was found with Sibbet's body inside it. The railway ran up the side road beside where number 31 stands today. At the time there was a similar terrace opposite but this has since been demolished.

To get there from **Newcastle City Centre** you must catch the bus from **Eldon Square Bus Station** to **Houghton-le-Spring**, then change there onto another bus to **South Hetton**, getting off at **Grey Horse Convenience store**. It is a one-minute walk from here in the direction the bus is heading.

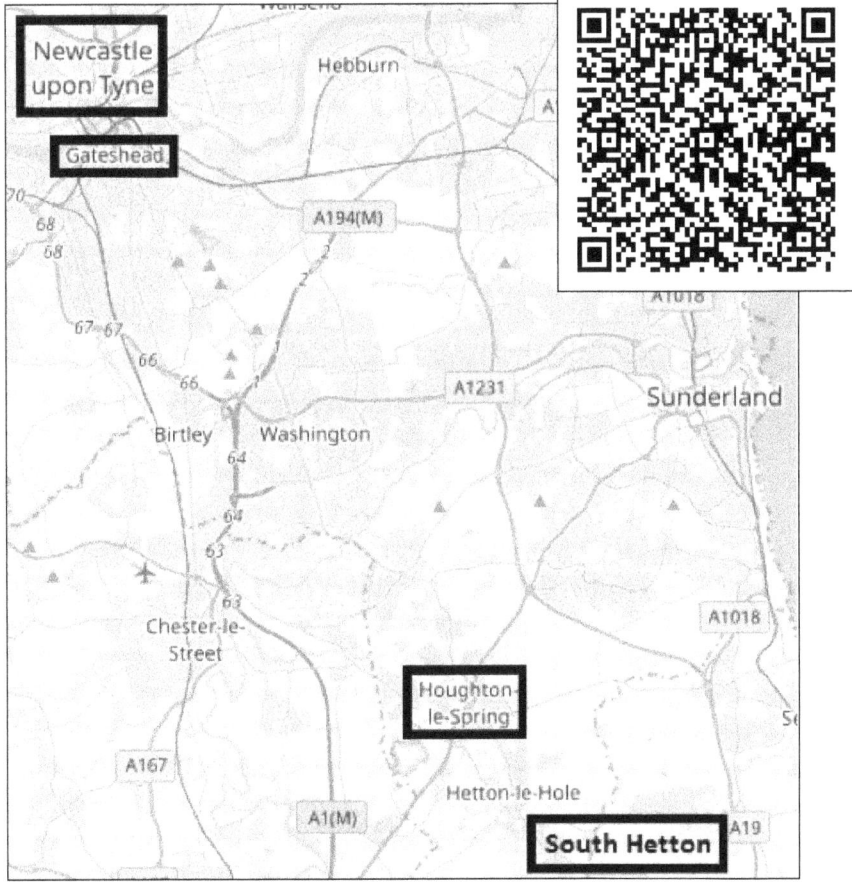

NEXT PAGE

SOUTH HETTON (CONT.)

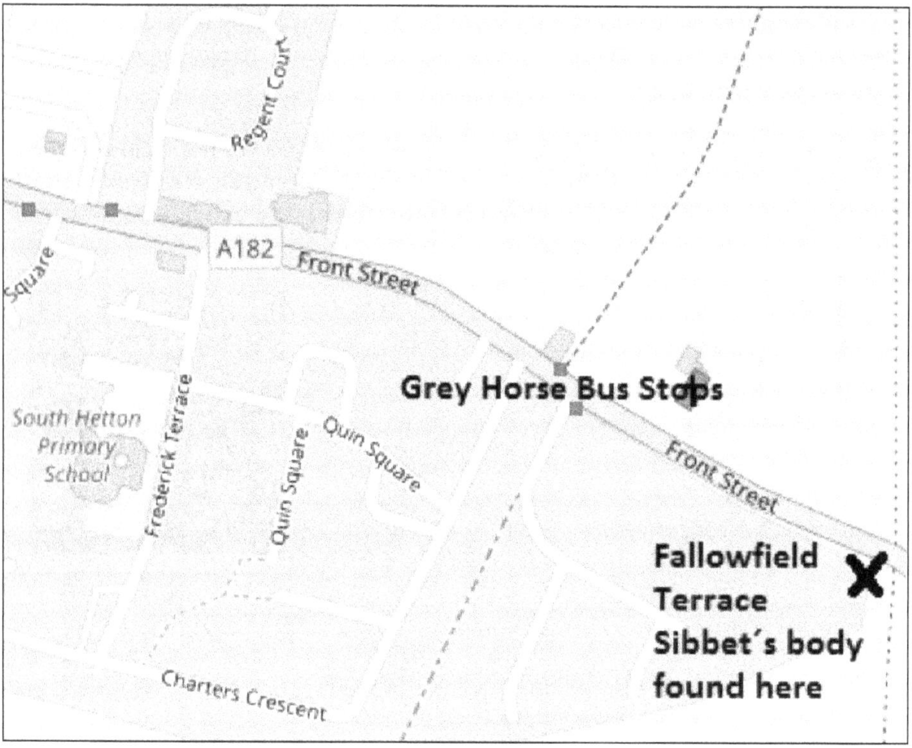

LA DOLCE VITA

Next, **back to Newcastle**, you will visit the location of **La Dolce Vita Nightclub**. These clubs were hugely popular in the 1960s around the time of the murder and attracted big names. It went into decline in the 1970s, finally closing in 2002. The location of the nightclub was originally **36-42 Low Friar Street**, which is in Newcastle City Centre. It is now a tall modern building.

From **St. John the Baptist Church** on the corner of **Grainger Street** walk along **Westgate Road** and take the second on the right, **Clayton Street West**. Next take the first left onto **Fenkle Street** and **Low Friar Street** will be the first on the right.

BIRDCAGE

From **Low Friar Street** it is not far to the location of another of the nightclubs involved in the story of the "One-Armed Bandit Murder." **The Birdcage Casino** opened in 1966, one year before the murder and is only a short distance away on **Stowell Street** in the city's **Chinatown**.

Continue up **Low Friar Street** to **Dispensary Lane** and walk along here, continuing along the footpath. This brings you out at **Stowell Street**. Turn right and walk along to find Nos. 20-22 which are on your left. This was the location of The Birdcage, later Stage Door Nightclub.

METRO RADIO ARENA

This route is especially recommended if the reason you are in Newcastle is to attend a Mark Knopfler concert at the **Metro Radio Arena**, as heading right by the **Quayside**, you will see a narrow street on your right, called **Shot Factory Lane**. That takes you to where the Metro Radio Arena is - a walk of about fifteen minutes. Once the concert is over, there's a nice route back to the city as the lights in the bridges make a very beautiful view and a pleasant walk too.

WHITLEY BAY

You can now go outwith the city limits once more and take a trip to the seaside and visit the locations associated with the famous Dire Straits song 'Tunnel of Love'. First head back to **Monument Metro Station** and take the yellow line to the coast.

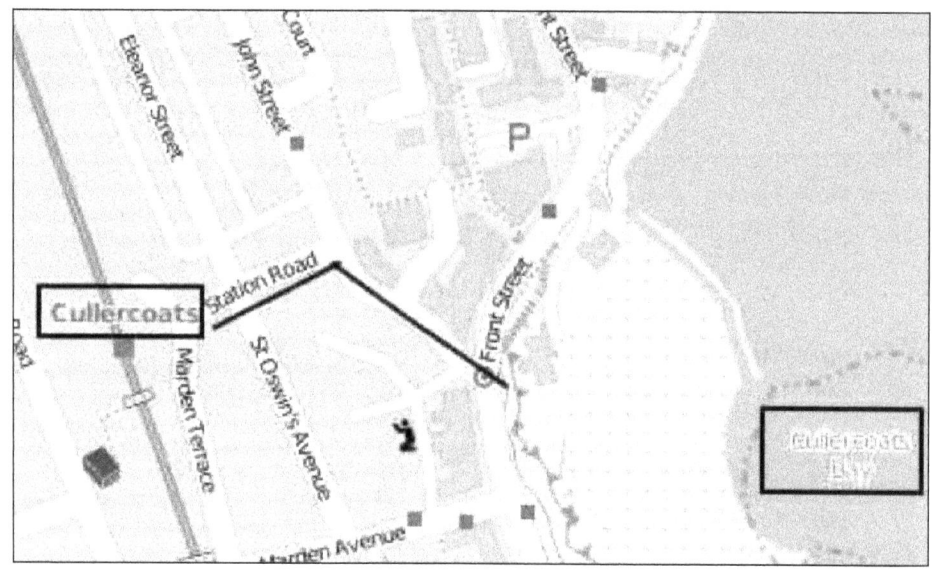

WHITLEY BAY (CONT.)

You will be using the Metro twice, visiting two bays mentioned in the 'Tunnel Of Love 'lyrics. The second stop is more important, as it is where the Spanish City amusement park used to be. The first stop will be at Cullercoats, twelve stops from Monument. Going out of the station go straight along Station Road, turning right at the second street, John Street, from which you can see Cullercoats bay.

Go back to the Cullercoats Metro station and continue to the next stop, Whitley Bay.

When you arrive at Whitley Bay, exit and walk straight along Station Road. After the intersection it turns into Esplanade Street. Continue walking until you arrive at the shore, walk along the Promenade, turning left until you arrive at the White Dome, the place where the Spanish City amusement park once stood.

3 LEEDS

In 1967, Knopfler left Newcastle to study journalism at **Harlow Technical College**. After finishing his studies he moved to Leeds with his girlfriend **Kathy White** to start work at the **Yorkshire Evening Post**; she was about to start teacher training in Leeds.

During these years working at the Yorkshire Evening Post, Mark developed his ability to create stories that would be of great help later in his career, writing the lyrics for his songs, as he has mentioned in many interviews. During his time at the newspaper, he reported on trials at the **Law Courts** which were held at the **Town Hall** in those days and also wrote about artists and musical events including **Jimi Hendrix, Pink Floyd, Johnny Winter, Yes, Humble Pie, John Mayall, Deep Purple, Leonard Cohen, The Doors** and a certain… **Steve Phillips**.

SITE OF THE BUILDING FORMERLY THE YORKSHIRE EVENING POST OFFICES

When covering one particular concert, at a pub called **The Peel**, he met **Steve Phillips**, a blues musician well-known in the local music scene and the two quickly established a relationship, playing gigs under the name **'Duolian String Pickers'**, derived from a guitar technique called 'fingerpicking' consisting of plucking the strings directly with the fingers, a technique which was very popular with some blues musicians, and also the brand of a resonator guitar, 'National Duolian' that they used in those days.

The pub, which changed its name to The Peel Hotel in 1976, used to house the longest bar in Leeds. It was known as "The Square" for many years before 2011, when it closed its doors and the building was sold. Nowadays (2016) it is a Sainsbury's Supermarket.

LEEDS TOWN HALL. THE LAW COURTS WERE HELD HERE WHEN KNOPFLER WORKED FOR THE NEWSPAPER

FORMER LOCATION OF THE PEEL, NOWADAYS A SAINSBURY'S SUPERMARKET

THE PEEL AS IT USED TO BE WHEN KNOPFLER PLAYED THERE. PICTURE: CLIFFORD STEAD

Steve Phillips was not only a brilliant guitar player but was also very skilled at building and repairing the instrument. Through the years, many of Knopfler's guitars would pass through his hands for various adjustments and painting. He also sold to Mark, what would be the most iconic guitar of Dire Straits' history, the **National Style O**, which would eventually be on the cover of the most famous Dire Straits album, 'Brothers In Arms'. Its metallic sound can be heard in some of the band's songs such as 'Wild West End', 'Portobello Belle', 'Romeo And Juliet', 'The Man's Too Strong' amongst others, and also in many songs of his solo career.

Mark and Steve played under the name **'Duolian String Pickers'** in many pubs including **The Peel**, **The Pack Horse** and **The Grove** where another local musician, **Brendan Croker**, often used to play in those days and with whom they would become friends.

THE PACK HORSE

Mark Knopfler playing the National Style O in Barcelona, 31st July 2015.
Picture: Julio Bricio

It was in **The Grove**, very close to the Leeds/Liverpool canal, in 1986, many years after those first musical steps, that the seed for The Notting Hillbillies was sown.

In 1986, after the very long '<u>Brothers in Arms</u>' Dire Straits tour, Mark was exhausted and decided to take some time away from songs, concerts and guitars. Steve then invited him to play, together with Brendan Croker, at The Grove in Leeds without any other reason than for pleasure. Mark accepted the invitation and he enjoyed the experience so much that over the years they played many more informal gigs of this kind. In 1990 Mark agreed to produce a record that Steve Phillips and Brendan Croker wanted to make together and after those years "having fun" playing blues, country and folk songs, the project developed until it became 'The Notting Hillbillies'. The album 'Missing... Presumed Having A Good Time' was released that year, followed by a small tour throughout the United Kingdom. The band continued playing in diverse charity concerts and small tours around the country, including two residencies at Ronnie Scott's in London and Birmingham in 1998 and 1999. In 2002 they performed their last concerts under the title 'Mark Knopfler And Friends', in which they played the first half of the show, followed, in the second half, by a small reunion of some of the Dire Straits members.

LEEDS / LIVERPOOL CANAL

The Grove Inn. Picture: David Gray

Inside The Grove -- The concert room

The City Varieties theatre, an 1865 Grade II listed building of special architectural and historic importance and a largely unaltered original interior, is one of the places Mark used to visit when writing reviews of some of the shows. During one of these, he interviewed '**The Ugly Sisters**', and he was so touched by them that he felt inspired to write some lines for a song that would take many years to be finished. That song, 'One More Matinee', which captures part of that conversation, was released on his second solo album, 'Sailing to Philadelphia' in the year 2000.

Between 1953 and 1983, this Victorian theatre achieved national fame as the venue for the BBC television programme 'The Good Old Days'. It is a rare surviving example of that era's music halls, the interior of which is a long rectangle, with boxes separated by cast-iron columns that can be seen in the 'Sailing to Philadelphia' video press kit, as Mark Knopfler and Steve Phillips are interviewed inside the hall.

In that same documentary, Mark Knopfler, Steve Phillips and Brendan Croker reminisce in another pub, **The Fforde Grene**, where they played together during the Dire Straits hiatus period. The Fforde Grene, which was located in the Harehills area of East Leeds, is now closed, but can be seen as it previously was in the aforementioned documentary about 'Sailing to Philadelphia'. One anecdote Mark mentions in that interview is that **Prefab Sprout** opened for them that day! Other famous bands that played there included **The Sex Pistols, U2, Simple Minds, The Rolling Stones** and even **Dire Straits** in 1978.

THE FFORDE GRENE IN 2005. PICTURE: ANDREA RASON

The Polytechnic is another venue where Mark played and also wrote his reports. On one of those occasions he attended a show by the band **Brewers Droop**, whom he had contacted several times previously, hoping for the opportunity to play with them. Some time after this meeting he had an audition for a bassist vacancy but they were so impressed by his guitar skills that they changed their minds and invited him to join the band as a guitarist. He remained with them for some months, touring and even recording some songs with them which wouldn't see the light of day until 1989.

Years later Dire Straits also played at the Poly during their first tour, supporting the American band Talking Heads.

Leeds Beckett University, formerly Leeds Polytechnic

Ron Watts (Brewers Droop): *"Mark Knopfler first came to my attention during the early days of the NBF (National Blues Federation). He was from the north-east and would write us letters, 'phone and send demo tapes. These were certainly good quality and I wish I'd kept them. The next time I saw Mark was when we played at Leeds and he came along to meet the band as he was a student at the university there. Mark was a nice lad and a great guitarist, but I'd forgotten all about him until Derrick left the band midway through recording our second album and I advertised in the Melody Maker for a new bassist. We'd arranged auditions for a day at the Nag's Head, and had about thirty applicants lined up. Mark was there, and when I pointed out it was a bass player we wanted he said "No problem. Stick your guitarist on bass and I'll do the lead". By now his playing was light years away from the tapes he'd sent the NBF so we hired Mark on the spot and brought in Steve Norchi to play bass".*[1]

During his time with Brewers Droop he played gigs with them all over the country. One of those concerts left him a memory which was put into a song many years later, in what would be his 2018 album 'Down The Road Wherever', entitled 'Matchstick Man'.

The story was mentioned in an interview with David Hepworth for Q Magazine, included in Myles Palmer's unauthorised biography released in 1993 and also during Knopfler's record 'Tracker' promotion when talking about the song 'River Towns'. In the press notes for 'Down The Road Wherever' Mark Knopfler said the following about the song:

[1] Hundred Watts: A Life In Music, Ron Watts. Edited by Heroes Publishing.

> **BREWERS DROOP**
> ARE PLEASED TO WELCOME TWO NEW MEMBERS
> **MARK KNOPFLER**
> AND
> **STEVE NORCHI**
> Come and see them with John, Ron, Steve and Bob at
> Cleopatra's, Derby, Thurs., 22nd November
> Queen Mary College, London, Fri., 23rd November
> Quaintways, Chester, Mon., 26th Nov.
> Agency and Management Big Bear, 021-454 7020

Add announcing first Mark Knopfler concert with Brewers Droop

"That's me, a young idiot with a guitar and a bag, climbing up into trucks and hitchhiking. I was trying to get back from a Christmas Eve gig in Penzance early on Christmas Day. I thought I'd hitch home. I don't think I really knew it was 500 miles from there."

"I got a lift up the old A1 and he let me off at a high crossroads in the Midlands. The sun was shining, there was snow everywhere and I could see for miles. There was nothing moving anywhere. I'm standing there with my guitar case and bag and this realisation of what I'd chosen to do with my life. To me, it was exactly what I wanted to do. It's just a snapshot of me then. From the air I would have been a tiny matchstick figure in this vastness of snow with his dream of being a musician."

At the beginning of 1970, Mark played in another venue in Leeds, **The Original Oak**, where **Mick Dewhurst** was starting a band called **Silverheels** who had just recruited Knopfler to join them. He put Mark in contact with **Dave Johnson**, a well-known bass player of the local scene, to try to convince him to join the band. That meeting would lead to the recording of the first Mark Knopfler original song.

THE ORIGINAL OAK

That first demo, of a folk song called 'Summer's Coming My Way', was recorded in The Harding Studio, a small recording studio in Bramley, Leeds, where local artists recorded their demos. The band consisted of Steve Phillips playing guitar and vocals, Dave Johnson playing bass and Paul Grainger playing drums. Grainger and Johnson were also part of Silverheels with Mick Dewhurst singing and Mark Knopfler playing guitar, but for this recording Mark decided to sing the song himself instead of Mick.

There exist only five or six copies of this demo, some of which were auctioned over the years. It's a real gem for collectors because of the small number and, of course, because it is the first song Mark recorded. The cover was a plain white sleeve and the label was also white.
Dave Johnson was interviewed for BBC Leeds radio[2] in February 2016 by Johnny L'anson about that demo:

"In January or February 1970, I was in the "The Original Oak" pub one night which was something like an HQ (head quarter) for music houses in those days, and a friend of mine Mick Dewhurst walks in and says: "I'd like you to meet this guy Mark Knopfler a friend of mine. We're forming a band and we need a bass player". Knopfler said: "I've heard you are a good bass player, David, would you like to join us?". I said: "well, really I am up with the guitar, I am not bothered".

And I thought "wow, this guy is good". So in the April Mark says: "I wanna do this disc" and we went to this studio, the Harding studio, in Bramley. Mark played us this song and it was the first time we had heard it. You know, we were there in the recording studio and he plays the thing to us and we sort of picked it up from there. I sort of put a bass pattern around it; Mick Dewhurst was our singer and was singing the vocals and Mark kept stopping and said: "no, Mick, I want you to do it like this, I want you to phrase it in such and such way". And gradually he took over and Mick went into the background and that's why Mark Knopfler actually finished up doing the vocal as well as the guitar part on the record. We still did something like 20 takes. It must have been. And finally, at the end, Mr Harding said: "you've long exceeded your hour, you know, I am going to have to charge you if you keep going". So we selected the best take and used that one.

Mark always said: "we are good enough to make it. Let's take the band to London" and us all cynics we just said: "Well, come on Mark, it's the '70-ies not the '60-ies. It doesn't happen like that anymore. You don't just go to London and make it overnight". And he went off to London. And I bumped into his first wife in '74 at a leaving do and she said rather ruefully: "Mark is down in London making it". Because of course at that time he hadn't made it. Then in 1978, this great record came up from a band called Dire Straits, Sultans of Swing. But the penny still had not drop with me until one of my work colleagues said: "this band Dire Straits, the singer and lead guitarist is a guy called Mark Knopfler. Didn't you use to play with him?". "Yeah", "Oh, wow, right". So I have been dying out ever since really."

The BBC site included a picture of the record on which can be seen all Dave's handwritten details about the recording, including the name of the song, the writer, musicians and the studio where it was recorded.

[2] Johnny L'anson interviews Dave Johnson, for BBC Leeds, February 11th 2016

Copy of demo owned by Dave Johnson,
picture by BBC Leeds.

Besides the venues already mentioned, which hosted folk and blues concerts in the 1970's music scene in Leeds, there are another two pubs in which it is likely that Mark Knopfler and Steve Phillips played, for example, The Fenton and The Eldon.

The Fenton

The Eldon

In **Woodhouse Lane** pedestrian subway there was a reference to one of the Dire Straits songs, written when Mark was living in London, but based in Leeds. 'In The Gallery' tells us about Leeds-based artist, **Harry Phillips**, father of Steve. Some of Harry Phillips' sculptures can be found at St George´s Church, Letchworth, Hertfordshire.

The reference to 'In The Gallery' was in the following panel, now removed by vandals.

THANKS TO ADRIAN RILEY, FROM ELECTRIC ANGEL DESIGN LLP.

The 'In The Gallery' panel was part of a project called **Leeds Song Tunnel**. According to their website:

"The artwork commissioned by Leeds City Council is part of the (Leeds First Direct) Arena project. The artwork is to provide visitors to the Arena with a sense of fun and anticipation as they walk through the subway to the Arena. Many of the song titles relate to the experience of attending a music event at the Arena. The desire was to represent Leeds popular music scene. The Song Tunnel idea and artwork was created by Adrian Riley."

LEEDS ARENA, MARK KNOPFLER PLAYED THERE ON MAY 18TH 2019 FOR THE FIRST TIME. PICTURES: DAVID GRAY

Mark and Kathy got married in 1972 when Mark was in his second year at university, studying for an English degree after leaving his job at the newspaper. Because of their economic situation, Mark started travelling to Kathy's family farm in **Dinnington** to work during the holidays, as mentioned in the chapter about Newcastle, consequently spending long periods apart from Kathy.

Mark Knopfler[3]: *"I married my sweetheart from high school when I was at university. When I left school I did one year's journalism training and two years on the paper, that's three years, then three years in university. So I was 23 when I got married. When I left university, I got a job in a professional band down here in London. I passed my first audition and played for a couple of months, then the band went bust. I didn't have a job, couldn't survive playing rock 'n' roll. So I went back home. She was a farmer's daughter from up there. Part of my surviving was just working on the farm for a bit. I'd done a lot of farm work, I used to work on the harvest there. The teaching happened after that period. I actually enjoyed the farm work. It toughened me up a lot. I've always done manual work, since I was a kid. Worked on building sites and in warehouses. Being unemployed when you want to work is the worst feeling in the world."*

The marriage didn't last for long[4] and in 1973, after finishing his English degree, Mark left Leeds to work in London as a teacher and to keep following his musical dreams, carrying with him experiences that would be reflected in songs that would be recorded five years later with Dire Straits such as 'Water Of Love', 'Setting Me Up' or 'Six Blade Knife', but that's another chapter… and another city.

[3] Q Magazine, 1991, https://web.archive.org/web/20010222155952fw_/http://www.knopfler.net/interview10.html

[4] Daily Mail, 1st March 1997

Leeds University

LEEDS MAPS

On arrival at Leeds by train, exit the station at the main exit / entrance. The route begins at the railway station which can also be used as a reference point when attending a Mark Knopfler concert, for instance.

The Peel former building & The Yorkshire Evening Post former building

After exiting the station from the main concourse, cross by the traffic lights and continue right along **New Station Street** to the junction with **Boar Lane**. At **Boar Lane**, cross the road and on the right at **number 63**, on the corner of **Bank Street** is the building where **The Peel** was located when Mark lived in Leeds, where he met Steve Phillips and where they played together. It is now a Sainsbury's Local.

Retracing your steps, turn right at **Albion Street**. At the junction of Albion Street and **Bond Street** is the building where the Yorkshire Evening Post was located when Mark worked there as a journalist. A more popular route, however, would be to exit the **station** at the main concourse and immediately turn left, crossing at the traffic lights to **Boar Lane**. After a short walk along Boar Lane, Sainsbury's Local (the original site of The Peel) will be found on the left.

MAP in **NEXT** page

Comes from **previous** page

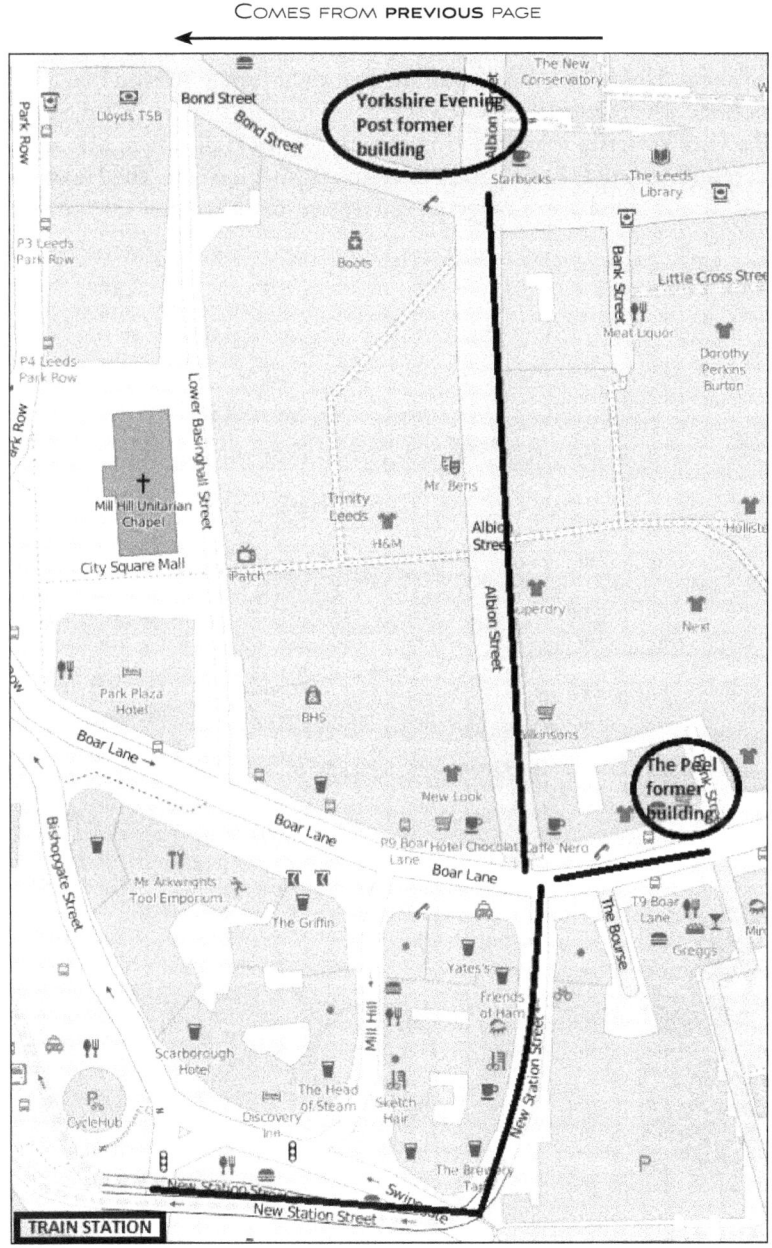

THE CITY VARIETIES & TOWN HALL

Continue along **Albion Street** and take the first right turn at **Albion Place**. Turn left at **Lands Lane** where, near the end on the right, is a small street called **Swan Street** where **The City Varieties** is located. To get to the **Town Hall**, where MK reported on trials etc, return to **Lands Lane** and proceed to the junction with **The Headrow**. Turn left at The Headrow and The Town Hall can be seen on the right.

Polytechnic (Beckett University)

Take the street at the right side of the Town Hall, **Calverley Street**, and turn down the third street on the right, **Portland Way**. Continue along to **Woodhouse Lane**, where **Leeds Beckett University** can be seen, and from where the route will continue.

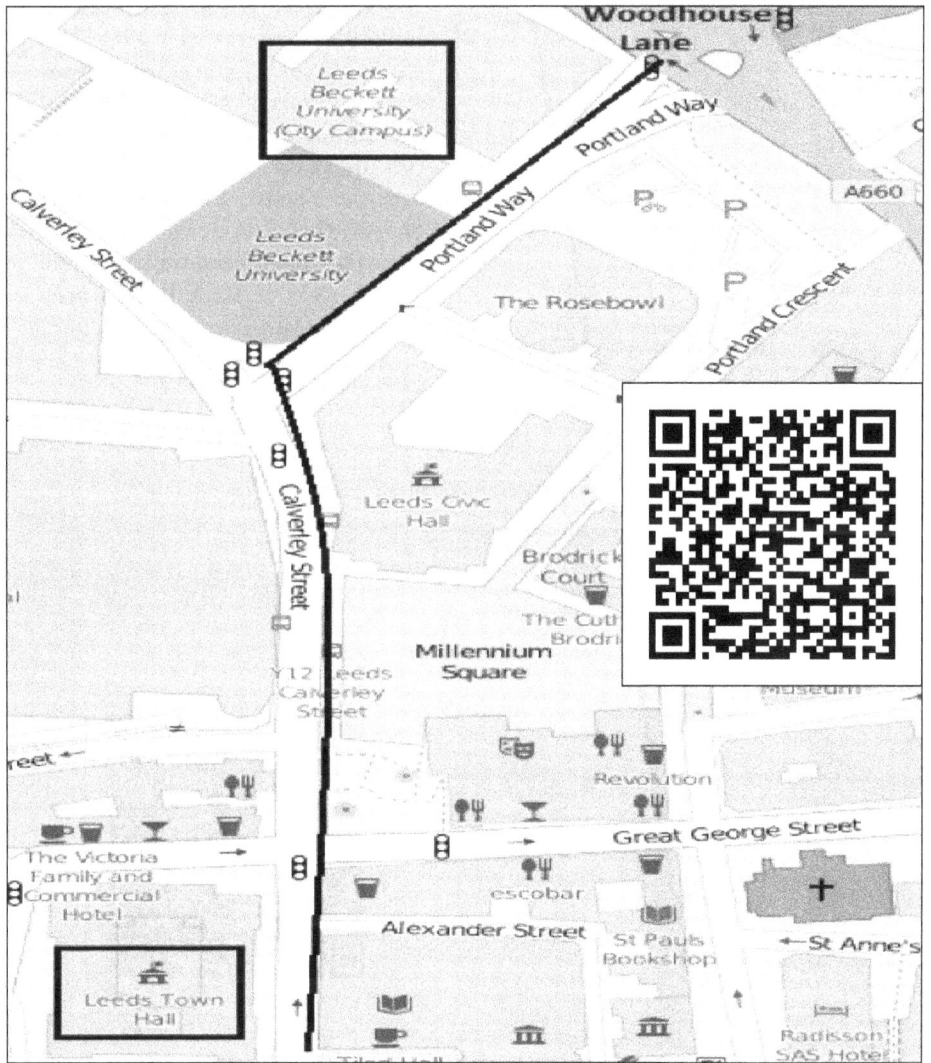

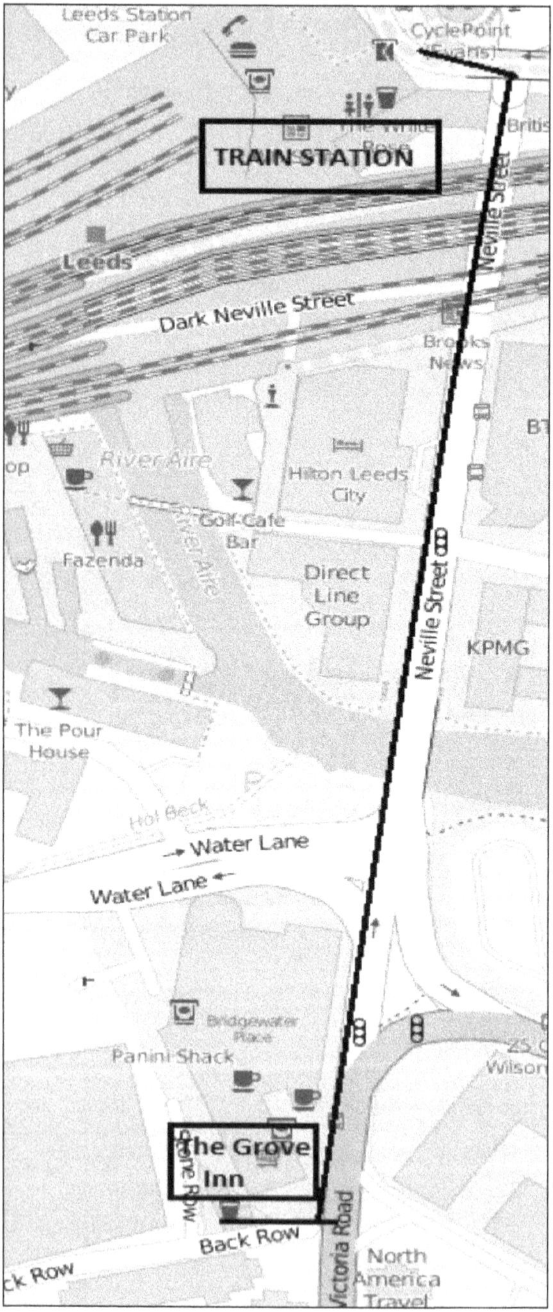

The Grove Inn

This is probably the most important place in the city relating to Mark's musical life in Leeds, as he not only played here, alone and with the Duolian String Pickers but this was also the place where The Notting Hillbillies were created in 1986. The starting point is again at the **railway station**. Walk along **New Station Street**, under the tunnel towards **Neville Street**, and cross the bridge over the **Leeds / Liverpool** canal. Shortly, the street name changes to **Victoria Road**. Keep walking until on the right is **Back Row**, where **The Grove Inn** is located.

The Fenton, Leeds University, The Eldon and The Pack Horse

Continuing along **Woodhouse Lane** you'll find **The Fenton** and **The Eldon** pubs, where it is very likely that Mark played during his years in Leeds. **Leeds University**, where Mark studied for his degree, is also on **Woodhouse Lane**. **The Pack Horse**, where the Duolian String Pickers played is across the road from the university.

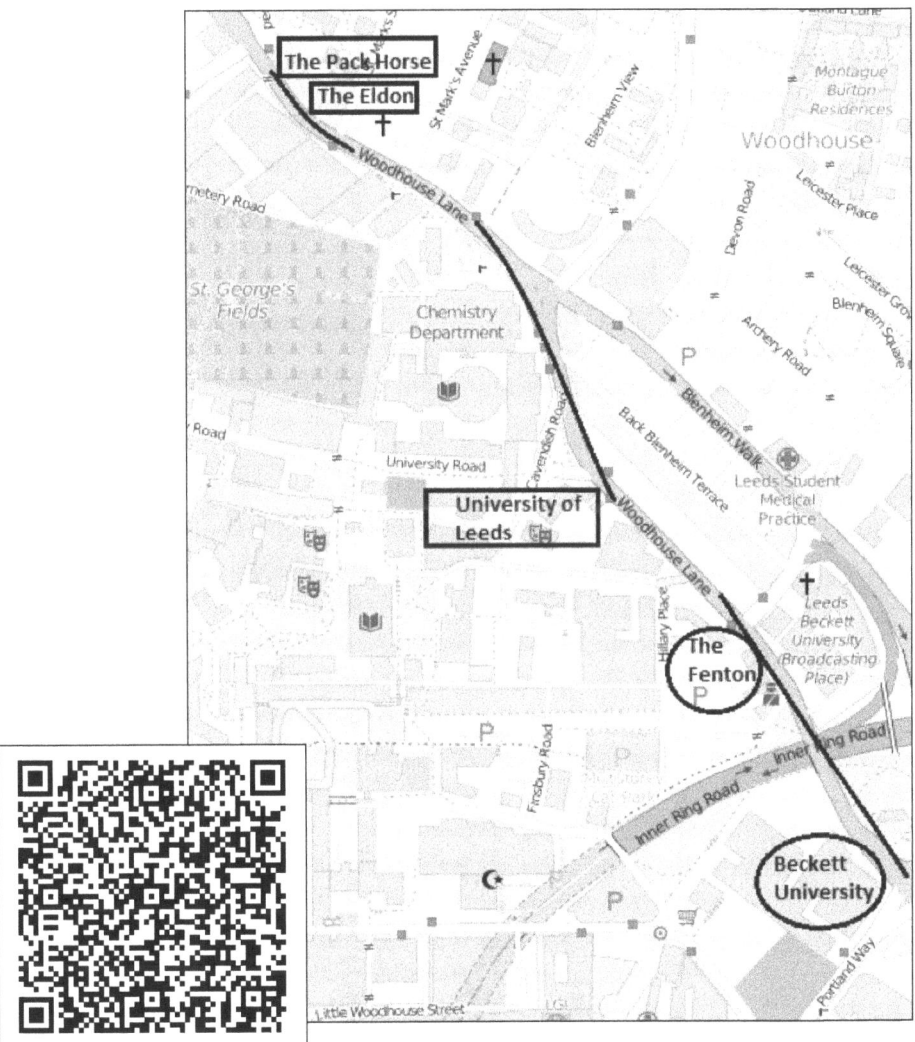

The Original Oak

From the **Pack Horse**, **The Original Oak** is a 25-minute walk along **Woodhouse Lane**, which changes its name to **Headingley Lane** after a short distance. It's possible to take the **bus, numbers 1, 6, 28, 97** and **x84** to the **Headingley Lane / Bainbrigge Road** stop and then walk about 2 minutes to the pub.

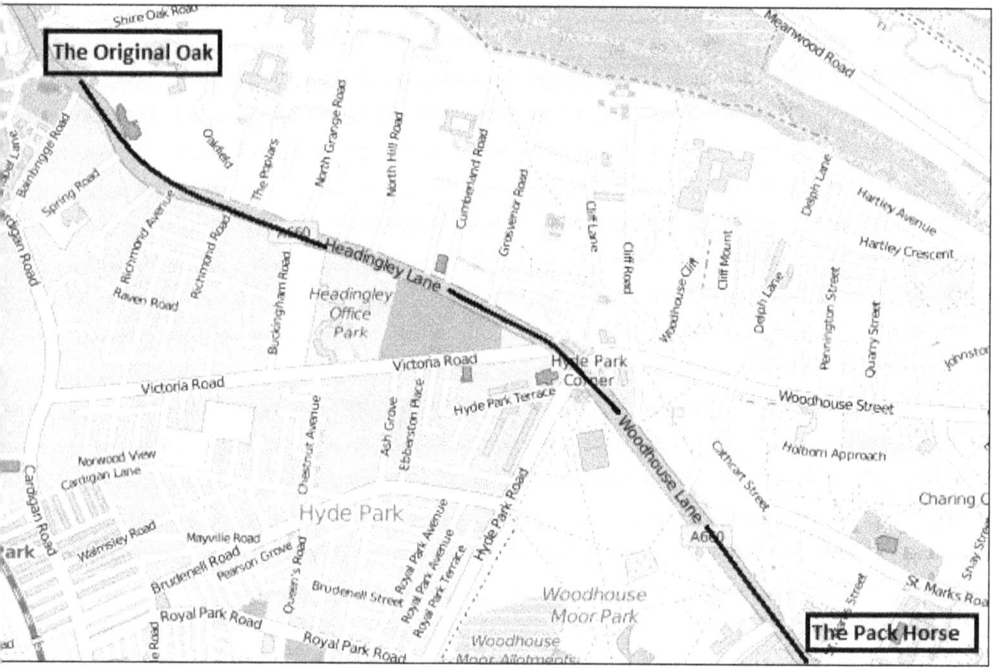

In The Gallery Panel

The subway links the adjacent **Woodhouse Lane Car Park** to the **Arena**, as well as the **City Centre**.

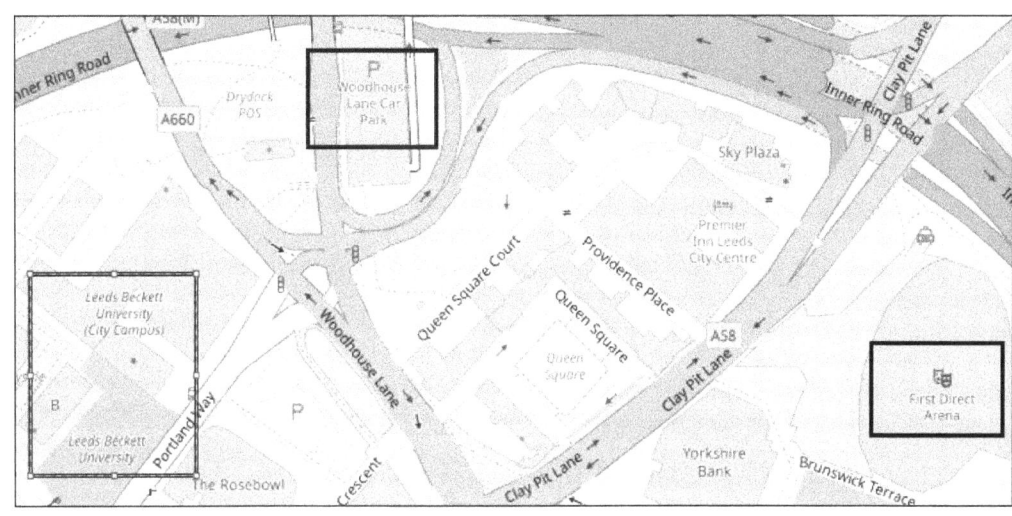

101

4
DEPTFORD & GREENWICH

In 1973, after graduating in English from Leeds University, Mark Knopfler decided to go to London in pursuit of his musical dreams. In the meantime, he took a job as a lecturer at **Loughton College** in Essex, whilst living in a rented flat in **Buckhurst Hill**.

It's during this time that he met **Dave Pask** and started playing with the **The Café Racers**. Also during this period, his younger brother **David** was living in London, and ended up sharing a flat with **John Illsley** in **Deptford, Lewisham**, on the South Bank of the River Thames.

The Knopfler brothers used to visit each other and it's in one of those visits that Mark met John. The brothers used to spend most of their time playing and working on songs and John joined them playing bass. In April 1977 Mark left his flat in Buckhurst Hill and moved in with them.

Announcement of a rock & folk concert listing "The Knopfler Bros" from 1975. Picture shared by Paul Smith, member of Antrobus, in Twitter. David Knopfler said about this gig in Facebook that they (Mark and him alone) probably played an acoustic set of songs: - "I think it was probably a four or five song set in the afternoon and from best recollection we did covers - probably "If I needed you", "Tattler", "Log cabin home in the sky", "Roll in my sweet baby's arms" -

John Illsley: *"I was looking for a flatmate as the rent was too much for me and I was a student at University in London. A friend knew David and we met, got on and he moved in. Mark used to come down to visit David and very quickly he and I became good mates, used to hang out a lot, play the guitar together and shared the same love of certain types of music."*

Deptford is very near to **Greenwich**, and living in the area inspired some of the songs that gave them success including 'Sultans Of Swing', which was originally written with an acoustic approach on Mark's National Steel guitar, about a band playing in a pub that the Knopfler brothers used to frequent at that time.

The lyrics describe the peculiar situation of a jazz band playing all kinds of songs to people who cared very little about the music. They called themselves the **Sultans of Swing**. According to a letter that a BBC production team sent in 2010 to the local newspaper Crosswhatfields[1] asking for some information about the place and the band, the pub was probably the **White Swan**, at **13 Blackheath Road**. That pub turned into a hotel years later and nowadays is closed, but in the building there are still signs of the hotel with a swan.

"White Swan Hotel" pictures by Jordi Benítez, David Barragués, Jordi Morilla and Jesús de la Torre

David Knopfler, about the place they saw the Sultans Of Swing mentions: *"It was my local pub in Greenwich when I was a social worker in Greenwich before I moved in with John in Deptford. It could perhaps have been The White Swan - sounds right - but it wasn't on Blackheath Road. I was renting in a house share in* **Ashburnham Road** *at the time and the pub was on* **Greenwich South Street** *- the busy main road it T-junctioned out of. The band was a trad swing band... calling themselves the "Sultans of Swing." We watched them for all of two songs before moving to the back room to play pool."*

There was a White Swan pub in Greenwich around that area in 85-87 Greenwich Road that unfortunately has been demolished; this is how it looked when it was still there, but already closed. (Next page)

[1] http://crossfields.blogspot.com.es/2010/07/dire-straits-documentary-photos-and-ear.html

It's also mentioned in the Dire Straits biography written by Michael Oldfield that the pub where they listened to the Sultans Of Swing was located at **Greenwich High Road** and was probably called The Swan or something similar. It's more likely that it was that one, and not the one located in Blackheath Road, especially because it's also mentioned in the book that the Knopfler brothers didn't know John Illsley at the time they saw the Sultans Of Swing at the pub, so they weren't living in Farrer House in Deptford yet.

Picture courtesy by "The Lost Pubs Project'" website

Deptford is connected to central London by train. London Bridge to the then terminus Deptford was the capital's first and oldest railway. Early on, it was extended from Deptford station across the fields as they were then, and those in Glenda Bogdanovs's photo (check page 106) are the original arches in use to this day. The main station to get to their flat, in a tenement building called **Farrer House**, is **New Cross**, actually it lies halfway thereabouts between Greenwich Station and Deptford Station in Deptford High Street, but New Cross is the station mentioned in a Dire Straits song that would be the first one to be released in a record, 'Eastbound Train' which talks about a woman that attracts the attention of the main character (probably Mark) during one of those journeys. The lyrics describe the stations and change of lines from Deptford to Buckhurst Hill so it's very likely that it was written after one of Mark's visits to David at Farrer House. That record was a compilation album called 'Front Row Festival' which was recorded live at the Hope and Anchor pub in Islington in winter 1977 and released in March 1978.

DEPTFORD

NEW CROSS STATION

MAPS OF TENEMENT BUILDINGS IN CROSSFIELD ESTATE, FARRER HOUSE IS NUMBER 5.
PICTURES: ÒSCAR PALLARÈS AND FRANCISCO JAVIER MATAS

Mark was still playing with The Café Racers from time to time, John Illsley and David Knopfler got to play with them in some concerts, but Mark wasn't happy with the band as they used to play mainly rock and roll covers and not any original material. The trio needed a drummer to complete the band, and Mark called up **David 'Pick' Withers**, who played for the Brewers Droop band. However, that wasn't how Mark and Pick met, as they didn't play in the band at the same period of time. They were introduced by a mutual friend who loaned Mark a tape recorder. Pick was playing drums and he left a good impression on Mark, who later called him to join the trio. Now a band of four, they started to rehearse together in their flat to prepare for what would be their first concert together...

PICTURE OF THE VERY FIRST CONCERT OF DIRE STRAITS AT THE FARRER HOUSE GARDENS, COURTESY OF GLENDA BOGDANOVS

This first concert was in a music festival that took place at the garden just next to their flat at Farrer House. In all Dire Straits tour dates it is noted that they played that concert under the name of Mark´s previous band, The Café Racers, but according to **Colin Bodiam**, who designed posters for some of the band concerts in Deptford during those years, they played as Dire Straits. David wore a T-shirt with the Café Racers logo so that must be why it was believed they played under that name.

In **David Knopfler**'s words: *"I was indeed wearing a Racers T-shirt. Pick proposed 'Dire Straits' as our name on the day of the concert which was on the grass outside Farrer House. We needed a name in a hurry for our first show – and it stuck."*

According to Michael Oldfield's book, their slot lasted around thirty minutes, during which they played 'Sultans Of Swing', 'Down To The Waterline', 'Southbound Again', 'In The Gallery', 'Wild West End', Brenda Lee's 'Sweet Nothin's' and some Ry Cooder songs.

David Knopfler mentions that a couple of his own songs might had been played by the band that day too: *"I don't recall exactly – But it would have been most of the songs that appeared on the first DS album plus a couple of songs of mine, 'Southside Tenements' and 'Sacred Loving'. We tended to do Chuck Berry's 'Nadine' as an encore song. I do recall doing 'Sweet Nothin's' but not so sure about Ry Cooder… possible we did one Cooder song … I used to sing 'The Tatler' with Mark as an acoustic duo – so it's possible we carried it over to the Straits first set but I couldn't swear to it. The electricity came from our flat – where we rehearsed and where I suspect the meter may have been doctored. The concert was well attended, had a wide variety of local bands performing, including several very punky ones and as far as I remember we performed reasonably well for a first outing."*

The audience didn't pay much attention to these unknown bands, so different to the others of the period. The festival ended with a local band that was already successful - **Squeeze**.

According to all official tour diaries, the concert took place on 9th July 1977, but in Squeeze tour dates of that period the date for that music festival features as **June 26th**, as the flyer, *courtesy of David from packetofthree.com* in the previous page mentions.

Again, according to Colin Bodiam, the Crossfield Estate Festival always happened on Sunday, so June 26th 1977 must be the exact date of that first concert.

Colin Bodiam: *"With a multitude of punk bands, they went on like an oasis of relative calm amidst all the chaos, around 4pm in the afternoon, Squeeze topped the bill around 10pm with lighting supplied by bikers from their machines."*

However, the most important fact is that the first gig that Dire Straits played, was in the back garden of their flat in Farrer House tenements building, and to mark that very special moment, in December 2009 a black commemorative plaque was attached by the PRS for Music, a society that takes care of musical heritage in the United Kingdom.

Actually, the place where the plaque can be seen wasn't the exact place of their first concert ever. The plaque is attached just next to the door of the apartment where they used to live, but the concert took place at the gardens at the back of the entrance door, from where you can see the 'Love Over Gold' wall.
Just in front of the wall with the Farrer House plaque is the 'Love Over Gold' wall.

Picture of the unveiling of the plaque, courtesy of Colin Bodiam, pictured between Mark Knopfler and John Illsley

It is said that there was a mural with that phrase which was the inspiration for Mark Knopfler to write the song, as he explained in a short interview filmed in this very same garden for the documentary to promote his second solo album 'Sailing To Philadelphia'.

This mural by **Gary Drostle**, was painted with the help of children of the area, with whom Mark Knopfler was involved.
When the painting was finished, a commemorative plaque was attached, with

PICTURE OF THE GARDEN WHERE THEIR FIRST CONCERT TOOK PLACE

a reference to Dire Straits, and the painting that inspired their song, and that also inspired the artist to paint the wall as we know it today. However, this plaque was stolen repeatedly and eventually it wasn't replaced, so when you visit the wall, you won't find the plaque. However, you can see how that plaque was in the picture taken in 2001 in the next page.

David Knopfler's song 'Southside Tenements', previously mentioned, also made reference to the love over gold writing in the wall: (*Some spray-can words 'bout love an' gold - remember them?*) and also about the arches of the bridge just next to the love over gold mural (*Take the shortcut home / Past the arches / by the railway / Where an' old friend swears that he could save me*).

Those arches appear as well in a Mark Knopfler song titled 'One Song At A Time' from his album 'Down The Road Wherever', which coincidentally is a line in the song, which talks about Mark's memories of his Deptford days from the point of view of his

Picture: Rafael Montero Sastre

managing to succeed in his musical career and leaving Deptford. In fact the year 1979 is mentioned in the song, which is the year when he bought a house for himself in London and left Farrer House where the band shared a flat, according to Mark in the BBC Arena documentary.

The song is divided between his own memories of Deptford and historical references to the area, mentioning the year 1979 in the first chorus and talking about the archways, the creek, the back lanes and the river boats from his days living there, and then in the next chorus referring to the year 1879 with historical references to the Deptford Dockyards, the slaving ports, Bristol and Liverpool ships, the execution dock and the hanging of mutineers.

On the way from New Cross Station to Farrer House, in Crossfield Estate, there is a

theatre called **The Albany**. It is the venue where Dire Straits played, according to all the official tour dates, their first concert under that name, on 28th July 1977, opening for **Squeeze**. The Albany suffered a fire in 1978 and it had to be demolished and rebuilt, being opened by Princess Diana in 1982.

Asked about the repertoire during those early gigs, David Knopfler answers: *"Mark and I had been working for a while on material in his bedsit in Loughton [NOTE: before they moved to Deptford], where I was squatting on his floor for a month or so until I found my first place to stay in SE London where I'd found a job as a social worker. Those became the bulk of the songs that appeared on the first DS album. ( ) We had 'Sacred Loving' and 'Southside Tenements' in the set, as I mentioned, which were credited solely to me - then there was a recognised co-write called 'What's the Matter Babe' but that wasn't written until some months later ( ) I loved working with Mark and he clearly had an exceptional gift for the guitar*

Picture: Òscar Pallarès

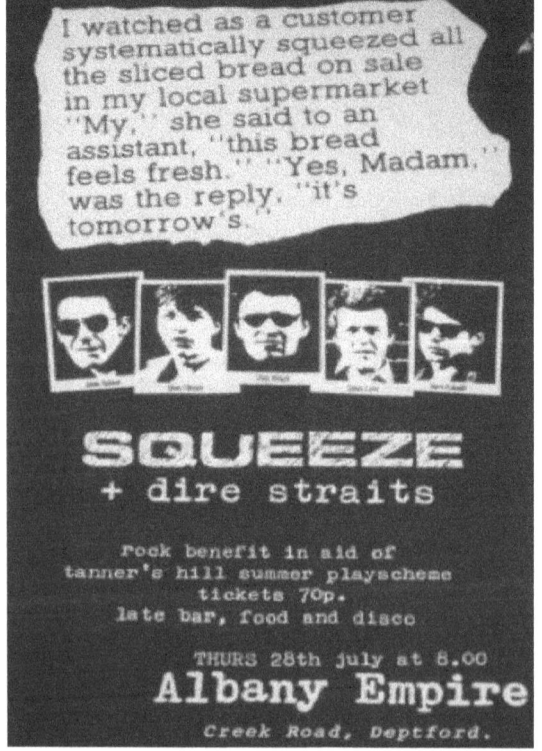

Poster courtesy of David from packetofthree.com designed and printed by Colin Bodiam.

without which none of us would have been likely to have found a record deal or commercial success ( ) though we were all in our own ways very focused on the same goals and on our band identity. As with so many bands there was a certain synergy and the whole was greater than the parts. ( ) <u>Southside Tenements</u>... I was a Social Worker in Deptford living on the Crossfields Estate SE8 so some of the lyrical references of the song are specific to the time and place."

Dire Straits played at the Albany Empire on several occasions during their Deptford days, as in the one referred to in tposter, which was **designed and printed by Colin Bodiam**.

The last time they played at the Albany was on 2nd July 1978, (the one mentioned in the poster that Colin Bodiam holds, in the picture with Mark Knopfler and John Illsley during the plaque unveiling at Farrer House) with queues around the building because of their increasing fame.

About those Deptford days. Colin Bodiam mentions that they played other pubs and clubs that are not mentioned in any articles, books or tour dates, such as one at the short-lived Broadway Queen club in Deptford. Eighteen people turned up with nine on the guest list.

Their flat wasn't really the best place to rehearse so they moved the instruments to a nearby location at Greenwich, not very far from Farrer House, called **Wood Wharf Studios**, a very nice place with windows looking out on the banks of the Thames, and very close to the esplanade where the **Cutty Sark** and **Gypsy Moth IV** clipper ships lay in their dry docks.

John Illsley: *"Great place to work, close to our council flat and cheap, wonderful view of the river. We did some good work* *there, used it a lot"*

In these studios Dire Straits rehearsed their songs before they went into a recording studio or started a tour from 1977 to 1986, their big 'Brothers In Arms' world tour being the final one prepared there.

This studio can be seen in the Arena series documentary of 1980 which comes as bonus material in the 'Alchemy' Bluray Disc and DVD, in the scenes in which they are rehearsing, in many of the early pictures of the band and also in the aforementioned documentary to promote Knopfler's second solo record 'Sailing To Philadelphia'.

Nowadays there is an apartment and office building where the the studio used to be,

JOHN ILLSLEY, MARK KNOPFLER AND PICK WITHERS WITH THE CUTTY SARK AND GYPSY MOTH IV AT THEIR BACK, WALKING BY THE RIVERSIDE TOWARDS THE STUDIO.
PICTURE BY ADRIAN BOOT / WWW.URBANIMAGE.TV

MARK KNOPFLER, INSIDE WOOD WHARF
PICTURE BY ADRIAN BOOT / WWW.URBANIMAGE.TV

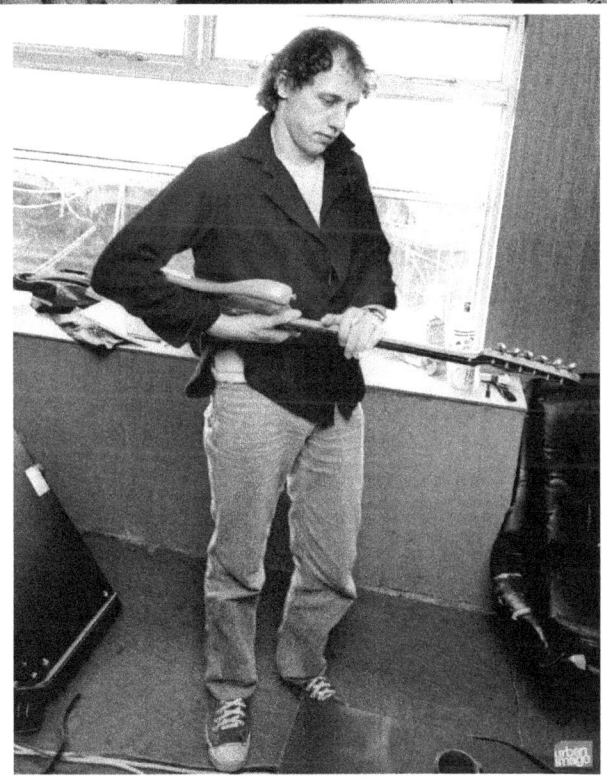

THE BAND AT THE BANK OF THE THAMES, DURING LOW TIDE, JUST IN FRONT OF THE WOOD WHARF STUDIOS AND NEXT TO THE STUDIO WINDOWS. ALL PICTURES BY COLIN BODIAM, TAKEN DURING "PORTOBELLO BELLE" FIRST REHEARSALS.

DEPTFORD

Videocaptures of how Wood Wharf looked in the 80's from a documentary called "Les Enfants du rock : Une Histoire Anglaise" by French channel: Antenne 2

Wood Wharf in 1979, "Screen capture from "Nationwide: Kate Bush on tour", from BBC1 TV, 1979

Wood Wharf studios in 2000, before being demolished, screen captures from the "Sailing to Philadelphia" video press kit, thanks to Brunno Nunes

Wood Wharf nowadays, an apartments block built where the studio used to be
Picture: Juan Pablo Bernardo

but the name remains visible and the spot where the studio used to be is where the white columns are.

Following the river path is the esplanade where the famous **Cutty Sark** clipper ship lies in dry dock, restored after a damaging fire in 2007. Of particular note is that she was built on the Clyde in a town called Dumbarton, close to Knopfler's birth town of Glasgow, in 1869. A "clipper ship" is simply a fast sailing ship.

The Cutty Sark was one of the clippers that used to carry the tea between China and London, and is mentioned in the song 'Single Handed Sailor', together with another famous clipper, '**Gypsy Moth**', whose complete name is Gypsy Moth IV. They used to be together at their dry docks in Greenwich (hence the '**dry dock town**' phrase in the song, together with the fact there are so many wharves in that part of the river) and because of their sizes, the big Cutty Sark and the small Gypsy Moth IV, they looked like the '**mother and a baby**', reference in the lyrics as well. During one period of time, the owners of the Gypsy Moth IV kept her at **Cowes** on the **Isle of Wight**, but nowadays it's owned by the **Gypsy Moth Trust** and usually is at **Buckler's Hard harbour**, near the **Beaulieu river**, in **southern England** but as she sails from time to time, it is better to check the trust website and locate where she is: https://www.gipsymoth.org/

'Single-Handed Sailor' is a song inspired by the story of **Sir Francis Chichester**, a sailor who was the first and fastest to navigate around the earth alone, on board the Gypsy Moth IV[2], using the clippers' route between Europe, the Far East and Australia that runs through the Southern Ocean to take advantage of the wind system known as The Roaring Forties.

Picture of the Gypsy Moth IV when in Greenwich, Oscar Pallarès

[2] Gypsy Moth story from "What's That Song About? Blog entry: http://www.rockremembers.com/2009/04/single-handed-sailor-dire-straits-1979.html?m=1

Gypsy Moth pub at Greenwich, just next to the Cutty Sark.
Picture: Juan Pablo Bernardo

Both clippers were very close to the Wood Wharf Studio so it's easy to understand that their history influenced Mark Knopfler to write the song about it.

David Knopfler: *"The song 'Single Handed Sailor' has a nicely sketched out, emotionally satisfying, lyric and a quite-demanding tune to perform too, with some jazz-influenced inflections. I probably wouldn't be able to figure it all out now.*

"Mark brought it, pretty much fully-formed, to rehearsals and I think, had written it overnight. I don't believe the slightly quirky and busy, rhythm part I added, after Mark showed me the trickier chords, really met full approval from either Mark or later our Producer, Barry Becket. I'm pretty sure if I'd been a session player, they would have insisted it was tidied up more and that I delivered something a little more consistent, spacey and disciplined but they generously let it go and it survived to make the cut, for better or worse. If memory serves, and often these days it doesn't, it was still performed in the live set when I left the band.

"It had a kind of rhythmic pace and economy that was simpatico to the sentiment of the song. Maybe I also liked it, in part, because I also found the River Thames at night, with its quiet barges moving, almost invisibly, through the dark, so quickly in and out of view inspirational... a place of excitement and beauty. And there was also the not unremarkable skill for just one person to be handling such a boat. I don't suppose those long sand barges are still around these days performing their industrial deliveries.

"That economical, almost romantic 'Eng-Lit' and half-journalistic style of narration worked for me. It wasn't commonly used by lyricists in the gracelessness of the punk era either. I wouldn't

be surprised if Mark wouldn't have tipped a nod to the way Ray Davis could mine treasure from the battered grime of Waterloo Station and bridge."

Along the Cutty Sark esplanade we have another element that is shown in the video clip of one of the most famous Dire Straits songs, 'Walk Of Life'. Released on their album 'Brothers In Arms' there are two videos: one more famous and orientated to the US market, with American football and baseball clips, the other one rather less known and orientated to the UK market, with a man busking in a tunnel and wearing the same kind of clothes that Mark Knopfler wore at the Live Aid concert. He was playing the National Style O guitar shown on the 'Brothers In Arms' cover, while people walking by threw coins into his guitar case or even stopped to sing along with the chorus of the song!

When you see the video it looks like an underground tunnel but it's not. It is in fact the **Greenwich Foot Tunnel** which passes underneath the Thames from the **Cutty Sark esplanade** to the other bank of the Thames. These tunnels are very common in this area of London as after Tower Bridge there are not any other bridges to cross the river, so the only way to access the other bank by car or walking is using the tunnels.

The Greenwich Foot Tunnel is one of the attractions of this esplanade as from the other side there are very nice views of the Cutty Sark , and the Old Royal Naval College.

PICTURE: DAVID MARTÍN

THE ENTRY TO THE GREENWICH FOOT TUNNEL AND THE CUTTY SARK. (ABOBE)
TUNNEL THAT CAN BE SEEN IN "WALK OF LIFE" VIDEOCLIP. (BELOW)
BOTH PICTURES BY DAVID MARTÍN.

PICTURE: JAVIER PELÁEZ

VIEWS OF THE CUTTY SHARK AND THE FOOT TUNNEL ENTRY
FROM THE OPPOSITE BANK OF THE RIVER.
PICTURE: JAVIER PELÁEZ.

To access the tunnel you have to go inside the domed building that can be seen in the pictures.
Not far from the Cutty Sark esplanade, is the **Royal Observatory**, the place that marks the meridian 0 or Greenwich Meridian, that offers also great views of London, including

DEPTFORD MAPS

NEW CROSS STATION, ALBANY THEATRE, FARRER HOUSE / LOVE OVER GOLD WALL

In order to reach **New Cross Station**, the easiest route is to take the underground train. On the underground, take the **Jubilee Line** (coloured grey on the London Underground 'Tube' map) and change at **Canada Water**, taking the train to New Cross. There is another station after this one called **New Cross Gate**, so don't get confused.

Going out of the station turn left, walking by **Amersham Vale** and in about 120 metres, turn right at **Douglas Way**. In 350 metres you will arrive at the location of the **Albany Theatre**.

Follow **Douglas Way** to the end of the street which leads straight into **Giffin Street**, which leads into **Deptford Church Street**. There you will see some tenement buildings like the one in the pictures. In one of these you will find a map with the name of the building, **Farrer House**, which you will find after going down the train bridge on your right.

There are some similar buildings close by. In case of any doubt keep walking straight ahead until you get into **Creekside**, where you will find the **'Love Over Gold'** wall and from there the Farrer House plaque is easily seen.

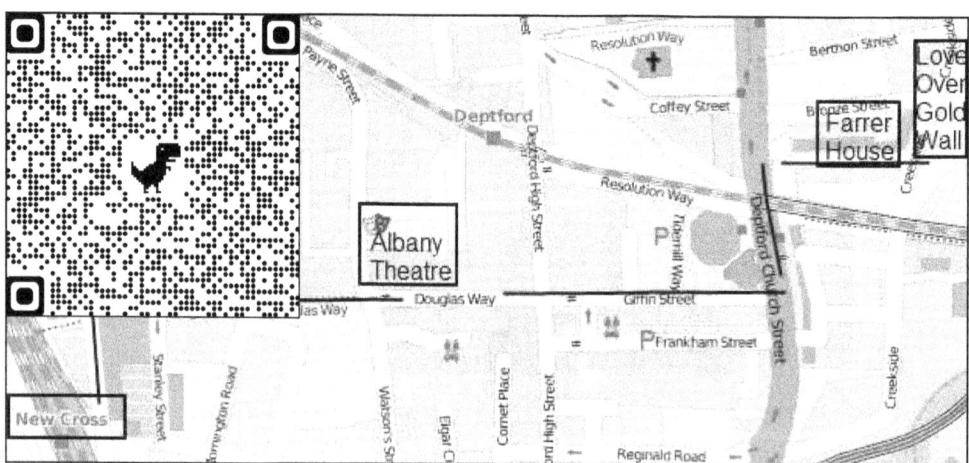

Wood Wharf / Cutty Sark / Foot tunnel / Royal Observatory

Following your trip, leave Deptford and walk towards Greenwich, along **Creekside** in the opposite direction to the train bridge (the arches), leaving that bridge behind you. Approximately three minutes later, walking by Creekside you'll come to **Creek Road**, and turn right. Now, walking across a bridge over the **Deptford Creek**, take the second street on the left after the bridge, called **Horseferry Place**, until you reach the River Thames. Just on your left, you'll see a building with the name **Wood Wharf**.

Following the path whilst enjoying the views of the Thames, you'll come to the next stop, where the famous **Cutty Sark** clipper ship lies in dry dock

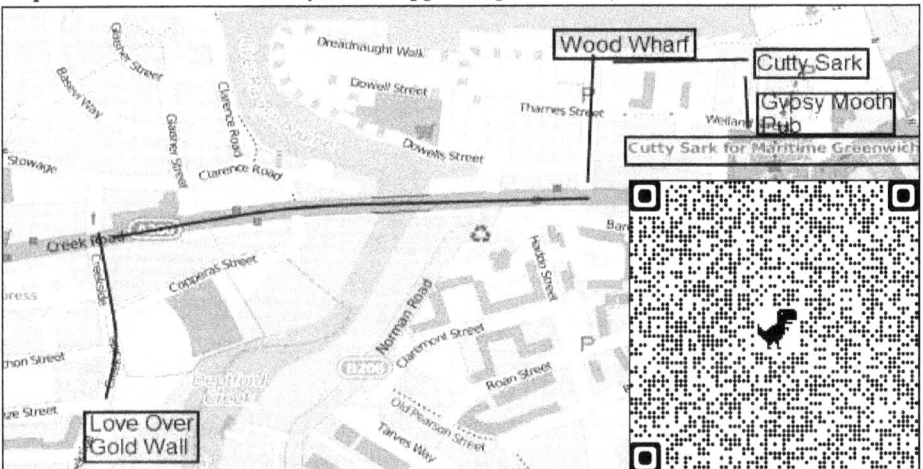

In the following map you can see where the Foot Tunnel entry is, to cross to the other bank of the river.

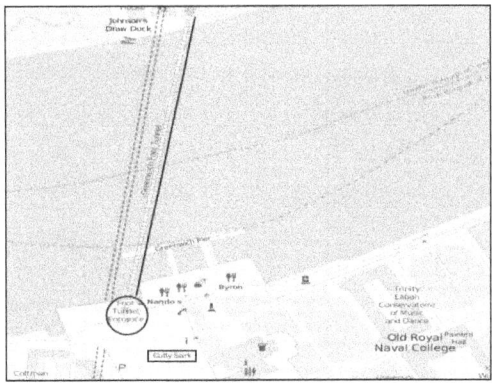

131

If you want to visit the **Royal Observatory**, cross **Greenwich Park** and climb the hill.

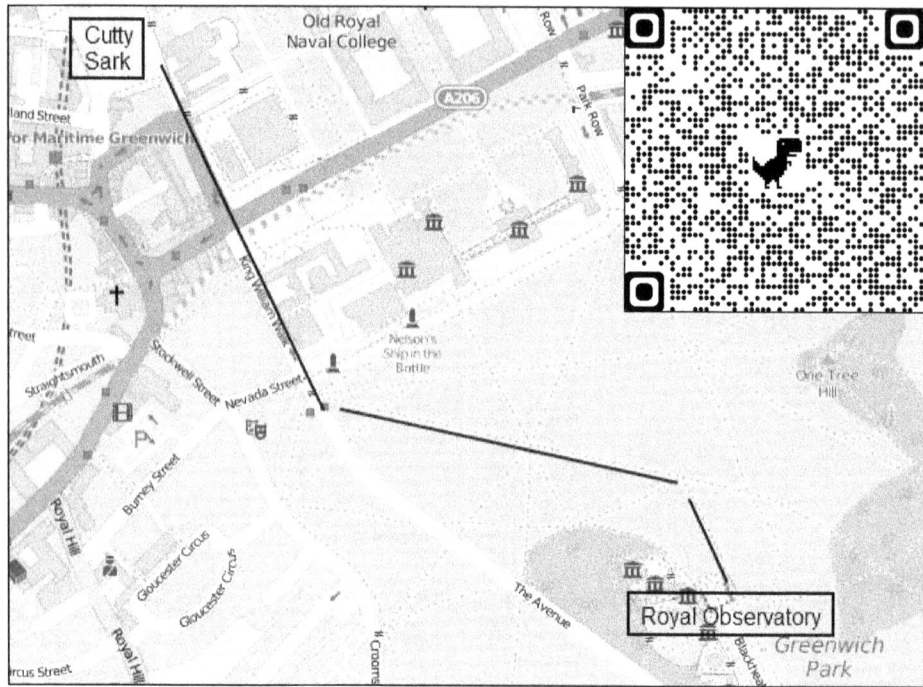

If you want to return to the city, take any of the tourist boats that depart from **Greenwich Dock** and enjoy the views sailing the Thames, or take the DLR line at '**Cutty Sark for Maritime Greenwich**' very close to the Gypsy Moth pub, then change to the **Jubilee Line at Canary Wharf**.

White Swan

In **Deptford**, if you would still like to see where the **White Swan** was according the BBC, the address is **17 Blackheath Road**. It can be reached from **New Cross Station** by going out, turning right and then turning left, walking along **New Cross Road** until it changes to **Blackheath Road**. Walking time is about twelve minutes. You can also get there by **DLR** to **Deptford Bridge**. The White Swan former location is about three minutes' walk from the station.

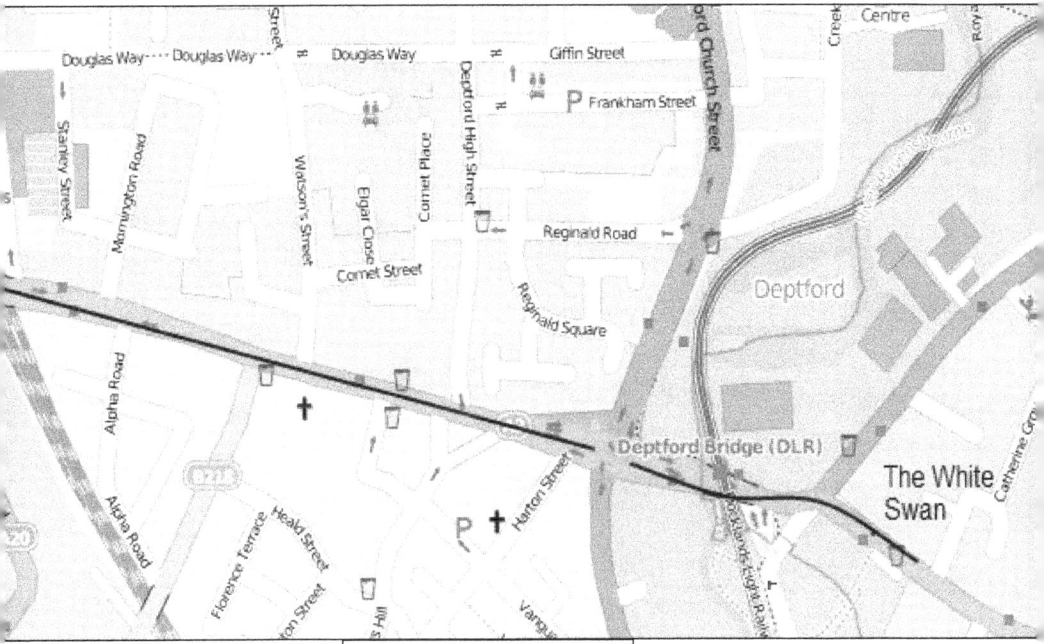

The White Swan mentioned in the Michael Oldfield book and also by David Knopfler, was located in Greenwich High Road 85-87. The fastest way to reach it is again Deptford bridge station, walk along Deptford Bridge until you get to Greenwich High Road. It's a 5 minutes walk

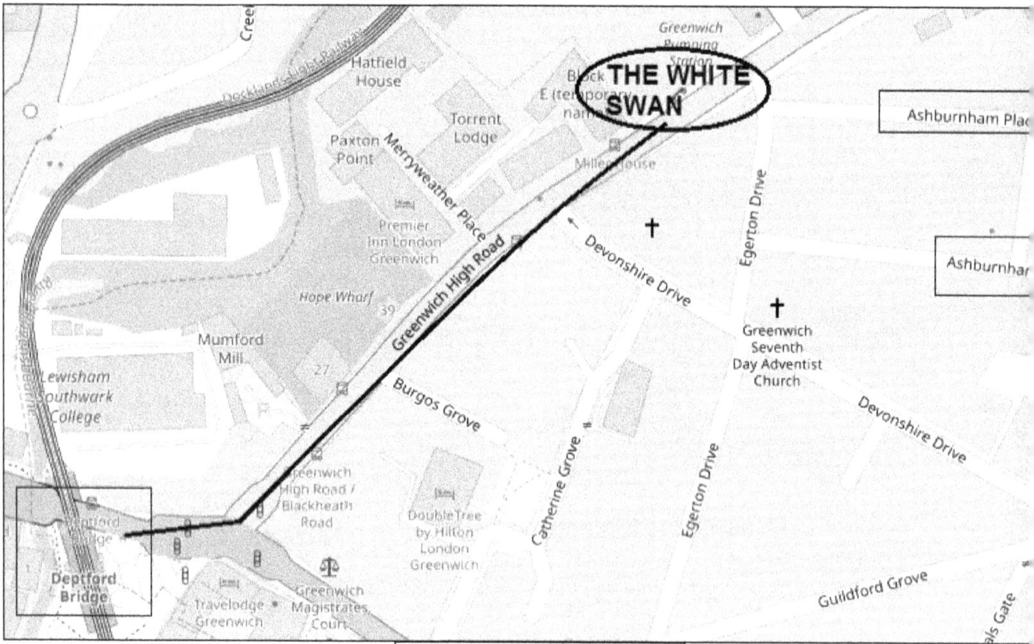

5 ISLINGTON

PICTURE: DAVID MARTIN

Islington is a borough in inner London and which is related to Dire Straits by two places that were significant in the early years of the band.

The first is the **Hope And Anchor pub**, one of the venues where Dire Straits used to play frequently during late 1977 and early 1978. This one is especially important since it's the place where the first released Dire Straits song was recorded.

As mentioned in the previous chapter, it was their song 'Eastbound Train', which was released in a double album entitled 'Front Row Festival', which was a festival that took place between Tuesday 22 November and Thursday 15 December 1977. The album reached number 28 in the UK albums chart. The album also included songs by bands such as *The Stranglers, The Pirates and Wilko Johnson.*

PICTURES: DAVID MARTÍN

The Hope And Anchor opened its doors in 1880 and was one of the first to embrace the punk movement in the 1970s. Amongst the names that played there are famous bands such as: *Joy Division, Madness, The Clash, The Cure, The Jam, The Ramones, The Pogues, The Police, Squeeze, The Stray Cats and U2.*

When entering the pub there are stairs going down to where the stage is located in the basement where the concerts take place. It's usually closed when there are no performances but if you ask the staff, there is a chance that they may let you go downstairs for a look. Going down you´ll see some concert adverts from the years when Dire Straits used to play there. Shown below and in the previous page.

PICTURES: DAVID MARTÍN

John Illsley: *"We played the Hand A (sic) a few times. It was a great vibe, very hot, very tight and very smelly. One night the right-hand side of the PA fell into the audience but it made no difference to the sound. In those days we had no roadies so after the gig we had to push all the equipment up through the hole in the ceiling where the beer barrels came in— really hard".*

PICTURE: ÒSCAR PALLARÈS

PICTURE: DAVID MARTÍN

Some fans that have been at the pub say that the double LP hangs on the pub's wall, but it is very unlikely that you will find any bar staff still there from when it was recorded.

This is the cover of the double album 'Front Row Festival', when the first Dire Straits song 'Eastbound Train' was released, later used as the B-side of the single 'Sultans of Swing' in almost all editions.

WARNERS ALBUM RELEASE:
"HOPE & ANCHOR FRONT ROW FESTIVAL"
VARIOUS ARTISTS

CHAS DE COLLIS, propped up at the bar, reveals the full facts about the **HOPE & ANCHOR FRONT ROW FESTIVAL**

The release of 'Hope & Anchor Front Row Festival' must surely establish this North London landmark as Britain's most famous rock music pub. Situated at 207 Islington Upper Street, just a two minute walk from Highbury and Islington tube station on the Victoria line, the pub ranks as one of the first in London to run regular rock gigs.

It was back in the early Seventies that people first started to talk about 'Pub Rock'. Of course, even at that time numerous pubs were featuring rock groups, but very few were emerging with any apparent aspirations towards greater success. The Tally Ho in Kentish Town was probably the first pub in London to specifically cater to a rock audience. Bands like Bees Make Honey and Brinsley Schwarz (with Nick Lowe) played regular gigs there, paving the way for Ducks Deluxe, Kilburn and The Highroads (fronted by Ian Dury), Ace and Chilli Willi, among others.

The Hope & Anchor was originally a jazz venue, but about this time started to feature rock bands on Fridays and Saturdays. When the Tally Ho changed landlords and discontinued rock in favour of Irish showbands the Hope quickly took over as North London's main pub rock attraction.

The rock policy was pulled into shape by Fred Grainger and Dave Robinson, who ran the gab on a shoestring not to mention a "devil-may-care" attitude.

The upstairs bar was dominated by at least the most interesting jukebox in London running a spectrum of sounds from Professor Longhair to Van Morrison to in-demand 'Pub Rock' singles.

Down in the cellar one could regularly catch The Stranglers, Graham Parker & The Rumour, Dr Feelgood, Steve Gibbons Band

WILKO JOHNSON BAND
THE STRANGLERS
TYLA GANG
THE PIRATES
STEVE GIBBONS BAND
XTC
SUBURBAN STUDS
THE PLEASERS
DIRE STRAITS
BURLESQUE
X-RAY SPEX
999
THE SAINTS
THE ONLY ONES
STEEL PULSE
ROOGALATOR
PHILIP RAMBOW

K66077

and The Kursaal Flyers, to list but a few. The pub even installed its own recording studio though this is now defunct.

As the years passed, Fred eventually quit the Hope to open a rock club in Brighton while Dave joined Jake Riviera in running Stiff Records. Albion Management and Agency took over the tenancy of the Hope in January of '77 under the auspices of bearded, genial landlord John Eichler. Since that time John has organised various benefits in order to keep the pub open in the light of numerous threats of closure from the brewery. The Front Row Festival grew from one of these ideas, with name bands returning to the pub and performing for only expenses. Ian Grant of Albion narrowed down a long list to a final 22 bands — all of which have played at the pub at one time or another. The an "ideas meeting" was called.

It would surely have been crazy with such an amazing collection of bands not to arrange the recording of the Festival be issued on a double album, and what an album! 17 Hope & Anchor bands live.

And so the Hope & Anchor continues with its policy of live rock, attracting a hard core of punters alongside the usual gaggle of A&R scouts. Latest news is that the upstairs restaurant to the pub is being converted into an after-hours membership club for tired record company execs, music biz hacks, DJ's and producers. And why not? Perhaps the best is yet to come.

The Hope & Anchor is situated on the corner of Upper Street and Islington Park Street in an up and never came part of North London. In the bowels of this establishment lies or rather lurks a black smoke-filled cellar of matey proportions.

This subterranean world's overlord is the bearded Fred Grainger, originally from good old Shoreham-On-Sea, a non commuter part of Sussex.

In the early years, jazz could be heard bubbling up through adjacent Islington drain pipes. Colds have been caught there by many from the late Phil Seaman to Jo-Ann Kelly.

The Hope has been father to such as Brinsley Schwarz (should have made it), Chilli Willi, the Ducks, Ace and the Bees and in the words of lesser commercials 'many, many more'.

The then Brinsley's manager and most pleasant person Dave Robinson moved in upstairs and with Grainger formed Upper Street Music and have filled their clammy kingdom with the most exciting sounds around.

'Hope & Anchor Front Row Festival' is an excellent example of what wafts up from the lovable black hole of Islington.

4 SIDES OF HONEST ROCKIN' AIN'T GONNA HURT AT 4 QUID 49p

Advert of the Front Row double LP release, picture by Alejandro García

There was some merchandise associated with the release of the LP of the festival, such as this nice t-shirt:

PICTURES: ALEJANDRO GARCÍA

The second place of interest is the studio where their famous demos were recorded - **Pathway Studios**. This was a studio with some history, founded by producers Peter Ker and Mike Finesilver, where not only Dire Straits had recorded, but also other artists such as *Elvis Costello, The Police, Madness and Squeeze*. Alas, the place is no longer a studio but a private apartment, although in a documentary produced by "**British TV Sky Arts 'Mark Knopfler Guitar Stories'**", John Illsley and Mark Knopfler visit the place when talking about Knopfler's Fender Stratocaster as well as the demos they recorded there. John Illsley, who presents the documentary, comments that the new owners have maintained the musical heritage of the place. In that same programme, one can see Mark Knopfler and John Illsley in the recording room.
OBVIOUSLY, AS A PRIVATE APARTMENT, IT CAN'T BE VISITED BEYOND THE MAIN DOOR.

This place is remarkable in Dire Straits' history because between June and July of 1977, Dire Straits went to Pathway to record the demos that gave them their first contract. In these sessions they recorded five songs, four of them written by Mark Knopfler ('Sultans Of Swing', 'Wild West End', 'Water Of Love', 'Down To The Waterline') and one by David Knopfler ('Sacred Loving').

That demo was sent to BBC Radio London DJ **Charlie Gillett** and when it was broadcast on his show **Honky Tonk**, people from various record companies started to call the radio enquiring about the band.

141

Both pictures: Miquel Martínez

David Knopfler: *"We recorded our first demos at an eight-track demo studio called Pathway – Chas Herrington was the sound engineer – and the five songs we focused on became known as the Honky Tonk Demos. They were 'Sultans of Swing', 'Down to the Waterline', 'Wild West End', 'Sacred Loving' and 'Water of Love'. I can't recall if there were outtakes from that session... There might have been a song or two that didn't get mixed – Now that I think about that – I recall a track I wrote called "T.RO.U.B.L.E Trouble (sic)" which I think we did one pass at. Mark was pretty decent at arrangements and my work frequently benefitted from his useful, critical insights. For demos we mostly went with first or second takes. You had a matter of a few hours to get it all done."*

John Illsley: *"I had been left a little money when my Grandmother died so we used that with the understanding that if we made any money I would be repaid – it was. As far as I recall, we did just those five songs."*

About 'Sacred Loving', in David's words: *"It had reggae inflections. I recall playing it at the Nashville in West London during a soundcheck when we were opening for Elvis Costello...a newly signed artist to Stiff Records, and he logged us from the back of the hall. I seem to recall nattering with a young Charles Shaar Murray too outside waiting for the doors to open to let us in to soundcheck and he was telling me about Stiff's marketing genius and their double-sized posters and I thought... that sounds like a plan!"*

"Sacred Loving" lyrics provided by David Knopfler:

Oh my love I wish I were strong
To carry your pain
If my hands were of a granite
I'd take all of your needs and never bend
They say, you'll be weakness only with passion
That goodness come only through fire
My wisdom is so wild eyed
A child is still with me, so is desire
Living and loving sharing just nothing
Waiting and praying just hoping for change
It's the way of the world, so uncaring
That a bad man needs good love is hard to explain
Sacred loving, without it there's just nothing
I feel so humbled by the ways I've lied
You ride with the winds, fly with your horses
And I hide from a devil howling inside.

David Knopfler ©1977

They returned there once again, in April 1978, to re-record 'Sultans Of Swing' for the single, as the record company wasn't satisfied with the version on the record, and wanted a version that sounded more like the demo recording, which is known amongst fans as the 'alternative Sultans of Swing'.

DIFFERENT VERSIONS OF THE 'SULTANS OF SWING' (ALTERNATIVE VERSION) SINGLE WITH 'EASTBOUND TRAIN' RECORDED LIVE AT THE FRONT ROW FESTIVAL, FROM GERMANY, THE NETHERLANDS AND SPAIN.

ISLINGTON MAPS

HOPE AND ANCHOR

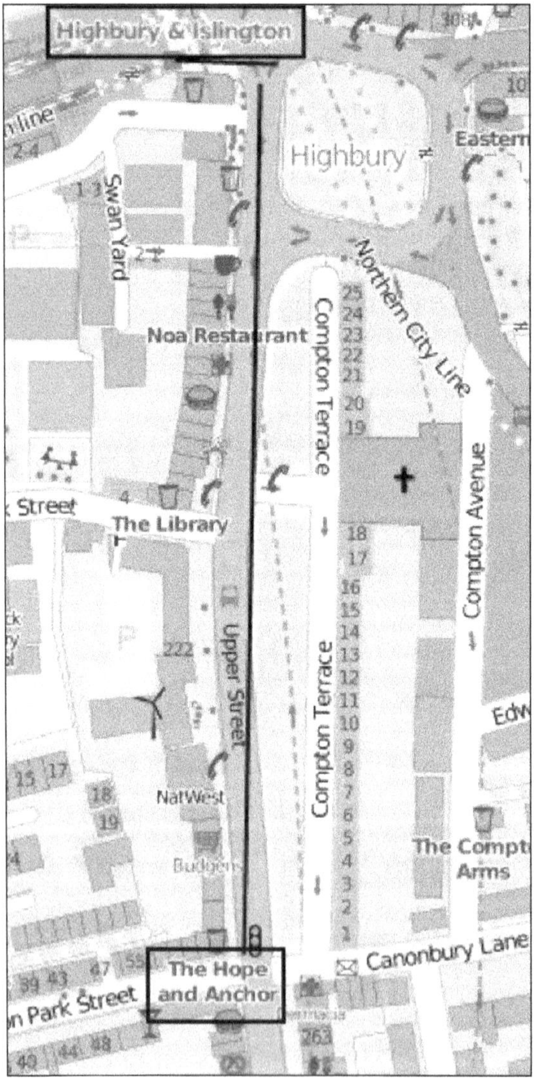

It is easy to get to the Hope and Anchor pub. It is still open and offers live music -Mark Knopfler's son Ben has performed here on drums with his band The Rocket Dolls. The tube stop closest to it is **Highbury & Islington**. When you exit, turn right and walk towards **Upper Street**. In a short five minutes' walk you will get to the Hope and Anchor, on the corner with **Islington Park Street**.

Pathway Studios

To get there, from the **Hope and Anchor**, go back to **Highbury & Islington** tube station, and from there take **St Paul's Road** and later turn left by **Highbury Grove** and walk until turning right by **Highbury New Park** and follow until it splits to the left and straight ahead, it turns into **Grosvenor Avenue**. What was Pathway Studio is located at number **2A**, in a driveway, as can be seen in the documentary when John Illsley and Mark Knopfler walk to the door, (in the picture beside the car), next to a tyre shop.

If going without previously stopping at the Hope and Anchor, stop at **Canonbury Tube station**, and turn left at **Wallace Road**, then later turn right towards **Grosvenor Avenue**, following the same directions mentioned above.

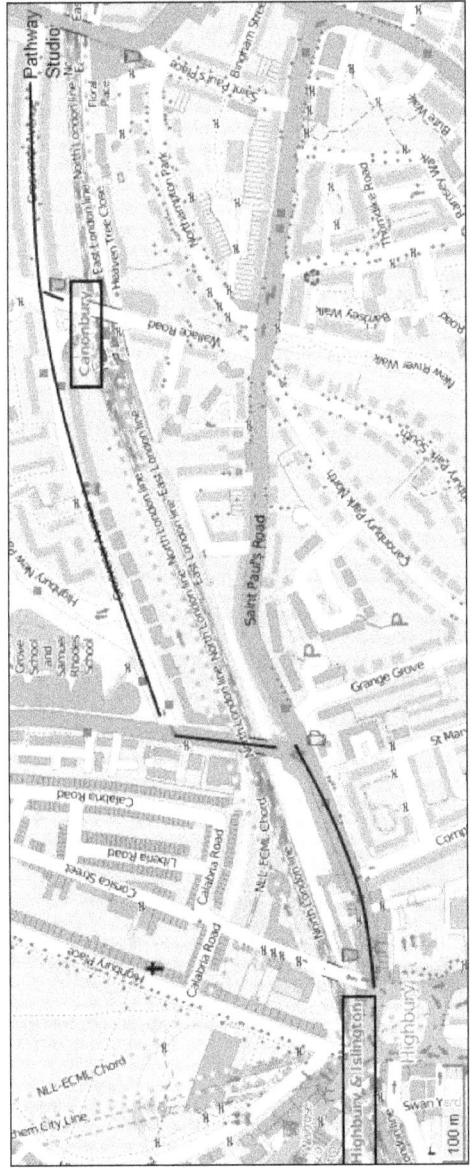

6 CLAPHAM

With a demo tape recorded and in their hands, the next step was to distribute it and wait to see what happened. John Illsley met Radio London DJ **Charlie Gillett** when John and his then girlfriend were opening a record store, so he was the first one to get a copy.

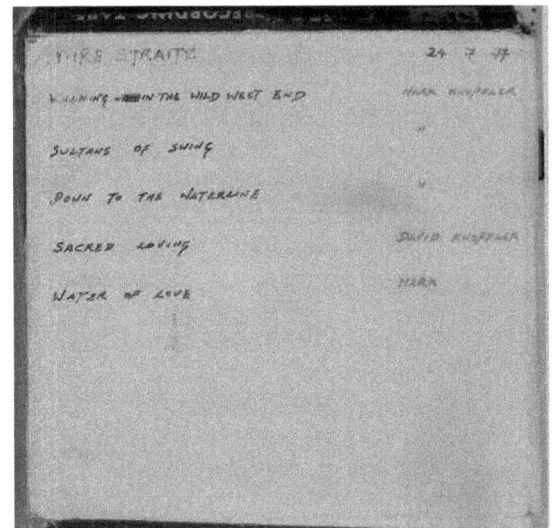

PICTURE OF THE DIRE STRAITS DEMO TAPE, PUBLISHED BY CHARLIE GILLETT IN HIS WEBSITE

Gillett was impressed by the songs and decided to play one of them, 'Sultans Of Swing', in his programme Honky Tonk on 31st July 1977. Twenty-eight songs were played on that Sunday programme and it was 'Sultans Of Swing' - the eighteenth song played that day between Bonnie Raitt's 'Good Enough' and 'School Is Out' by Ry Cooder - that caught the attention of most of the artist and repertoire personnel of London. They immediately started to call the radio station to enquire about that band who "sounded like an American band".

PICTURE: ANDRA NELKI

John Illsley: *"Mark and I were shifting furniture for some cash so missed the first time but we heard it the next week, then went to meet Charlie to get a view."*

In the Sky Arts documentary '**Mark Knopfler Guitar Stories**', Mark and John talk about the Gillett show and they mention that someone in the **Oxford Arms** pub (32 Church Street, Deptford) told them that 'Sultans Of Swing' was played on the radio that day. The Oxford Arms was mentioned in David Knopfler's song 'Southside Tenements', that was played by Dire Straits during their early concerts and was released on David's sixth record, 'The Giver'" in 1993.

> *"Sleepwalkin' to The Oxford Arms*
> *No-one noticing warehouse alarms*
> *Slamming dominoes in the back bar*
> *Safe from harm, by The Tenements*
> *The Southside Tenements"*

The Oxford Arms changed its name to **The Birds Nest** and still exists in the same location. There is a story about its being the pub where the Knopfler brothers saw the band called The Sultans Of Swing as it's very close to the Farrer House apartment, but when that happened, as mentioned in the Deptford chapter, the brothers didn't yet know John Illsley and David wasn't living in Deptford yet but in Greenwich, and Mark visited.

THE BIRDS NEST, PREVIOUSLY KNOWN AS "THE OXFORD ARMS".
PICTURE: OLAF BAUSCHAT

After that success, Charlie Gillett played '<u>Sultans Of Swing</u>' once more and the rest of songs during the following Sunday's programme and then on 11th September, Gillett asked Dire Straits to play at the **Honky Tonk Summer Festival** at **Clapham Common** with two other bands: Rico and The Darts. The concert was broadcast live by Radio London.

They played in the **Clapham Common bandstand,** constructed in 1890. It is the largest bandstand in London and a Grade II Listed Building. In 2006 it was restored and still hosts many musical events from July through to September annually.

Poster courtesy of Alejandro García

Andra Nelki attended that festival in a professional capacity as a photographer and took pictures of the performance which have appeared in some books, newspapers and records including the 'Record Store day' special release on double vinyl of four of the five songs included in the demos, called 'The Honky Tonk Demos' in 2015.

Andra Nelki: *"the band who played before Dire Straits was a popular afro-Caribbean musicians band (Rico) and the crowd watching was 90% black faces and very enthusiastic and Dire Straits were a bit intimidated about following them onto the stage. Much of the audience wandered off when they saw DS getting up on stage but some stayed and enjoyed them too."*

John Illsley: *"We played most of the songs from the first album. I think we were on stage for about 30-40 mins, no sound check, I remember not being able to hear what everyone else was playing as the monitors were pretty poor but we did ok."*

The following pictures are all courtesy of Andra Nelki:

CHARLIE GILLETT STANDING BEHIND MARK

Charlie Gillett. picture: Andra Nelki

Note that Mark's Fender Stratocaster is not painted red yet!

Gillett had a name in the radio world in London. Previously to his Honky Tonk programme he wrote for Rolling Stone and New Musical Express among others. In 1970 he wrote a book called 'The Sound of the City: The Rise of Rock and Roll' and was also the first one to play in his programme demos by other artists such as Graham Parker and Elvis Costello.

In 1980 he moved to Capital Radio and went back fifteen years later to Radio London and the BBC until he died in 2010 after a long illness.

With the exposure the band received from airplay on Radio London and performing in the Honky Tonk Summer festival, the band continued playing gigs and earning a reputation that would lead them to the next step - signing a record deal.

CLAPHAM MAPS

CLAPHAM COMMON

There are two tube stations close to **Clapham Common park,** where the bandstand is located: **Clapham Common** and **Clapham South**, both on the **Northern (black) line**.

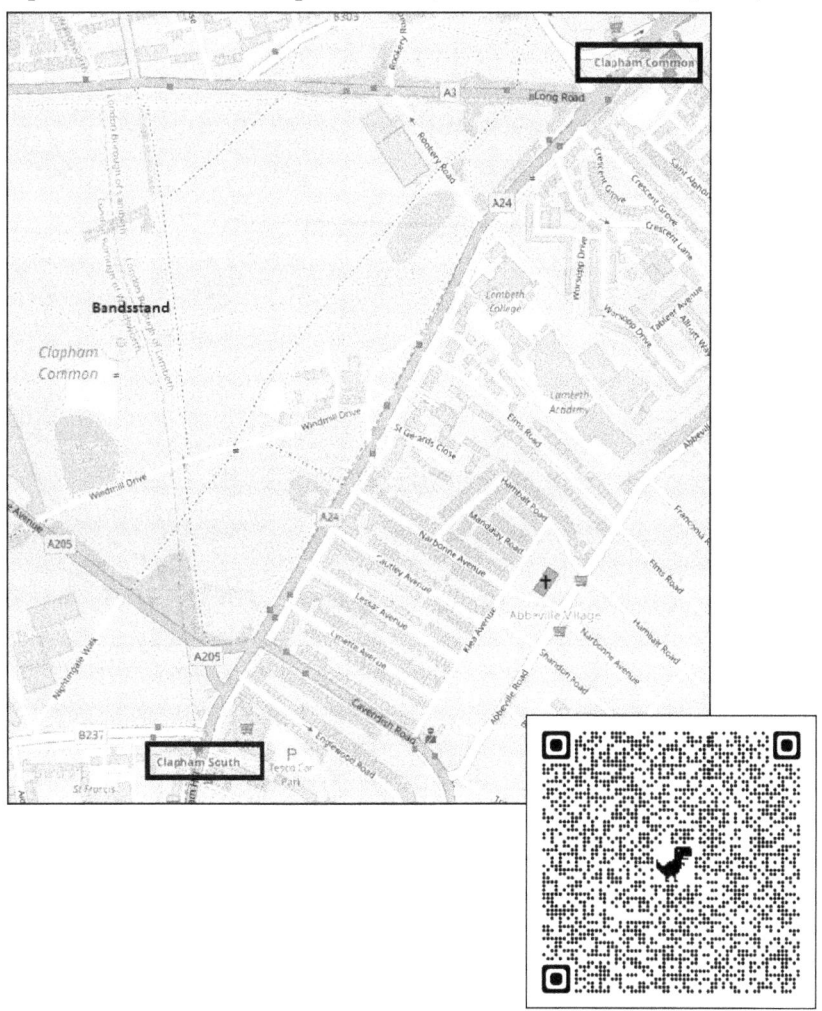

Oxford Arms / The Birds Nest

In Deptford (Chapter 4), it is close to **Farrer House** and the "Love Over Gold" wall, just following **Creekside**.

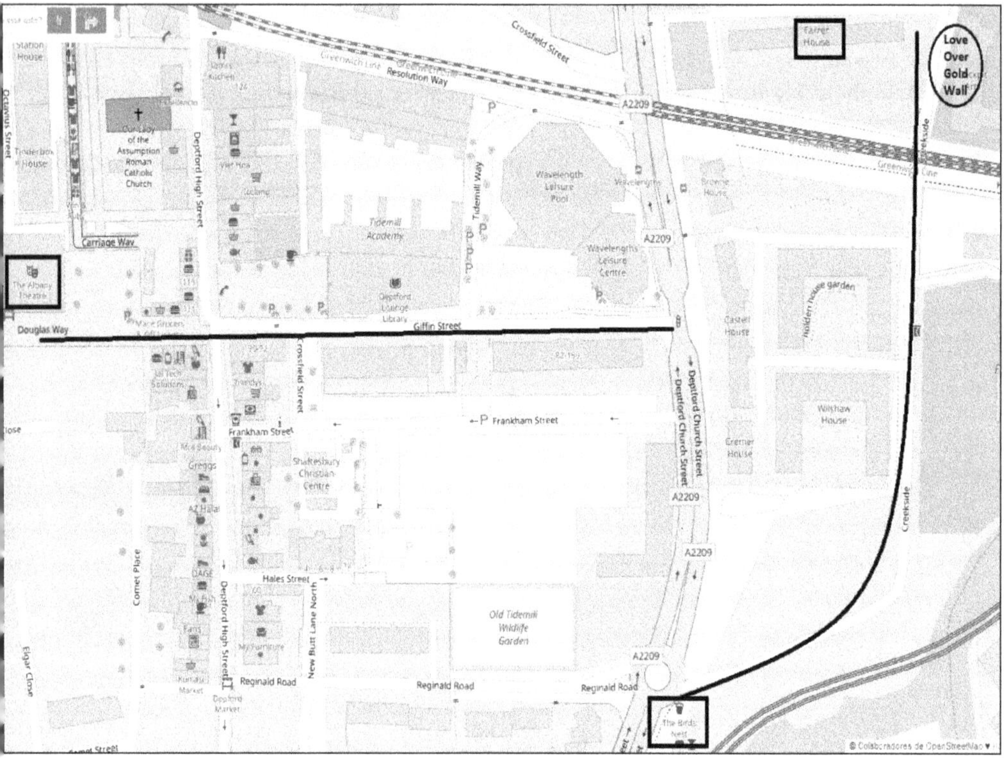

7 CAMDEN

PICTURE: JOSÉ IGNACIO CORBALÁN

Camden Town, in **Chalk Farm**, North London, is one of the most visited areas of London, with two of the most famous markets in London: **Camden Market** and **Camden Lock**. It's also the place where an old music venue can be found - **Dingwalls**. It's one of the places that Dire Straits used to play in their early years and where they got their first record deal.

Over the years the Dingwalls name disappeared from Camden Lock and it was called Jongleurs, or Lock 17. Nowadays you will find the three names. Jongleurs offers Comedy Nights, Lock 17 is a restaurant and Dingwalls is a concert venue.

DAINGWALLS STAGE NOWADAYS
PICTURE: JOSÉ IGNACIO CORBALÁN

On 13th December 1977 **John Stainze** sent **Ed Bicknell** to Dingwalls to listen to the band live and to sign them for his company **Vertigo Records**, from **Phonogram**. Bicknell arrived when the show was already started and liked the band's style so much that he told Stainze he wanted to represent them.

When the concert finished he went backstage to meet the band, and when he entered the backstage area he stumbled into Mark Knopfler's guitar, but despite that he convinced them to go to his office next day where he offered them a contract. They accepted and the first thing they did was to go on tour across the United Kingdom as the support band for **Talking Heads**.

They had fifty minutes to open their shows and shared the hotels with them, travelled together and even used the same equipment. It was a great improvement in their career. Including little details such as having the chance to soundcheck and sharing the stage with Talking Heads in songs such as 'I'm Not In Love', 'Psycho Killer' and 'Gloria'.

David Knopfler wrote a song during that tour that was played by Dire Straits some years later, called 'Bernadette'. It was performed some nights during the North American tour in 1979 but was never recorded by the band and it wasn't until 2016 that David decided to record and release a version of it, as part of the unreleased and rare songs included in his double album 'Anthology Vol 2 & 3'.

Talking Heads members were more than surprised to know that a band without a record released took so much care with their instruments, changing strings, drums, heads and cleaning guitars and bass everyday, when they, with a record out and a certain name, rarely changed their strings.

During that Talking Heads tour they played in a venue close to Camden Lock, **The Roundhouse**, where big stars from all over the world still play nowadays.

PICTURE: JOSÉ IGNACIO CORBALÁN

Camden Lock is one of the stops of the tour made by boats along the **Regent's Canal**, and that Canal is featured in the so-called 'alternative' version of the 'Tunnel Of Love' song, in a particular scene some Dire Straits record sleeves can be seen floating on the water.

CAMDEN

LITTLE VENICE, FROM WHERE THE BOATS DEPARTS TOWARDS CAMDEN.

SCENES OF THE "TUNNEL OF LOVE" ALTERNATIVE VIDEO CLIP

REGENT'S CANAL AND LITTLE VENICE SIGN

CAMDEN MAPS

DINGWALLS

Getting to Dingwalls is really easy. The tube stop is **Camden Town** and when exiting the station, turn right and walk towards **Camden High Street** until you reach the bridge over the canal. Camden Lock is on the left and Dingwalls is just next to it.

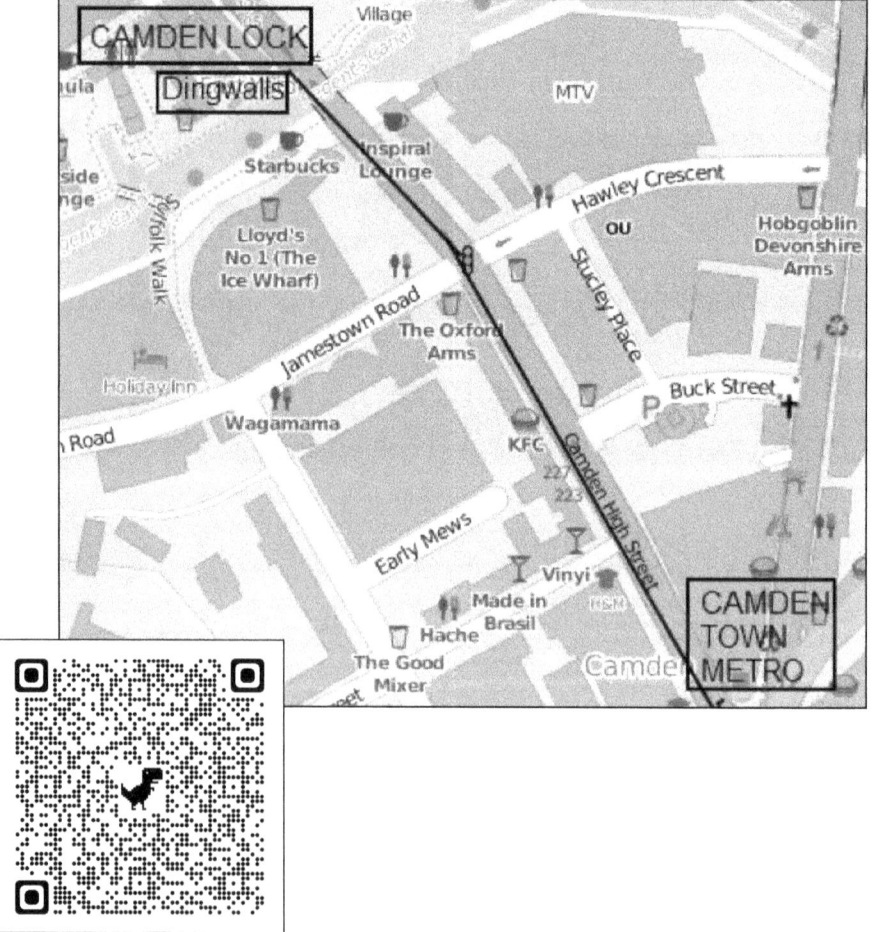

THE ROUND HOUSE

From the inside of **Camden Lock**, exit at the **Stables gate** and walk towards **Chalk Farm Road** until you get to the **Roundhouse**, which is very close to the **Chalk Farm tube stop**.

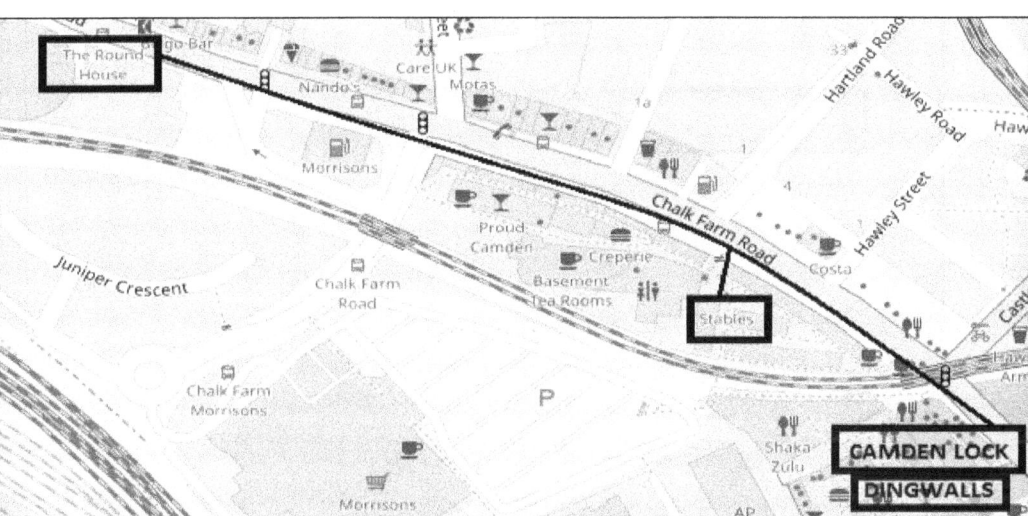

LITTLE VENICE

You can get to Camden by canal, a pleasant trip that is not particularly well known to tourists, by taking one of the boats that sail the **Regent's Canal** to **Camden Lock**. The boat departs from **v**. To get there, take the Bakerloo (brown) Line and stop at Warwick Avenue. When exiting, turn left and walk towards Warwick Avenue until you get to the waterside where the boat departs. During this pleasant trip, you will pass close to the famous London Zoo, where some of their birds can be seen. When the trip ends, the boat docks in Camden Lock, next to where Dingwalls is located.

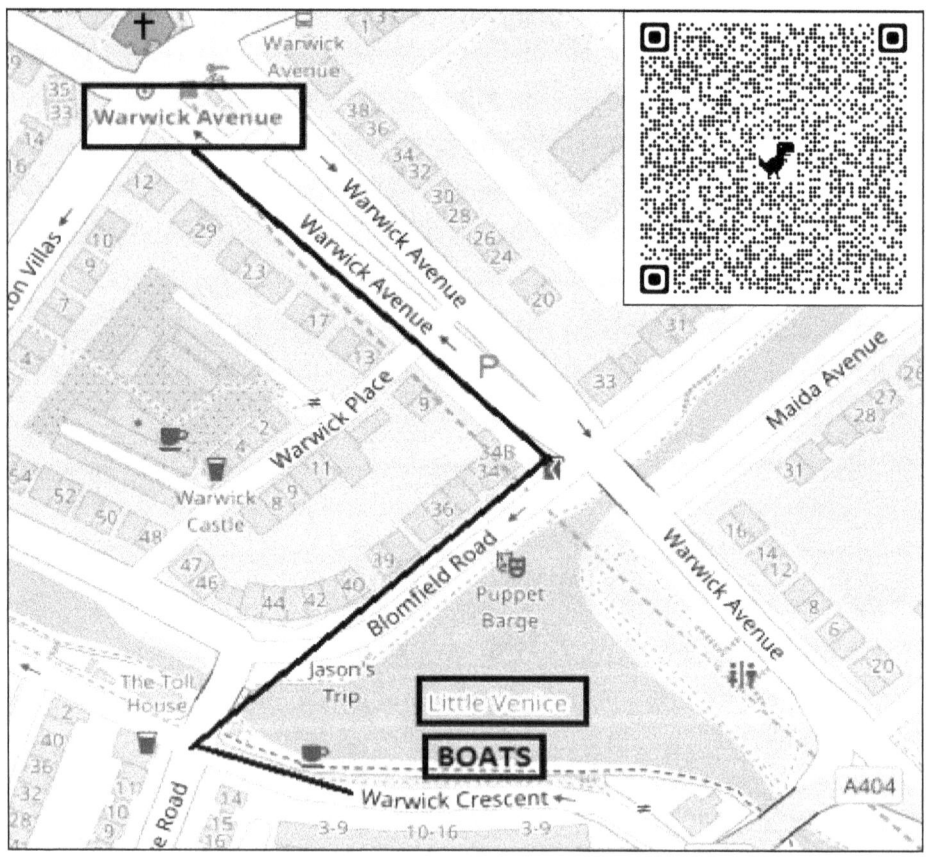

8 WEST END

PICADILLY CIRCUS

After the Talking Heads tour, Ed Bicknell managed to organise a few more tours for Dire Straits supporting **The Climax Bluesband** and **Stix**, then other shows opening for artists such as **Gerry Rafferty**. In the meantime, they continued playing their own gigs in the London area.

One of those places where the band used to play was **The Rock Garden**, a venue that used to be in the famous **Covent Garden square**. The Garden was closed in the late 2000's and today there is an Apple Store in the same place.

PICTURES BY ALEJANDRO GARCÍA

IN BOTH PICTURES THE SAME DOOR CAN BE SEEN. THE FIRST PICTURE IS FROM 2006 AND THE SECOND FROM 2013.

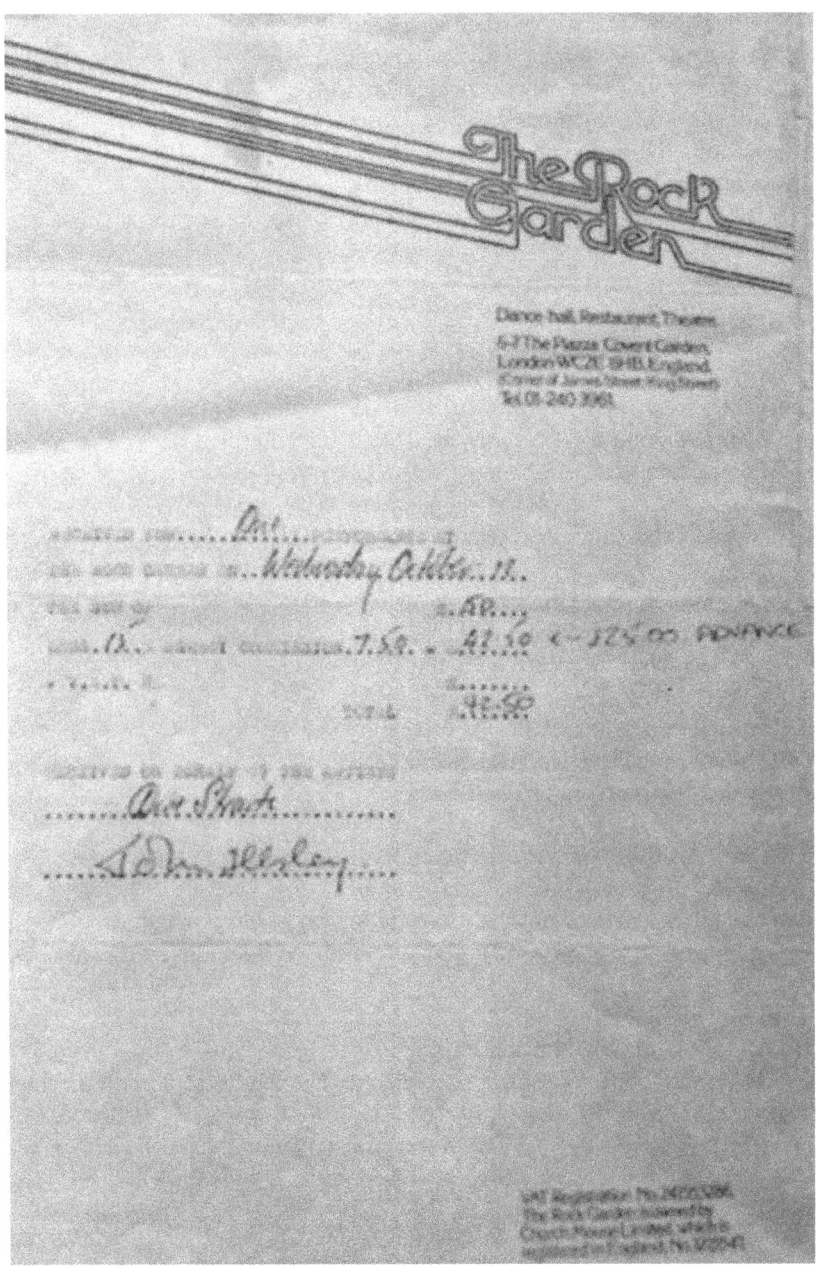

Contract signed between the Rock Garden and John Illsley in the name of Dire Straits

Covent Garden is on the eastern border of the famous **West End**, also known as Theatreland, as there are many theatres where most of the musicals and plays are put on. This interesting area of London is the main subject of one of the songs recorded by Dire Straits in their demos, where Mark Knopfler talks about wandering around some of the places of what he called the '**Wild West End**'.

The song starts with "*Stepping out to Angelucci's, for my coffee beans*". **Angelucci's** was an old coffee shop. The real shop is no longer there as they moved many years ago to Finchley, North London. For many years the canopy with the name remained at the ice-cream shop where Angelucci's used to be, but now it's gone.

In the same street, but in front of where Angelucci´s used to be, there is another place that has a relation to Mark Knopfler's career some years after 'Wild West End' was written. That place is **Ronnie Scott´s Jazz Club**. Many legends of jazz and blues music have played there over the years, including **The Notting Hillbillies**.

Ronnie Scott's is still open and offering a good schedule of concerts, so if you're interested in attending any of these, check out their website as booking is required.

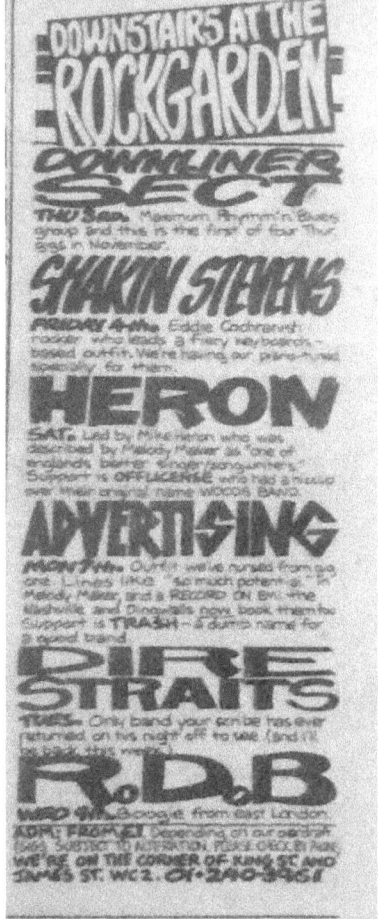

ROCK GARDEN ADVERT FROM MELODY MAKER, PICTURE BY ALEJANDRO GARCÍA.

From 20th July to 1st August 1998, and from 19th to 24th July 1999, The Notting Hillbillies played what were to be their last official concerts [but they still played four more!] in Ronnie Scott's, sharing the stage with legendary musicians such as *Lonnie Donegan* (singing and playing guitar), *Chris Barber* (playing trombone), *Chris White* (saxophone), *Bobby Valentino* (fiddle), *Dave O'Higgins* (saxophone), *B.J. Cole* (pedal steel) and *Pat Crumley* (saxophone).

Also mentioned in 'Wild West End' is the **Barocco bar**. It used to be located at 13 Moor Street, only two minutes' walk from Frith Street. Not far from Moor Street,

PICTURE: ÒSCAR PALLARÉS

PICTURE: JOSÉ IGNACIO CORBALÁN

CHINATOWN.
PICTURE: JOSÉ IGNACIO CORBALÁN

during the early years of the band, Mark Knopfler and John Illsley attended an exhibition they didn't like at all at a local art gallery. That made Mark think about **Harry Phillips**, father of Steve Phillips, who was a sculptor. This inspired his writing of a new song called 'In The Gallery'. That gallery was located in the West End, not far from the spot where the Barocco bar used to be. Unfortunately the gallery no longer exists.

John Illsley: *"The gallery was on the corner of Shaftesbury Avenue and Charing Cross Rd. and being looked after by a friend of MK's. The work was very cutting edge, but dreadful and self-conscious. Mark wrote the song on the way home in the back of the cab.*
We just couldn't believe the stuff that was in this gallery, bits of string, bricks piled up in a corner, garbage cans strewn all

over the floor. We got to the flat, and Mark stayed writing in the back seat. So I went upstairs and made myself a cup of tea. Thirty minutes later, he finally came in. 'I just finished this song,' he said. And that was 'In the Gallery'. He wrote the whole thing between Shaftesbury Avenue and Deptford.''[1]

SHAFTESBURY AVENUE.
PICTURE: JAVIER PELÁEZ

Shaftesbury Avenue is precisely the next location to be mentioned in Mark's walk in the **Wild West End**. It's where most of the theatres are located, as well as many restaurants, shops and other places in the lyrics which have their main entrance on this avenue, one of which is **Chinatown**.

Following Shaftesbury Avenue there is another one of the sightseeing parts of London, a meeting point in the heart of the city, not only for tourists, but also for Londoners: Piccadilly Circus. A short walk from there, another famous location in the city hosts the inspiration for another of the early Dire Straits songs, **Trafalgar Square**, and the song 'Lions'.

[1]Rolling Stone, November 21, 1985. By Ken Tucker, David Fricke: https://www.rollingstone.com/music/music-news/dire-straits-the-rolling-stone-interview-110732/

Its name commemorates the 1805 Battle of Trafalgar which took place in the Napoleonic War against France off the coast of Cape Trafalgar, Spain. Nelson's Column at its centre is guarded by four monumental bronze lions sculpted by Sir Edwin Landseer.

The statue on top of Nelson's Column is made from Craigleith sandstone from Edinburgh (subject of one of the next chapters) It was put onto a ship at Leith docks and shipped down to London. Craigleith (an area in north Edinburgh) stone was the most prized in the country and had a worldwide reputation owing to its containing quartz, making it very hard and durable - ideal for building and carving. Nearly all of the New Town in Edinburgh is built from this stone. An extension of Buckingham Palace was built from Craigleith sandstone too.

PICTURE: JAVIER PELÁEZ

It's those four lions and the magic of the place during sunset that inspired Mark Knopfler to write the song 'Lions', one the last songs that would be written prior to entering a recording studio for what would be the biggest of the many steps happening later to Dire Straits as a band.

In Trafalgar Square lies one of the most important museums in the city, **The National Gallery**, and surrounding Nelson's column, tourists frequently climb onto the lions to have their photograph taken.

NATIONAL GALLERY, AT TRAFALGAR SQUARE

From Trafalgar Square, the famous Great Clock of Westminster (aka "Big Ben," which is actually the nickname of the bell in the clock but has been adopted for the tower too) can be very seen very clearly. From the square, passing the Admiralty Arch and walking by The Mall, at our left we'll find St James's Park and at the end of The Mall, the famous Buckingham Palace, which is the London residence and administrative headquarters of the British monarchy.

Also from Trafalgar Square instead of walking under the Arch, going by Whitehall Avenue you'll find other important sites of interest to tourists, such as Horse Guards Parade, and Downing Street, the official residence of the Prime Minister of the United Kingdom. At the end of Whitehall there is Parliament Square, with the Houses of Parliament at one side with Big Ben, and at the other side, Westminster Abbey. Just in front of Big Ben, across the river, there is the London Eye, also known as The Millennium Wheel, and the London Aquarium, accessible through County Hall.

Trafalgar Square, Nelson Column and the Big Ben

Buckingham Palace and Victoria Memorial

West End

St James's Park with the London Eye behind

Admiralty Arch

WEST END MAPS

COVENT GARDEN

The closest tube station is **Covent Garden** on the **Picadilly (blue) Line**, which is usually very busy with tourists. To avoid that problem, **Leicester Square station** on the **Northern (black) Line** could be an alternative. From Covent Garden tube station, take **James Street** and going down to **Covent Garden** you'll find the building where **Rock Garden** used to be on your right, which today is an Apple Store. If using **Leicester Square tube station**, go left walking by **Cranbourn Street / Long Acre** and when arriving at **Covent Garden station**, take **James Street**.

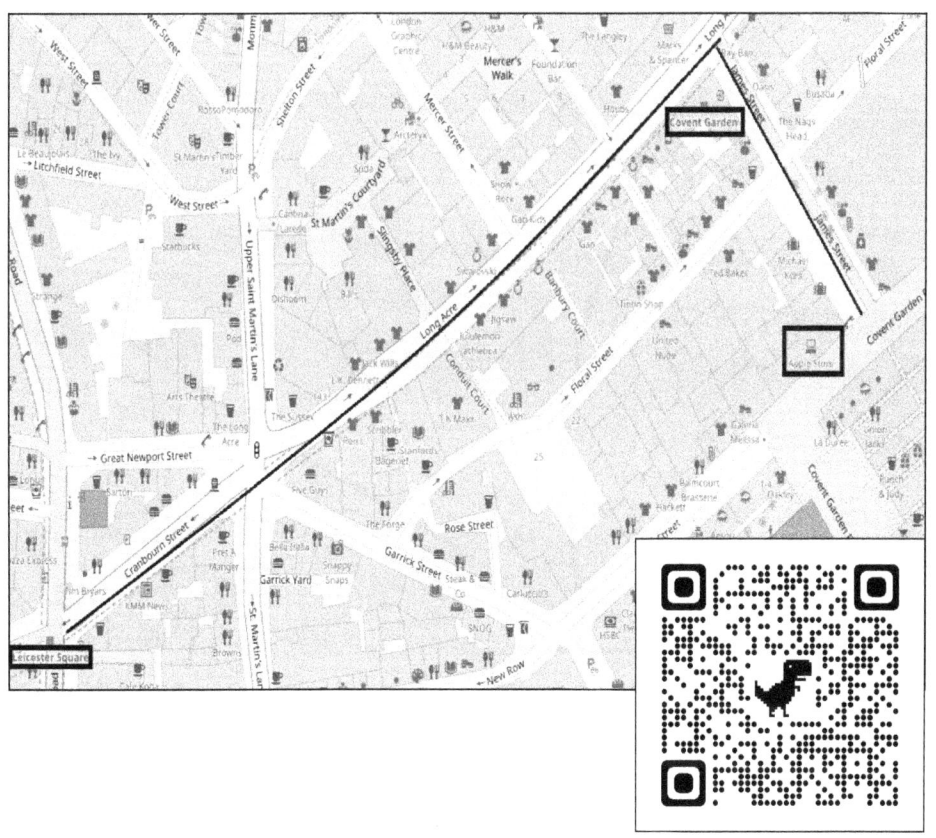

175

In The Gallery / Angelucci's
/ Ronnie Scott's / Barocco Bar

From **Covent Garden** go back to **Long Acre / Cranbourne Street**, go back to **Leicester Square tube station** and turn right by **Charing Cross Road** until it crosses **Shaftesbury Avenue**. At that **junction** is where the **gallery** that inspired the '<u>In The Gallery</u>' song used to be. A little bit further is **Moor Street**, which was the location of the **Barocco Bar (13 Moor Street)**. Turning left by **Old Compton Street** you'll find **Frith Street** on the right, where **Ronnie Scott's** stands, and in front, the ice cream shop that used to be **Angelucci's**.

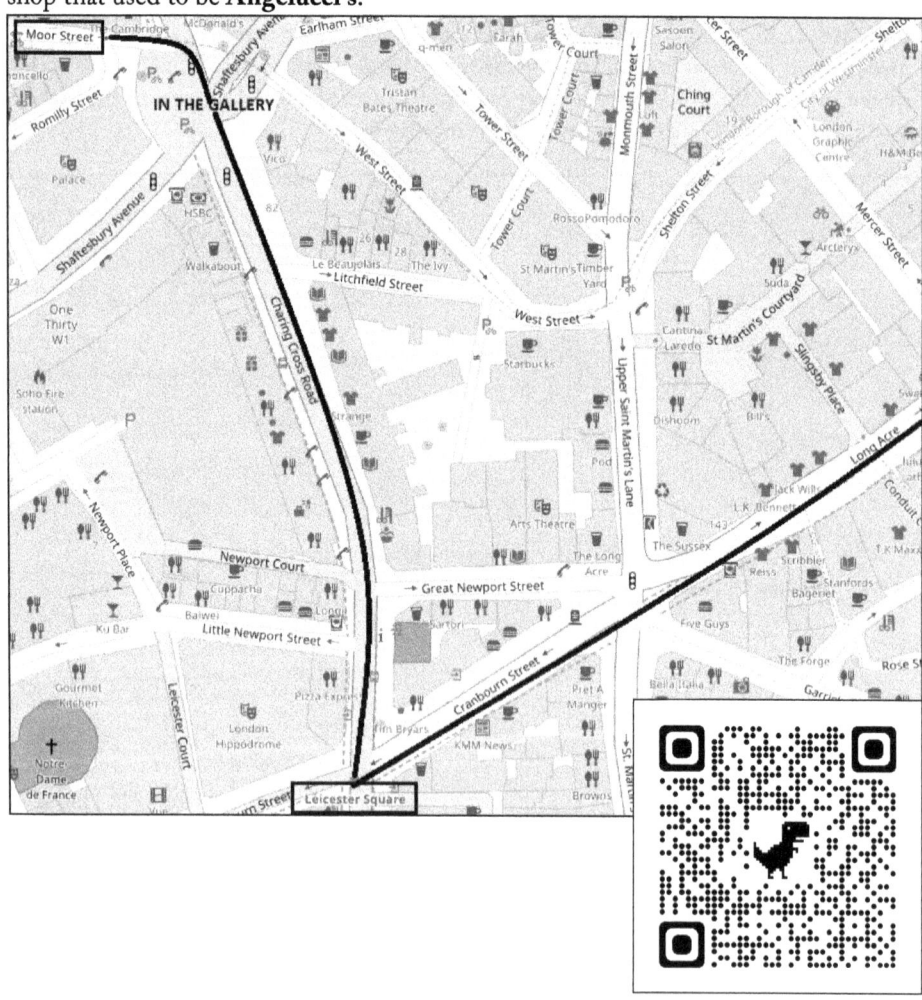

WEST END MAPS

In The Gallery / Angelucci's / Ronnie Scott's / Barocco Bar (II)

CHINATOWN

From **Frith Street**, return to **Shaftesbury Avenue** and then turn right, walking in the direction of **Piccadilly Circus**. The first street you will find on the left is **Macclesfield Street** and from there, the entrance to **Chinatown** can clearly be seen.

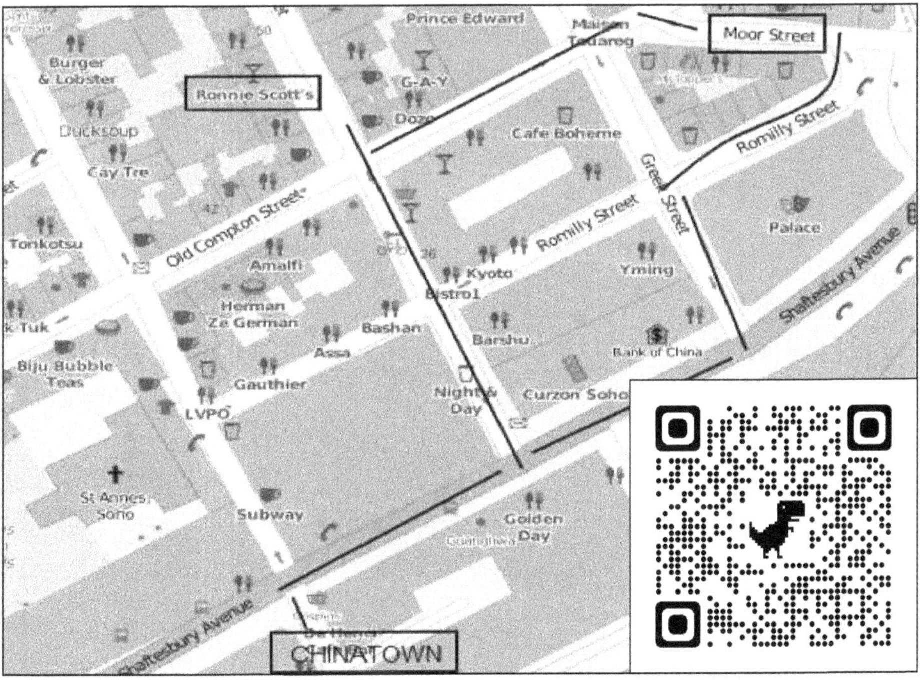

LIONS

Walk along **Shaftesbury Avenue** towards **Piccadilly Circus**. From there follow **Coventry Street** and then **Haymarket**, turn left at **Cockspur Street** and you'll find yourself in front of **Nelson's Column** and the **lions**.

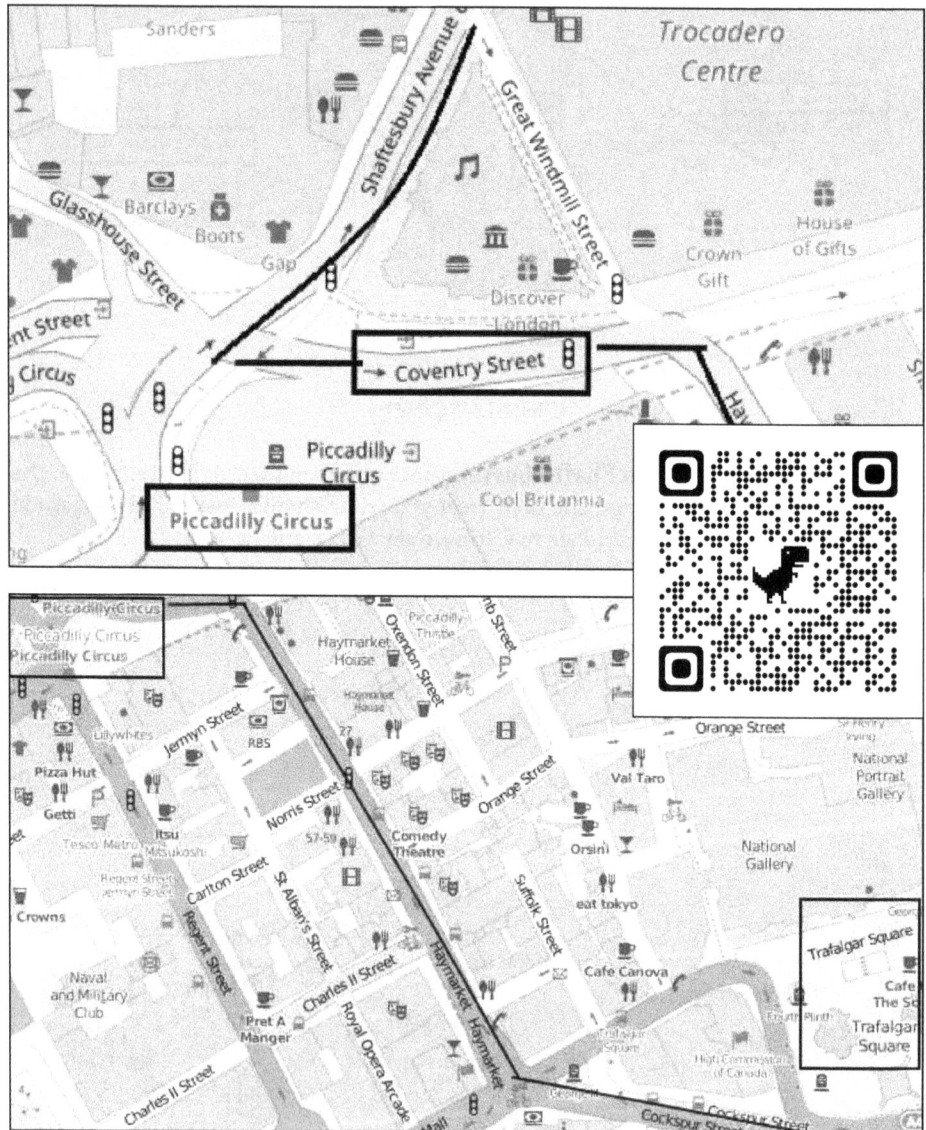

BUCKINGHAM / WESTMINSTER

For **Buckingham Palace**, take **The Mall** from the **Admiralty Arch** for **Westminster**, passing by the **Horse Guards Parade, Downing Street, Houses of Parliament, Big Ben, Millennium Wheel and Westminster Abbey**, take **Whitehall Avenue** and follow it straight.

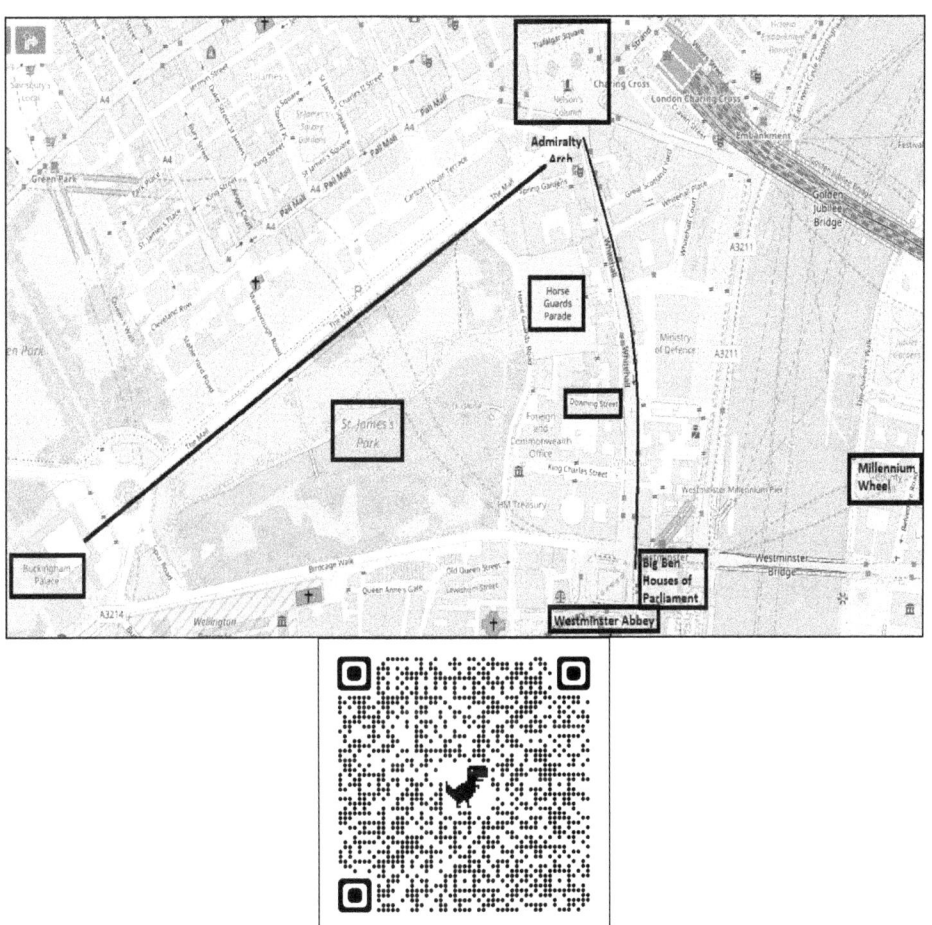

9
NOTTING HILL & HYDE PARK

PICTURE: ÒSCAR PALLARÉS

The band had proved their worth at live gigs and it was time to cut their first record. The chosen studio was located in Notting Hill, a district in West London, within the Royal Borough of Kensington & Chelsea. **Notting Hill** is known for hosting the annual Notting Hill Carnival and **Portobello Road Market**.

It is also known by the 1999 movie of the same name, 'Notting Hill', with Hugh Grant and Julia Roberts in the leading roles and for the 1971 film 'Bedknobs and Broomsticks' starring Angela Lansbury. Many of the scenes from 'Notting Hill' were filmed in Portobello Road and the famous fruit and vegetables market can be seen, along with some of the antiques stores.

Basing Street Studios, named for the street in which it was located, was established by Chris Blackwell, the founder of Island Records. It has also been known in the past as Island Studios and SARM, which was its last name. The studios were built inside a former church. In 2013, its last owner, **Trevor Horn**, decided to close the studio and sell some of the recording material before moving to another complex, Sarm Music Village, operating not far from Basing Street, at Ladbroke Grove, also in the Notting Hill area.

Basing Street Studios, under its different names, hosted some legendary recording sessions such as *Led Zeppelin's 'IV', Jethro Tull's 'Aqualung', 'Do They Know It's Christmas' by Band Aid*, recorded prior to the famous Live Aid concert, and recordings by many other artists such as *Queen, Bob Marley, The Eagles, The Rolling Stones, Genesis* and Guy Fletcher's former band *Roxy Music* etc.

PICTURE: JOSÉ IGNACIO CORBALÁN

PICTURE: JAVIER PELÁEZ

Between February and March 1978 Dire Straits recorded their first album, produced by **Muff Winwood**. It could be recorded so quickly as most of the songs had been a part of their live repertoire for a long time. Only 'Lions' was written shortly before entering the studio.

John Illsley: *"It was the first time we had been in a proper recording studio, so overwhelming in some ways but we got used to it , and most of the tracks went down live as we were gigging a lot and so we just set up and played. The whole thing took three weeks I think. Enjoyed working with Muff and Rhett Davis - a great engineer."*

In 2005, the **BBC** produced a **documentary called 'Brothers in Arms'**, talking about brothers who played together in rock bands. In the section about the Knopfler brothers, Ed Bicknell, David Knopfler and Muff Winwood can be seen talking about the relationship between Mark and David during the first years and the recording of the first record. Muff, who also played bass with his brother Steve in the Spencer Davis Group says that he suggested they record a couple of David's songs during the recording of their first album, but Mark wanted to focus on his own stuff, which was what they were playing live.

In 1998, Mark Knopfler would come back to these studios, as **Sarm West Studios**, to record the Metroland film score.

During the recording of their first album, Dire Straits members used to go for a drink in a nearby pub, "**Finch's**" (now the **Duke of Wellington**) in **Portobello Road**, where Mark met the landlady and wrote a song about her. That song was rehearsed and included soon after in their set. The song was 'Portobello Belle' which would feature on their second album, 'Communiqué' that would be recorded in Nassau between November and December 1979 with producers Jerry Wexler and Barry Beckett, who play piano as well in some of the songs.

Today, inside the Duke of Wellington pub there is a reference to this:

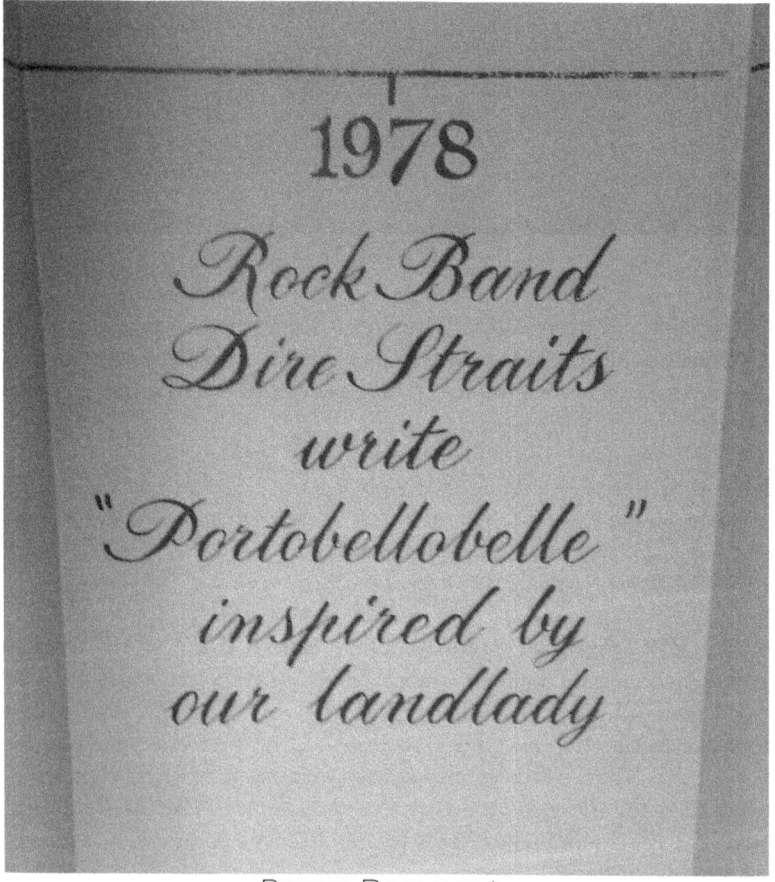

PICTURE: DAVID MARTÍN

NOTTING HILL / HYDE PARK

PICTURE: JUAN PABLO BERNARDO

PICTURE: DAVID MARTÍN

The Finch's landlady was **Rita Carty** and her daughter **Roisin Carty** gave this account:

Our Mum, Rita Carty, was landlady at The Duke of Wellington from 1968 to 1978. She came from Cavan in Ireland - hence all the Irish references in the song. Our parents divorced in the early 70s so our mum ran the pub on her own for the next six or so years (and even when our Dad was around she was very much in charge).

Everyone on Portobello knew and loved her. She had a reputation for being strong in running the pub (which was rough at that time) and bringing up her daughters single-handedly. She was petite and very beautiful (picture Jean Simmons or Elizabeth Taylor). The blind man mentioned in the song was Blind Bob. He used to sing outside our pub and was a regular customer.

Our Mum remembered that Mark Knopfler was a customer in the pub. She liked the song but wasn't so happy about the line "She ain't no English Rose" because at first she thought it meant she wasn't good looking! But we played the song a lot and we're very proud of it.

She inspired the song but it isn't a direct description of her (for example she never wore fingerless gloves - that's what the fruit and veg sellers would wear... and there were plenty in Portobello alongside the antiques shops selling Victoriana).

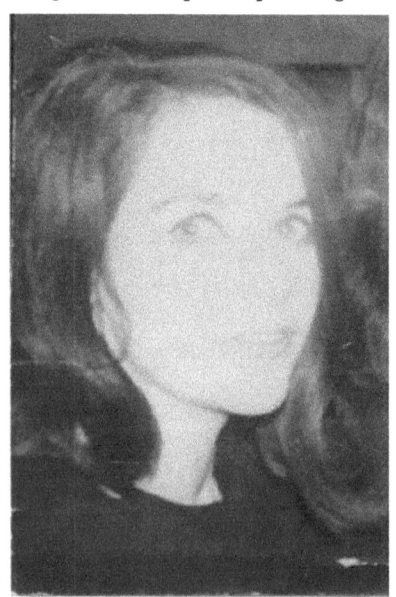

RITA CARTY, THE "PORTOBELLO BELLE". PICTURES COURTESY OF THEIR DAUGHTERS ROISIN AND MAIREAD CARTY

Also in Notting Hill and not very far from Portobello Road was the location of the office of **Ed Bicknell's Damage Management**. The agency managed Dire Straits from 1977 until they disbanded in 1995 and also Mark Knopfler's solo career until 2000, when Ed Bicknell and Mark Knopfler decided to take different directions and the office was closed.

At the start of Dire Straits' career, the office was located in 10 Southwick Mews, in Paddington, not long from Hyde Park and Marble Arch.

FORMER OFFICE OF DAMAGE MANAGEMENT
IN LAMBTON PLACE 16

Pictures of Damage Management office in 1999,
by Christian Almstrom

ENTRY TO SOUTHWICK MEWS, PLACE OF THE FIRST OFFICE OF DAMAGE MANAGEMENT. COURTESY OF IGOR SALMI

When a fan hears 'Notting Hill', immediately Knopfler's 'other band' springs to mind - **The Notting Hillbillies**.

In many interviews, Mark made references to a little recording studio set up in his Notting Hill house. It was where the Notting Hillbillies project was born when he was producing a record for **Steve Phillips** and **Brendan Croker**, old friends from his journalist days in Leeds. For this project he asked the help of **Guy Fletcher**, keyboardist of Dire Straits and collaborator with Mark Knopfler in many of his solo projects. That project evolved until it turned into a band that took its name from the London neighbourhood where Mark Knopfler lived and where the music was being recorded. According to some of the promo interviews for his second solo album, 'Sailing to

Philadelphia', in the year 2000, one TV programme for **Norwegian television NRK1** called '**Meeting in Holland Park**' in which Knopfler mentions that he "*used to live there, but now has moved to Chelsea*", the studio was located at **Holland Park Mews**, which is the street that can be seen in that interview. Also in many recent interviews about his own professional recording studio, **British Grove Studios**, he mentions that he used to have a studio in a little mews in Notting Hill.

Holland Park Mews is a cobbled street approached through its own arch off Holland Park in the Royal Borough of Kensington and Chelsea. Part of the Holland Park Conservation Area, all the properties are Grade II Listed Buildings and very well preserved. Originally used as the coach house/ stable accommodation for the main houses on Holland Park, their primary purpose nowadays is residential.

Some of the other projects recorded in his home studio were the film scores for 'The Princess Bride', 'Last Exit to Brooklyn' and the final overdubs of almost all his solo records after the main recordings were made in Nashville. Many parts of the Mark Knopfler and Chet Atkins 'Neck and Neck' album were recorded in that home studio, in a small room that inspired Studio 2 in the professional British Grove Studios, owned by Mark Knopfler in Chiswick, where Mark Knopfler and Guy Fletcher work alone giving shape to his new songs before the band arrive at Studio 1 to complete them.

Hyde Park is undoubtedly the most famous park in London and is located not far from Notting Hill. At one of its entrances there are two places related to songs written by Mark Knopfler: **Marble Arch** and **Speaker's Corner**.

Marble Arch is a white marble triumphal arch, originally designed by John Nash in 1827 to be the state entrance to the cour d'honneur of Buckingham Palace (also by Nash), but it was relocated in Park Lane in 1851 and nowadays stands on a large traffic island at the junction of Oxford Street, Park Lane and Edgware Road, isolated from the traffic.

The story in the song 'Madame Geneva's', published in Mark Knopfler's fifth solo album 'Kill To Get Crimson' in 2007, makes reference to the area around **Marble Arch**, a place where prisoners used to be executed by hanging. At that time it was known as **Tyburn Gallows**. That name comes from one of the tributaries of the Thames, the Tyburn Brook, which today runs completely beneath the streets of London. Knopfler also talks about **Gin Lane**, although this was the name of a print created by the famous 18th century artist William Hogarth to support the Gin Act and which was actually set in Bloomsbury, another part of London. 'Gin Lane' showed terrible scenes of public drunkenness and crime.

Speakers' Corner is one of the main entrances to **Hyde Park**, located close to the corner next to **Marble Arch** and a part of the park where those who wish to talk to the public and express their ideas and spark debates, often standing on soap boxes, or whatever, to be seen by everybody, may voice their opinions. Usually, Sunday is the day when most people can be found speaking, but it's normal to find them any day. There is total freedom of speech as long as there is respect for everyone's beliefs and there are no fights. It's common to see policemen around but they don't interfere, allowing everybody to give their speeches freely. This place is mentioned in the Dire Straits song 'Industrial Disease' from the 'Love Over Gold' album, where Knopfler makes a reference to *'two men say they are Jesus, one of them must be wrong'* which gives a good impression of the spirit of Speakers Corner.

PICTURE: JAVIER PELÁEZ

At the opposite part of **Hyde Park**, beyond the **Serpentine lake**, is one of the most iconic music venues in London (and famous worldwide) the **Royal Albert Hall**. Meeting point of Mark Knopfler fans, not only from Europe but from all parts of the world, this venue was the one chosen by Knopfler to play in London once he began his solo career, with so much success that he usually plays several nights in a row, with a record of six consecutive sold-out nights in his 2010 and 2013 tours.

Notting Hill / Hyde Park

The Royal Albert Hall

THE ALBERT MEMORIAL

The **Royal Albert Hall** opened its doors in 1871 and since then has witnessed performances by the best orchestras in the world, and concerts given by the biggest stars of rock such as *Jimi Hendrix, Led Zeppelin, Pink Floyd, Deep Purple, Bob Dylan, Eric Clapton* etc, including Mark Knopfler who played there for the first time in 1987, as part of the band in an Eric Clapton tour.

It was born from Prince Albert's idea of building a venue where art could have a place for all the citizens. Construction began in 1867, but he died before its completion. Queen Victoria ensured that construction continued and that there was the construction additionally of a memorial to her husband, so today there is a statue of Prince Albert looking directly towards the hall, known as the Albert Memorial.

The Royal Albert Hall was designed by Captain Francis Fowke, an architect/engineer who specialised in iron-framed buildings; it has distinctive large open galleries and spaces. Another building with similar construction methods he designed was the Royal Museum in Edinburgh, built 1861-6 and now the National Museum of Scotland (see Edinburgh chapter).

Over the years it has featured in popular culture and been used in some famous films such as 'The Knack' starring Michael Crawford and Rita Tushingham, and also in both of Hitchcock's versions of 'The Man Who Knew Too Much' where the interior is filmed.

PICTURE: JAVIER PELÁEZ

NOTTING HILL / HYDE PARK

MARK KNOPFLER AND BAND, PLAYING AT THE ROYAL ALBERT HALL, MAY 2015

Some pictures of the Royal Albert Hall decorated to welcome Mark Knopfler and his fans in 2010 and 2013

NOTTING HILL & HYDE PARK MAPS

NOTTING HILL

The conventional route that is recommended suggests going on a Saturday as it's the day when the antiques market takes place on the street in Portobello Road (during the week you will find only the fruit and vegetable market). Start at the **Notting Hill Gate tube stop** on the **Central (red) Line**. When exiting, turn right and then turn right again onto **Pembridge Road. Portobello Road** is the second street on the left.

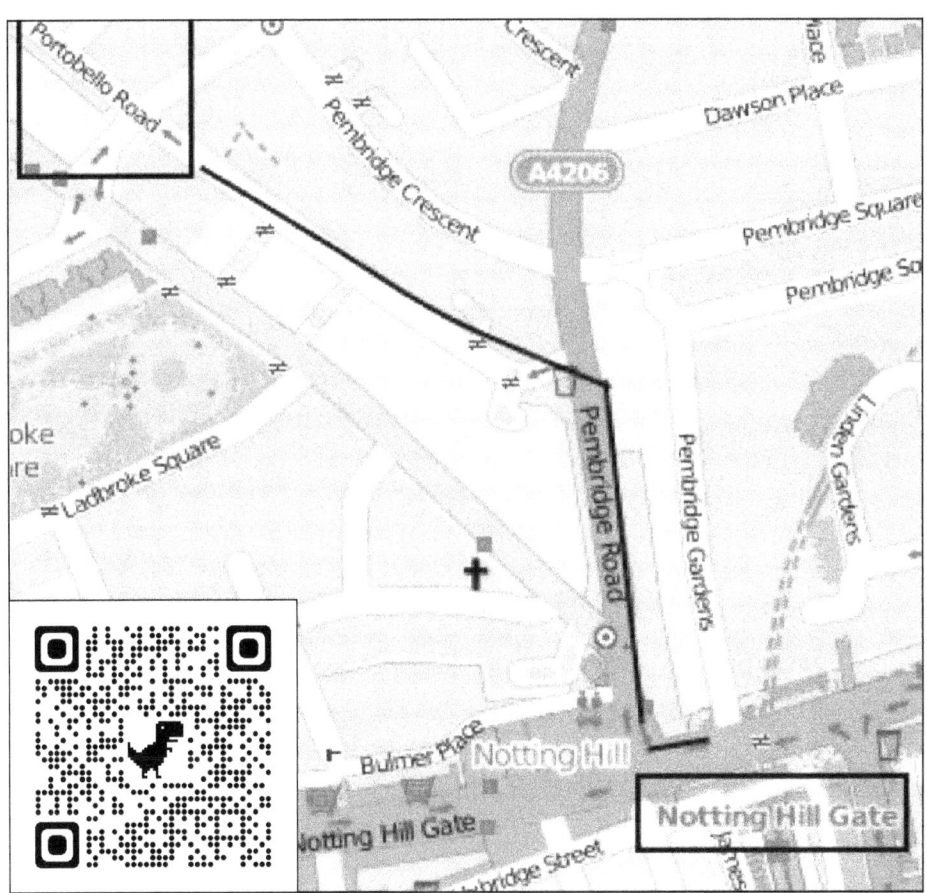

DAMAGE MANAGEMENT

Turn right on the second street that crosses **Portobello Road**, which is **Westbourne Grove**. Walk along Westbourne Grove until you get to **Lambton Place**, which is the second street on the right. The office used to be at **number 16**.

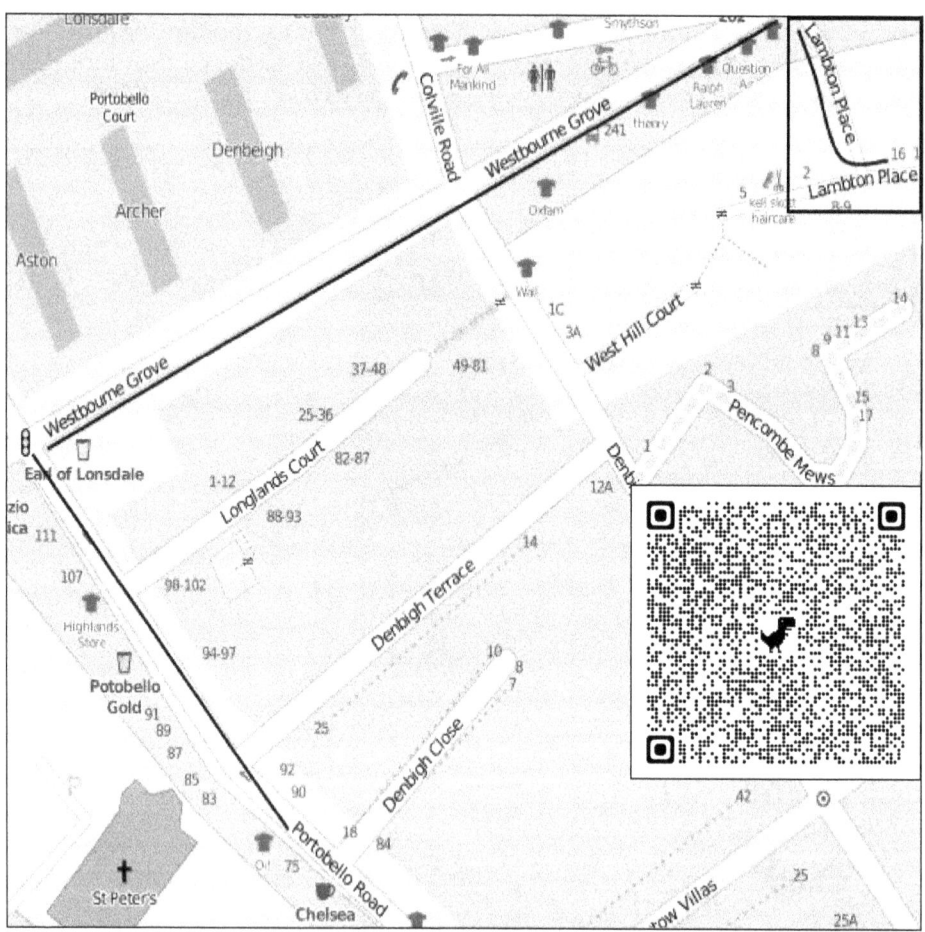

DAMAGE MANAGEMENT IN SOUTHWICK MEWS

From **Marble Arch**, take **Edgeware Road** and turn left in **Sussex Gardens** and then take **Norfolk Place** at your right and you'll see **Southwick Mews** entry.

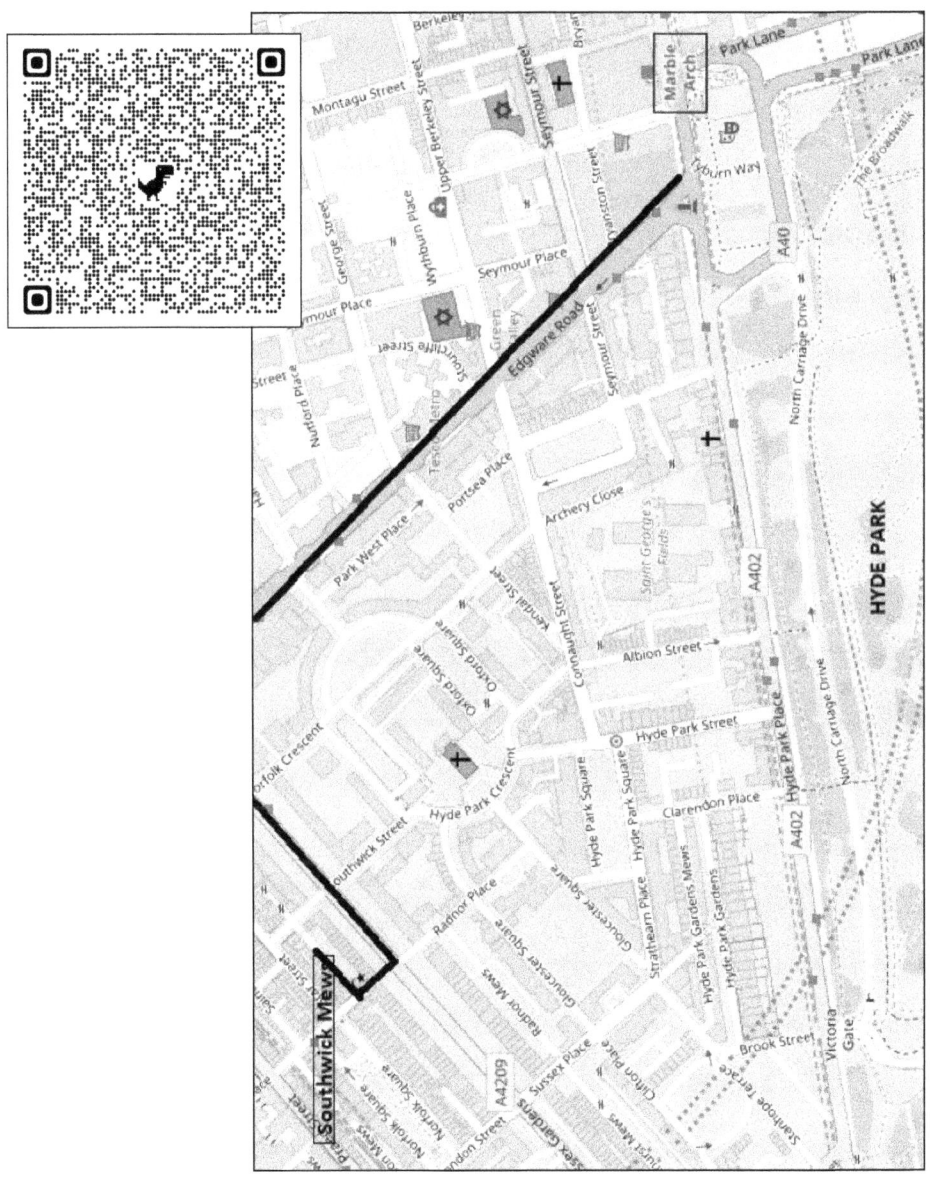

DUKE OF WELLINGTON

Go back to **Portobello Road** and in a short three-minute walk you will find the **Duke of Wellington pub**, where the landlady inspired Mark Knopfler to write 'Portobello Belle', on your left.

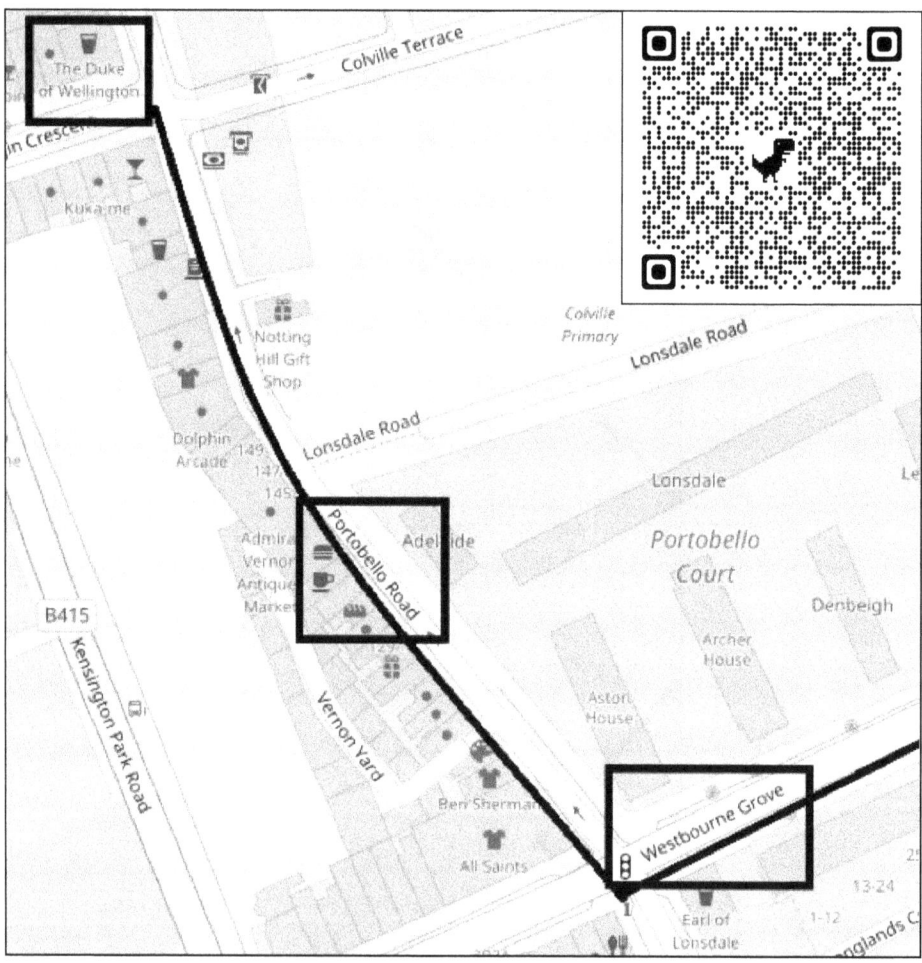

BASING STREET

Continue your route going back to **Portobello Road** and enjoying the market until you cross **Westbourne Park**. Turn right and the first street on your left is **Basing Street**, which is where one of the most prestigious London studios, owned by Trevor Horn, was once located. It existed under different names, Sarm West Studios being the last one.

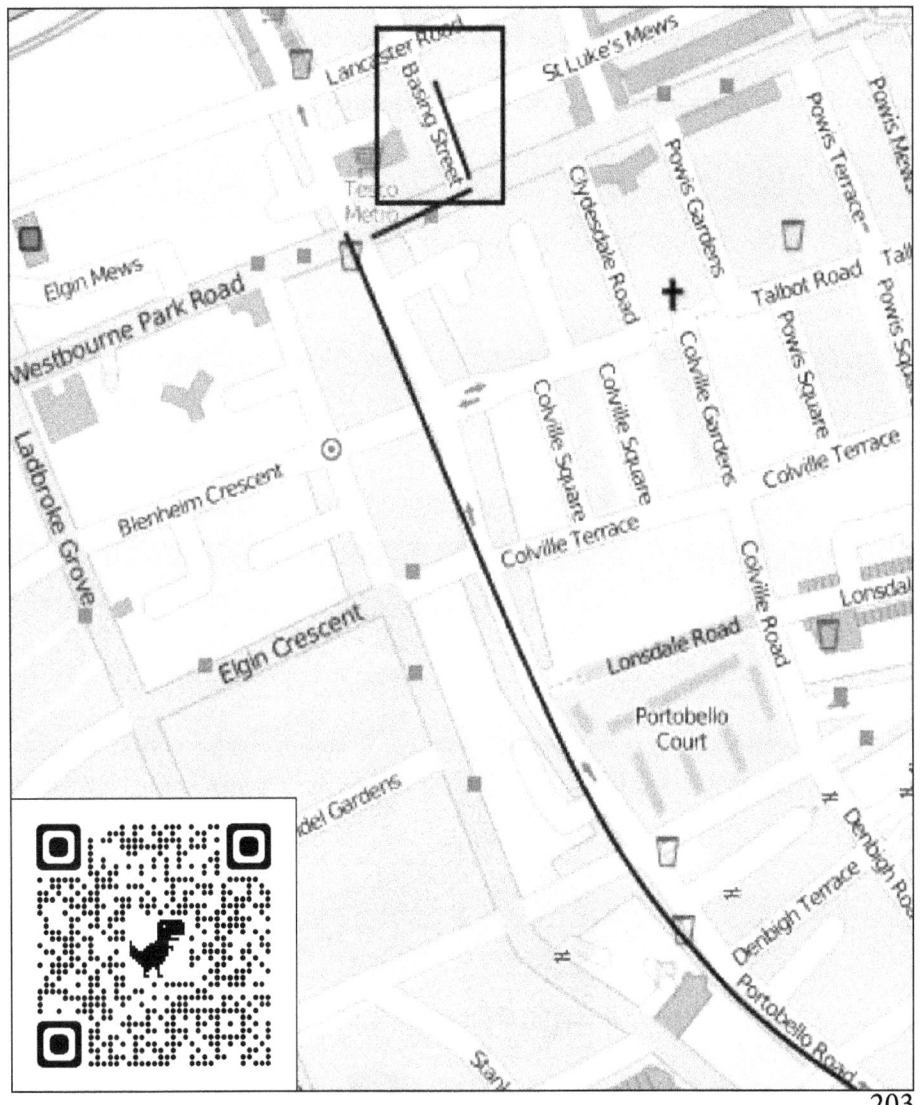

MARBLE ARCH / SPEAKER'S CORNER

The easiest way to get there is taking the **Central (red) Line** to **Marble Arch tube station**, which is just next to Hyde Park.

ROYAL ALBERT HALL

Enjoy a pleasant walk through **Hyde Park** on your way to the **Royal Albert Hall**. You will find a lake named **The Serpentine** that you will cross by the bridge and then follow the road until you are opposite the **Albert Monument** and the theatre.

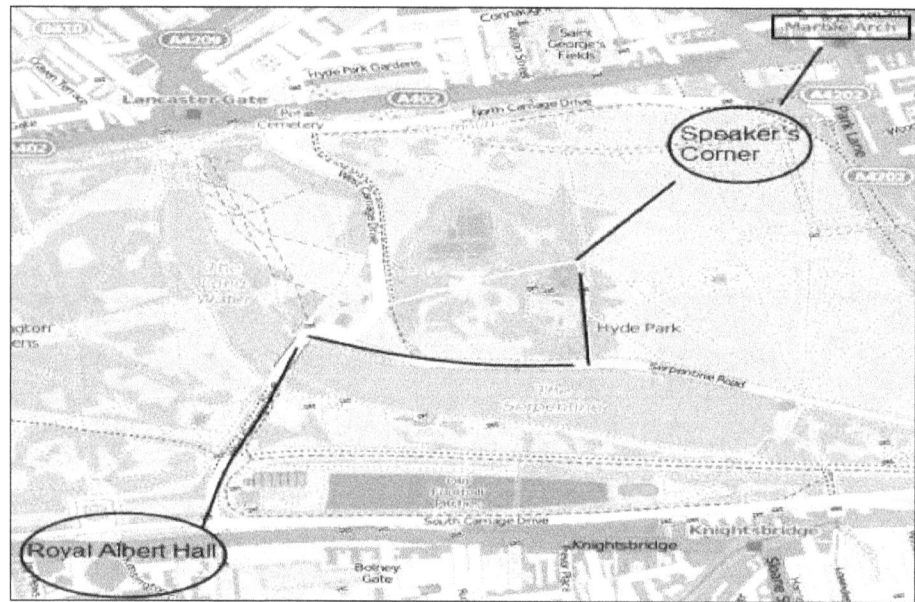

HOLLAND PARK

Holland Park tube station can be reached using the **Central (red) line** as well. Walking towards **Holland Park Avenue** and depending whether you go right or left you'll have to turn at Holland Park or at **Holland Park / Abbotsbury Road**. You'll find the small entry to **Holland Park Mews**.

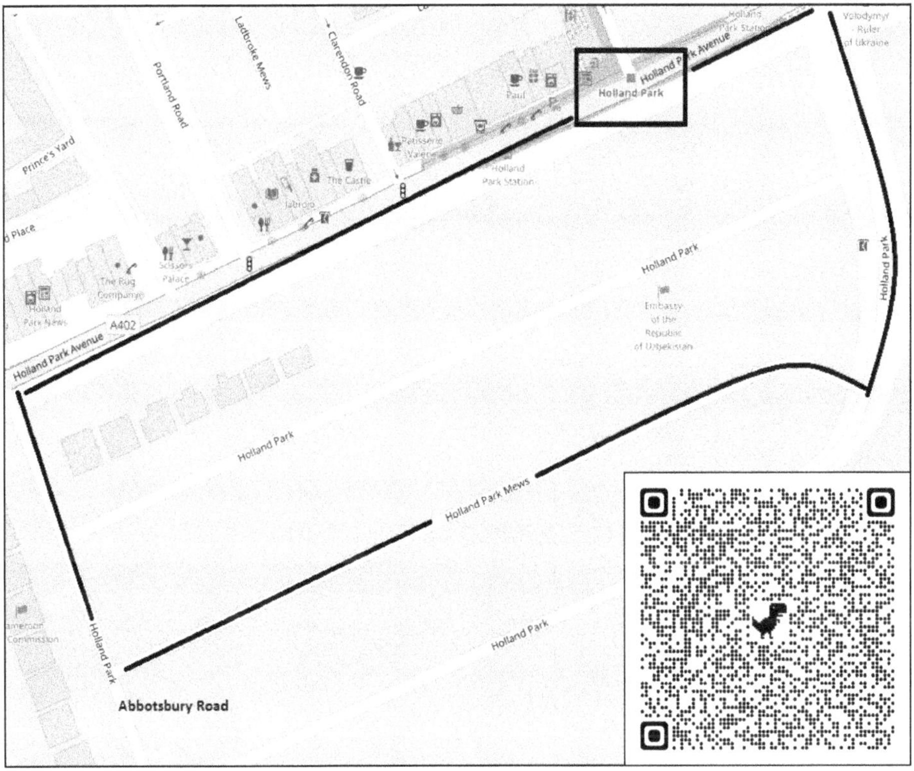

Note that Marble Arch / Notting Hill Gate and Holland Park are on the same tube line, and also Shepherd's Bush, which is the subject of another chapter.

10 NEW YORK

PICTURE: JOSÉ IGNACIO CORBALÁN

Although 'Communique', Dire Straits' second album, was a commercial success the general opinion of critics was that it was too similar-sounding to the first record, so Knopfler decided to find a producer to provide a more hard-edged sound, including the introduction of a piano. This is why producer **Jimmy Iovine** was contacted; he then recruited **Roy Bittan**, keyboardist of Bruce Springsteen's E Street Band for the recording. In June 1980 they entered the **Power Station Studios** in New York to record their third album 'Making Movies', starting a relationship between The Big Apple and the band including Mark Knopfler. They would return to record their next album 'Love Over Gold'; the first excursion into the world of film soundtracks by Knopfler for 'Local Hero'; produce and play on the album 'Infidels' by **Bob Dylan** and also to record and mix parts for what would be the biggest hit of all for Dire Straits, 'Brothers in Arms'. Additionally he met two people who were important in his personal and musical life: **Lourdes Salomone** and **Rudy Pensa**.

Three pictures of Avatar Studios, formerly known as Power Station Studios, by Dan Molda

Mark Knopfler recording in Power Station Studios
(1982-83 Tour programme)
Pictures: Guido Harari

Lourdes Salomone was an employee of **Power Station Studio** at the time and during the recording of 'Making Movies' she and Mark met and started a relationship. On 10 November 1983 they were married in a Register's office in Chelsea, London and as a wedding gift Mark bought her a house in **Greenwich Village on Bank Street, New York**[1].

From that moment, they lived between London and Manhattan, until the couple divorced in the early '90s, settling Knopfler at his London residence full-time.

According to an interview with Scott Spencer, from Rolling Stone magazine, Knopfler said *"At that time, I was living half the time in New York and half in London. I think Bob (Dylan) quite liked walking the streets of Greenwich Village again. He used to come round to our house on Bank Street armed against the cold in a fur hat, long blue cashmere coat and biker boots. I'd make a pot of coffee and we'd play pool."*[2]

Pictures: Dan Molda

[1]http://www.grandlifehotels.com/culture/the-best-little-block-in-the-world-bank-street/ GrandLife Blog, Peter Foges
[2]http://rollingstoneindia.com/mark-knopfler%E2%80%99s-second-act/2/ September 9, 2008 Scott Spencer, Rolling Stone India

Pictures: Dan Molda

As the observer Mark absorbs everything that surrounds him. Over the years living in the Big Apple he got the inspiration to write some of his songs, such as 'Money for Nothing', emerging from a conversation he overheard among the employees of an appliance store, where every television was tuned into MTV, criticising the appearance and lifestyle of the musicians who appear on the screens. He sat in one of the kitchens of the store to take notes of it all to write what would be the lyrics of one of the biggest hits of that album. The video clip for this song featured animations representing those workers, talking to each other in the appliance store. While Knopfler has never mentioned the name of the establishment, it could be one of the chain **PC Richard & Son**, very popular in the city at that time.

In the notes accompanying the compilation of Dire Straits' 'Sultans Of Swing' published in 1998, music journalist **Robert Sandall** speaks with Mark Knopfler on the origin of many of the group songs and specifically of 'Your Latest Trick'. He explains the bike rides via **9th Avenue** from the studios to his home in **Greenwich Village** after a long night of work which served as inspiration for the lyrics. The large garbage trucks, the taxis, the lights, the bustle of the streets down to to his house in **Bank Street**[2], etc form the basis to start writing one of the most important songs in the history of the group.

One of the biggest concerns arising from the tours was the harm suffered by their Fender Stratocaster guitars. Given the need to find a model that could replace them

[2] http://rollingstoneindia.com/mark-knopfler%E2%80%99s-second-act/2/ September 9, 2008 Scott Spencer, Rolling Stone India

9TH AVENUE. PICTURES: DAN MOLDA

and avoid further damage, Mark met **Rudy Pensa**, owner of the **Rudy Music's Stop** store on 48th Street between the first visit of the band in 1979 and 1980. Argentine by birth, Rudy had arrived in New York in 1978. His establishment soon gained a high reputation, specialising in vintage guitars and also in the construction and repair of guitars. It's where Knopfler would find one of his favourite guitars until Dire Straits disbanded, the Schecter. Rudy was asked by him also to build some guitars with specific characteristics, and this is how Mark met the luthier **John Suhr**, who worked in the shop and helped in the repair and development of new models.

The first they developed together was called R Custom, several of which were used in the recording and tour of 'Brothers In Arms', to be named Pensa Suhr in the late

PICTURE: ELIAN POUPARD
RUDY'S MUSIC STOP ORIGINAL SHOP

'80s, and when John left in 1990 to practise independently, Rudy continued to work on new instruments under the name Pensa Custom.

The best-known model would be the **Pensa Suhr MK**. On the Guitar Stories documentary Mark and Rudy reminisced over the romantic story that it was designed on a napkin in a coffee shop in New York. The objective was to combine the type of clean sound of a Stratocaster with the most powerful from a Gibson type, to avoid frequent guitar changes during concerts. From then until the end of the group's history it was the main guitar during the recording and tour of the album 'On Every Street', the band's last album. Its debut was at the **Prince's Trust Benefit Concert** on 5th and 6th June 1988 at the **RAH** in London where Mark appeared as a member of the *Eric Clapton band*, along with *Elton John*, and later at the concert for **Nelson Mandela's 70th Birthday** at Wembley Stadium on 11th June 1988 with Dire Straits, where Clapton played guitar accompanying the band. This was preceded by two warm-up mini concerts on 8th and 9th June where it was also used.

John Suhr gave his own version in the forum "TheGearPage.net"[3]: *"Mark Knopfler's was an interesting story. Naturally I don't remember it the way Rudy does, something about designing on a paper napkin... I already had a good portion of it built before we decided it was for Mark. In fact you can see the body as I was working on it in an old D'Addario add. ( ) Knopfler's was the most challenging since I had less than one week to paint it and build it for the Mandela concert, I was scared it would stick to the case!"*

"I already had begun the carve, it was just something I wanted to do. ( ) When I was in the carving process Rudy decided it would be a great guitar for MK for the Mandela Concert. They went out to lunch and talked about details like pickup colour etc but otherwise it was

[3] https://www.thegearpage.net/board/index.php?threads/any-pensa-suhr-owners-out-there.393313/

PENSA-SUHR GUITARS ADD.

pretty much already set in stone. Mark had some extra ideas like tapering the headstock but I explained it was too late. He also didn't like the rings not matching the pickup colour and wanted Ivory colour so I mounted the humbucker from the back so no ring was used. He decided the bridge should be locked to the body since he had no intention of using the tremolo really but enjoyed the stability of a locking setup. ( ) Rudy Pensa was the store owner and ran the business end, I did all repairs and building but I was only an employee there and we had no real factory".

New models under the name Pensa Custom have been built and used by Mark during his solo career in different albums and tours, always with a similar design and sound that make them easily identifiable.

Due to the business success, in December 2009 Rudy opened a new branch in **Soho**, at **461 Broome Street**. Unfortunately, in 2015 the 48th Street store was closed, like many other businesses dedicated to musical instruments that were in the area, so today this new store in Soho is the only one still in operation.

ALBERTO FERNÁNDEZ BURGOS

PICTURES: ELIAN POUPARD
RUDY'S MUSIC STOP AT SOHO

Picture: Elian Poupard

Picture: Dan Molda

Picture: Dan Molda
Rudy's Music Stop at Soho

John Suhr

John Suhr has designed and built a lot of guitars for a lot of people we all know. Like the list at left. And he strings his Pensa-Suhr guitars with D'Addarios for "consistently superior sound quality no matter what kind of music the players play."

D'Addario Strings & John Suhr: equipment for the major players.

D'Addadrio add, mentioned by John Suhr, with the body of the Pensa Suhr

During those first visits to the original store, Mark became friends with one of the workers in the shop, **Jack Sonni**, who also played guitar in some local bands. During the recording of 'Brothers In Arms', **Hal Lindes**, rhythm guitarist with Dire Straits, left the group and Mark offered Jack the opportunity to be a part of the band. He agreed and travelled to the island of **Montserrat** to participate in the sessions that were in progress at **Air Studios**. Later it was decided he would continue in the group and participate in the forthcoming world tour and this is how Jack Sonni became a guitarist with Dire Straits during the period of biggest success for the band.

Jack Sonni: *"We had become very close friends while meeting at the guitar shop during the recording of 'Making Movies'. We hung out, played guitars, drank, argued about music and drank some more. He sat in with my band when he was in town. I got 'phone calls from around the world while he was on tour to talk, bitch and shoot the shit. Like friends do. The idea of me playing in his band never came up until early December 1984*[4]*. I'd been in New York City for almost ten years chasing the rock star dream and it nearly killed me — literally. So I quit. In my head, it was done. I was working behind the counter in a guitar shop and had decided to go back to school for my main passion—writing. Fordham had accepted me already. Then just a couple days after I received my acceptance letter, I got a call from Mark Knopfler of Dire Straits to come and join him on the road. I was literally in the store one day, on the road the next. Caught up in the whirlwind, the heady seduction of performing on stage with my idols was a powerful thing."*[5]

It was also thanks to his friendship with Rudy that Mark discovered **Monteleone guitars**. Amazed by the beauty of them, he asked to meet the person who built them, visiting the luthier's workshop in **Islip, Long Island**, where he constructs his instruments one by one, completely handcrafted.

[4] http://jacksonni.com/thirty-years-on/
December 2014, Jack Sonni, Jack Sonni´s website
[5] https://reneejohnsonwrites.com/2015/04/15/jack-sonni-rocker-writer-gentleman-chef/ April 15, 2015, Renee Johnson, Renee Johnson writes blog.

As a result of this meeting, **John Monteleone** began working on a guitar for Knopfler and during the process, sent Mark a series of e-mails in which John spoke about the different phases of the construction. These e-mails were the inspiration for the lyrics of the song 'Monteleone' recorded on his album 'Get Lucky', which also marked the debut of the guitar by his rhythm guitarist Richard Bennett. The instrument would be named the **Monteleone Isabella,** in honour of one of Knopfler's daughters.

MONTELEONE'S GUITARS AND MANDOLINS MONTELEONE DISPLAYED IN RUDY PENSA'S SHOP. PICTURE: ELIAN POUPARD

All those years in New York created memories that have come back to Mark, reflected in his songs, as in the case of '<u>Radio City Serenade</u>' which is part of his double album '<u>Privateering</u>'. The Statue of Liberty is mentioned various times during the song, referred to as '*The lady with a light*' or "*The lady by the sea*" amidst '*the crosstown horns*'. The Hudson river features in the lyrics as well - "*I got you a river view*" and of course the theatre that gives name to the song, the **Radio City Music Hall** and '**The Rockettes**' ('*my beautiful Rockette*'), which is a precision dance company that performs at the Radio

Radio City Music Hall.
Picture: Elian Poupard

City Music Hall, especially during the Christmas season, when they play five shows a day, seven days a week.

"Radio City Serenade" is not the only time *"The Lady with a light"* appears in a Knopfler song. In the song "On Every Street", from the last Dire Straits record of the same name, there is also a mention in the lyrics: *"and the fireworks over liberty explode in the heat"*. During some promotional interviews in 1991 Knopfler was asked about its relationship with New York and he confirmed that "liberty" is a reference to **Liberty Island**, where the famous **Statue of Liberty** is located, and that the *"fireworks exploding in the heat"* is a reference to the fireworks on 4th of July.[6][7]

Both Dire Straits and Mark Knopfler as a solo artist played several times in the city, including at the **Radio City Music Hall** itself, with the band during the 'Brothers in Arms' tour along with the famous saxophonist *Branford Marsalis* as a guest on several songs. He also played there on the 'Shangri-La' tour in 2005 and the following year on tour with *Emmylou Harris*. In 2001 promoting the album 'Sailing to Philadelphia' and during the 'Tracker' and "Down the Road Wherever" tours in 2015 and 2019 they performed twice at the **Beacon Theatre**, where he had played with Dire Straits in 1980. In 2008 on the 'Kill To Get Crimson' tour at the **Rumsey Playfield auditorium in Central Park** and the **United Palace Theatre** during the "Get Lucky" tour, premiering the song 'Monteleone' live, John himself was in the audience that night with Rudy Pensa. The **Bottom Line**, the **Palladium** and **Madison Square Garden** have also played host to Dire Straits live over the years. The last one hosted the last show of the "Down the Road Wherever" tour (and maybe the last Mark Knopfler concert on a big tour format) with Bonnie Raitt.

[6] Q magazine 1991:
https://web.archive.org/web/20010222155952fw_/http://www.knopfler.net/interview10.html
[7] 4MMM FM. Brisbane, Australia, 10th November 1991:
https://web.archive.org/web/20010222155639fw_/http://www.knopfler.net/interview11.html

Top: Beacon Theatre, 2015 Elian Poupard
Bottom: Madison Sqare Garden, 2019. Alberto Fernández Burgos

It might be another reference to the city in the song 'So Far Away' from the album 'Brothers In Arms.' Although it is not specifically mentioned, he talks about separation, about missing loved ones, home etc, and this is perhaps the reason the videoclip for the song shows images of the **Manhattan skyline**, probably symbolizing the yearning that is encapsulated by the lyrics. Related to this, in an interview in "The Age" in 1986, his wife Lourdes joked about one of the phrases of the song where he sings "you've been in the sun and I've been in the rain" with journalist Bill Flanagan, saying, "*Hey, who has been in the sun and who's been in the rain ?" I've spent all winter in New York fighting with plumbers while you were in Montserrat!*"[8]

Finally, we have several references to New York in the lyrics of 'Tunnel of Love', a song whose main source of inspiration is the amusement park, the '**Spanish city**' near the English city of **Newcastle Upon Tyne**. Three amusement parks that today no longer exist are mentioned in the song together with the Spanish City: **Steeplechase Park** in the area of Coney Island in Brooklyn; **Palisades Park**, on the cliffs of the same name on the Hudson River between New Jersey and New York and **Rockaways Playland**, on the beach of the same name in Queens, New York.

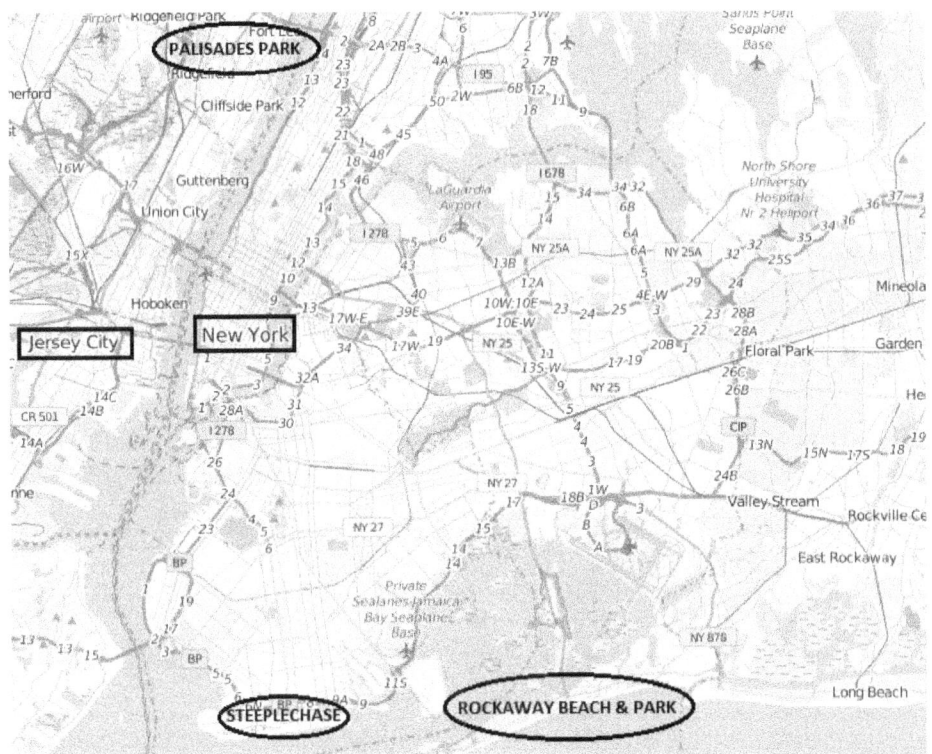

[8] Musician, September 1985, by Bill Flanagan:
https://web.archive.org/web/20080527141355/http://www.knopfler.net/interview48.html

NEW YORK MAPS

POWER STATION

Start your route from the old Power Station Studios, nowadays the **Avatar Studios** on the **441st of West 53rd Street**. The closest underground stop is the **7th Avenue** one.

From there to recreate Mark Knopfler's bike rides from the studio to his house that inspired him to write 'Your Latest Trick', walk by **9th Avenue**, that you will leave occasionally to visit other places mentioned in this chapter.

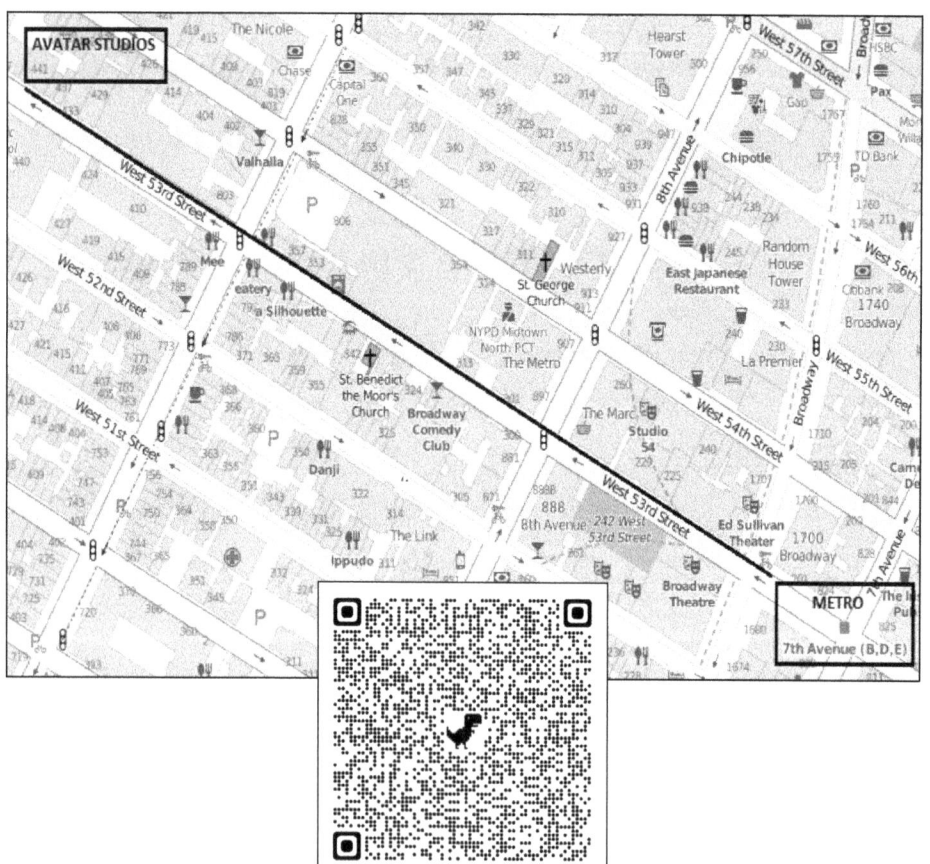

RADIO CITY MUSIC HALL

At the junction between **9th Avenue** and **50th Street** turn left and continue walking until the cross with **6th Avenue,** also known as **Avenue Of The Americas,** where you will find the **Radio City Music Hall.**

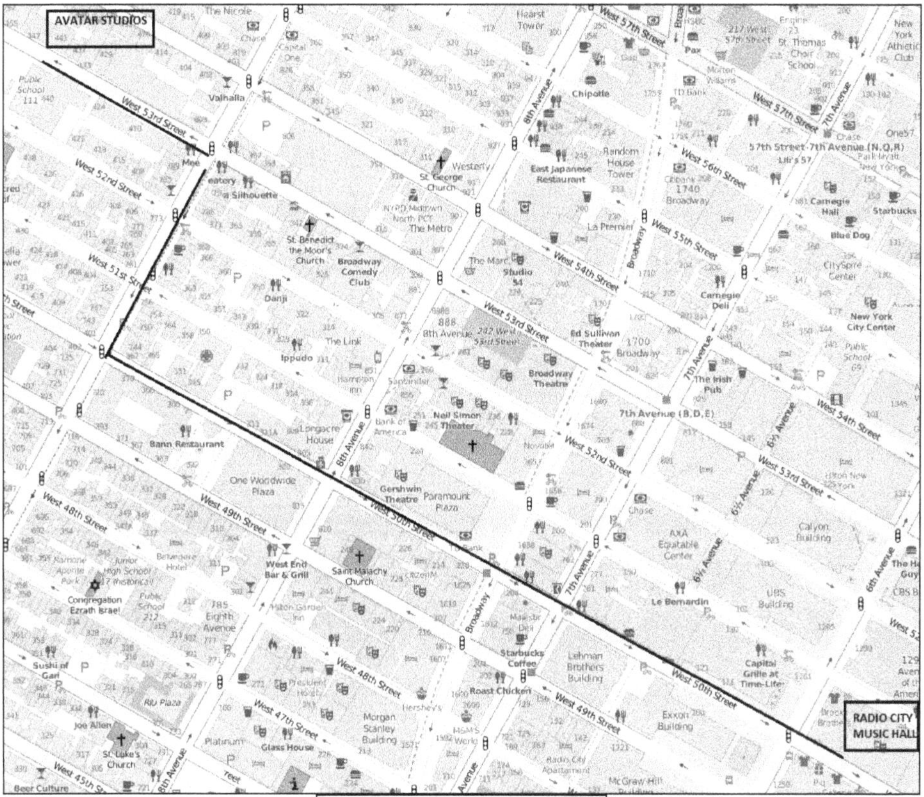

RUDY'S MUSIC STOP

From the **Radio City Music Hall**, keep walking by **6th Avenue / Avenue of the Americas** until the junction with **48th street** and turn right by that street. After some minutes walking, at the **number 169** you will find the place where **the original Rudy's Music Shop** used to be. Although it's closed, it's very likely that the marquees and signs are still there unless the property is rented or sold.

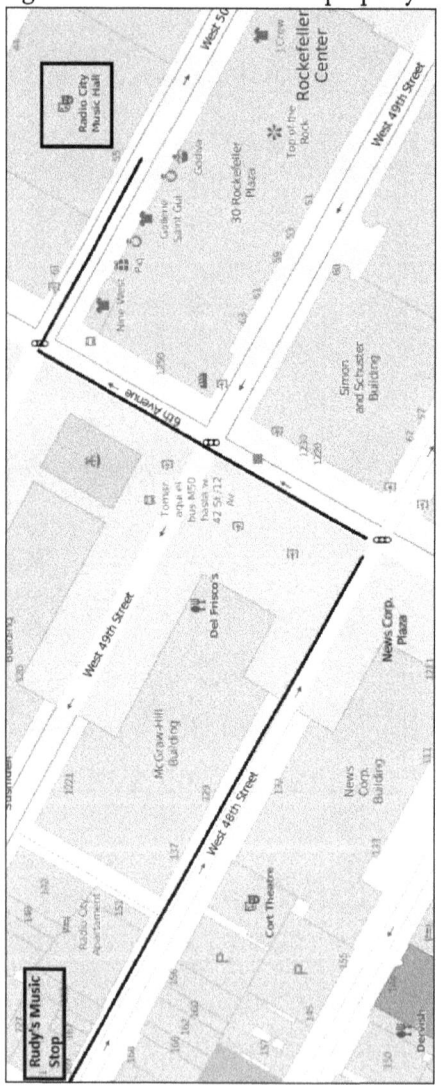

MADISON SQUARE GARDEN

Go back to **9th Avenue** walking by **48th Street**, and keep walking until the junction with **Muhammad Ali Way**, then turn left until you reach the **Madison Square Garden**.

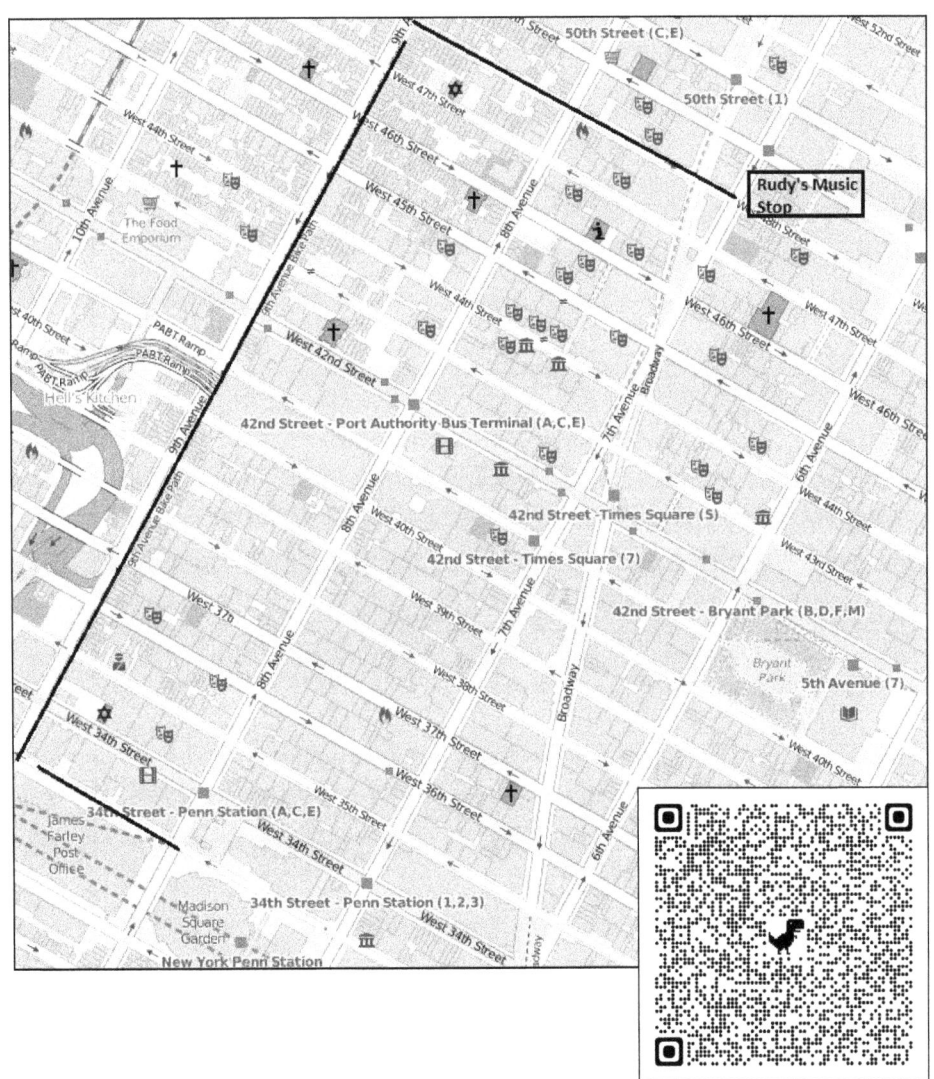

BANK STREET

Back to **9th Avenue**, keep walking about thirty minutes to get to **Bank Street**. When it crosses with **15th Street** you will find **Hudson Street**. Head by that street and five junctions later turn left and take **Jane Street**. Continue walking and after the cross with **8th Avenue** turn right to walk by **West 4th Street**. The second junction will be **Bank Street** and head there turning left, as Mark Knopfler's house was in that part of the street

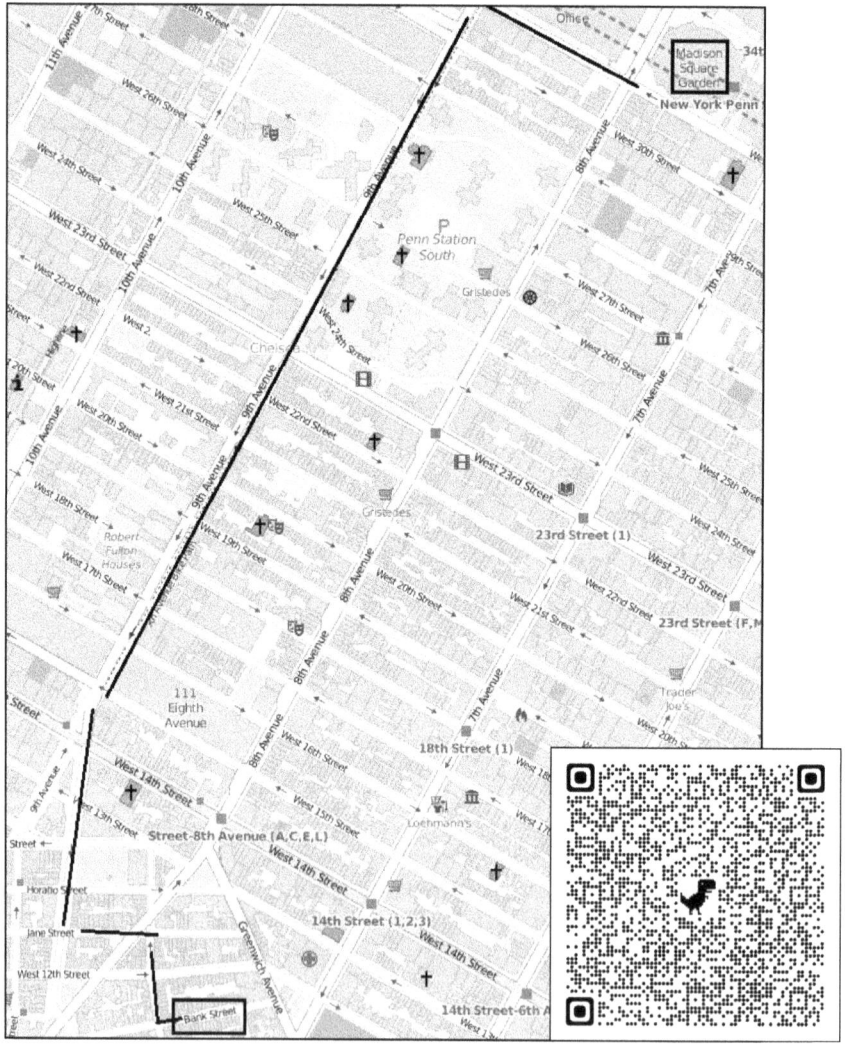

RUDY'S MUSIC SOHO

It takes almost thirty minutes on foot from **Bank Street** to the **Rudy Pensa** shop in Soho. Walking by **Bank Street** in the opposite direction until you reach **Bleecker Street**, turn left and walk until it crosses with **6th Avenue / Avenue of the Americas**; continue by that one and the sixth street on your left is **Broome Street**. The shop is at number **461**.

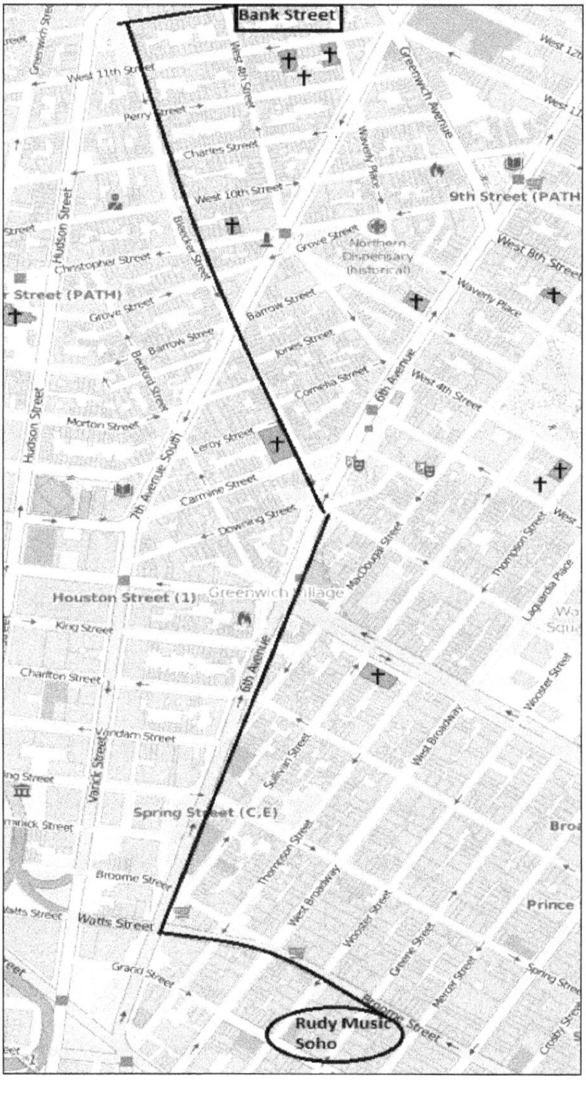

BEACON THEATRE - RUMSAY PALYFIELD

This theatre where Dire Straits and Mark Knopfler have played over the years is close to the underground stop at **72nd Street**. Walking by that street you can get into **Central Park** and then go on towards the **Rumsay Playfield** where Knopfler played in 2008.

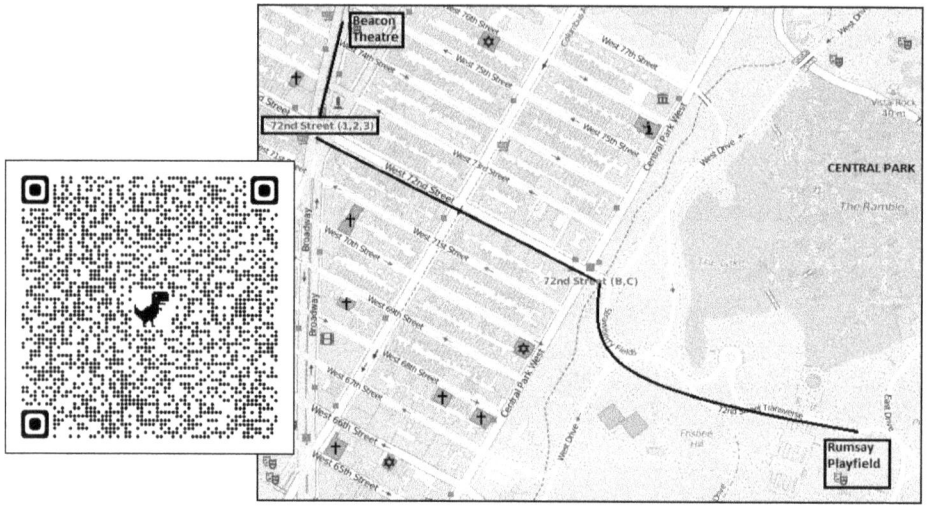

UNITED PALACE

Mark Knopfler played at the United Palace during the 'Get Lucky' tour in 2010 and the closest **underground stop is 175th Street**.

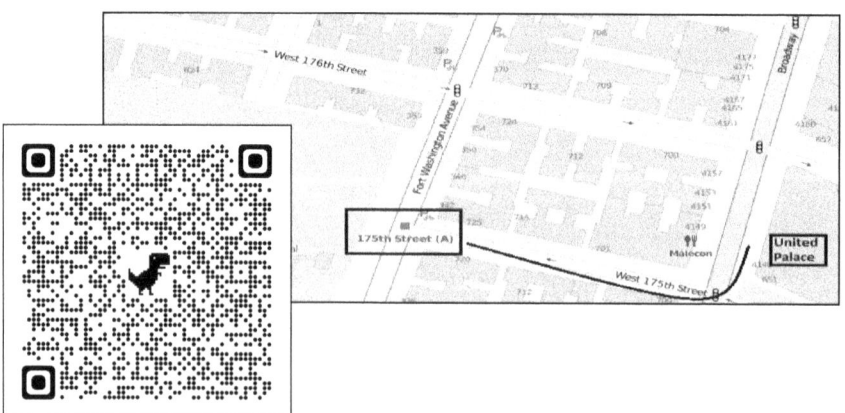

11 PENNAN

Over the course of Knopfler's career he has been involved in many projects with some eminent artists and shown his adaptability in performing differing musical genres. In early 1982 Knopfler's manager wrote to film directors indicating he would be interested in composing a film score. Later that year he was approached by producer **David Puttnam** with regard to writer-director **Bill Forsyth**'s new film 'Local Hero', a film about the determination of an American oil company to buy a Scottish village so that an oil refinery might be built on the site. Forsyth had had success with 'Gregory's Girl' the previous year so this was a good opportunity for Knopfler to secure his first soundtrack with an up-and-coming film director.

Like Knopfler, Forsyth was born in Glasgow and the film would also be set in Scotland. Location filming would take place mainly on the west coast around **Arisaig**, **Morar** and **Lochailort**. Most of the beach scenes were filmed around **Camusdarach** near Morar. Lochailort was the location of the church where the villagers gathered. The village that doubled as the fictional town of Ferness was the tiny village of **Pennan** in Aberdeenshire.

Picture: David Perbal

Pennan is a small fishing village, one of many along the Aberdeenshire coast and it's where the majority of the scenes of the film were shot as the village and its inhabitants have a key role in the film.

One of the locations featured several times in the film is the **harbour pier**. In some scenes the main character, played by American actor Peter Riegert, chats with the fishermen who are painting their boats and in another one, very special as Knopfler was asked to write a particular melody for it, a Russian tourist arrives at the village in his boat. The current harbour pier was constructed between 1902 and 1904, the previous one having been destroyed by a heavy storm forty years earlier. A repair was made to this only a few years before 'Local Hero' was shot.

The film itself is a rather low-budget affair, typical of Forsyth's films but created with the art of the filmmaker's craft at its heart. Comparisons will be made with other British films such as the Ealing comedies, especially 'Whisky Galore!' The actors are not famous Hollywood names, except for Burt Lancaster. Most are Scottish actors. This was also the case in 'Gregory's Girl'. The list of Scottish actors is familiar to any Scot, with the wonderful character actor Fulton Mackay, future Dr Who actor Peter Capaldi, Taggart star Alex Norton and the legendary comedian Rikki Fulton.

Another person who appears in the film in a cameo is our very own **Alan Clark**! He appears as a member of the **Acetones**, alongside the well- known guitarist Alan Darby. The Acetones are a group that perform in the Ceilidh scenes, recorded at the **Hilton Women's Royal Institute Hall at Banff**, a nearby town. Darby has played with Eric Clapton, Van Morrison (who provided guest vocals on 'The Last Laugh' from Knopfler's 'Sailing to Philadelphia' album) and many other artists. Another member of the group is Knopfler's then manager **Ed Bicknell** on drums, although he doesn't appear on film.

Many scenes feature a **red telephone box** that plays a key role in the film. There is a particularly special moment in the film when the main character calls his boss, played by Burt Lancaster, to explain to him about the Northern Lights that are happening while they talk. **The Northern Lights**, also called the Aurora Borealis, is a light phenomenon caused when solar wind from the sun collides with magnetic particles in the Earth's atmosphere, and it is visible in northern Scotland during autumn and winter seasons when the sky is clear.

The telephone box is not the actual one in the film - that was just a prop. In fact there

Northern Lights picture at Pennan Harbour, courtesy of Monika Focht, owner of the Pennan Inn BnB&Gallery"

NORTHERN LIGHTS PICTURE AT PENNAN HARBOUR, COURTESY OF MONIKA FOCHT, OWNER OF THE PENNAN INN BNB&GALLERY"

wasn't one in Pennan at all but tourists kept turning up expecting to find one, so they built one anyway, although at a more secluded location. The location shown in the film was unrealistic for stormy Scottish weather!

The hotel featured in the film was shot using some of the houses in Pennan and the

interior was filmed in **The Ship Inn at Banff**. Sadly, it has now closed down and they've applied for planning permission to turn it into dwellings.

When you visit Pennan you will find a lovely hotel named **Pennan Inn Bnb&Gallery**,

THE SHIP INN, IN BANFF, LOCATION OF THE INSIDE OF THE HOTEL IN THE FILM. PICTURE BY OLAF BAUSCHAT

PICTURES OF THE INSIDE OF THE SHIP INN IN BANFF, WITH REFERENCES TO THE FILM BY OLAF BUSCHAT

which has a commemorative plaque about the film, and the 'phone box' is located just in front of the hotel.
The beach on which the Ben Knox character lives in his small shack - he happens to be

Courtesy of Monika Focht, owner of the
Pennan Inn Bnb&Gallery

INSIDE THE PENNAN INN, PICTURE: DAVID PERBAL

INSIDE THE PENNAN INN BNB&GALLERY, WITH REFERENCES TO THE FILM AND THE MUSIC SCORE. PICTURES BY OLAF BAUSCHAT AND DAVID PERBAL.
(RIGHT, ABOVE AND NEXT PAGE).

the owner of the beach - is not in Pennan but on **Camusdarach Beach**, in **Morar** on the west coast, where most of the beach scenes were shot. This is also near **Lochailort**, the location of the church where the villagers gathered. It is called the Polnish Chapel in reality and located roadside, just off the main A830.

The relationship between Knopfler and Forsyth proved fruitful, Forsyth winning a

CAMUSDARACH BEACH AND THE CHURCH USED
FOR THE VILLAGERS' GATHERING

CAMUSDARACH BEACH, THE PLACE WHERE THE BEN KNOX
CHARACTER'S SMALL SHACK WAS IN THE FILM

CAMUSDARACH BEACH, BOTH PICTURES BY DAVID PERBAL

Lochailort, Polnish Chapel

This is the place that appears in the 'Local Hero' soundtrack cover

BAFTA for Best Director and Knopfler earning a nomination for Best Score for a Film. They also collaborated once more in the 1984 film '**Comfort and Joy**'. Knopfler would continue to compose soundtracks throughout his career using mostly musicians he was working with at the time, either with Dire Straits or as a solo artist. John Illsley, Alan Clark, Hal Lindes and Terry Williams all played on the 'Local Hero' soundtrack album. Knopfler also used **Gerry Rafferty** on vocal on the track 'The Way It Always Starts' **Tony Levin** on bass and **Mike Brecker** on saxophone between others.

It is interesting to note that the soundtrack would make more money than the film itself and the end theme, 'Going Home' would become an iconic anthem, leading out the **Newcastle United** football team at every home match. Both this and 'Wild Theme' would become a staple as the last song at live concerts of Dire Straits, Mark Knopfler and even The Notting Hillbillies.

On 3rd May 1996, during his first solo tour to promote the 'Golden Heart' album, Mark Knopfler played at the **Capitol Theatre** in **Aberdeen**. Prior to the show he paid a visit to Pennan and unveiled the plaque attached to the Pennan Inn hotel. The Press and Journal newspaper published an article by Marion MacKay with a nice picture of Mark in the telephone box.

Early in 2018 it was announced that there would be a **musical** based upon the film.

Picture: Marion MacKay

David Greig, artistic director of the **Royal Lyceum Theatre, Edinburgh**, worked on the musical based on the story and characters from the 'Local Hero' film, in cooperation with Bill Forsyth and also Mark Knopfler, who created the songs and lyrics for this stage version and direction by **John Crowley**.

Premiered at the Royal Lyceum Theatre in Spring 2019, with previews from 14th

LOCAL HERO

BOOK BY
BILL FORSYTH AND DAVID GREIG
MUSIC & LYRICS BY
MARK KNOPFLER
BASED ON THE SCREENPLAY OF THE ORIGINAL FILM
WRITTEN AND DIRECTED BY BILL FORSYTH

Advert used for the musical at the Royal Lyceum Theatre of Edinburgh

Queuing for one of the Local Hero Musical representations at the Lyceum in Edinburgh. Picture by David Gray

Inside The Lyceum Theatre. Picture by Janet Woodward / The stage. Picture: Jose Luis Gómez del Pozo

Pictures: Thomas Allesch

The live band and the cast of the Local Hero Musical. Pictures by José López Talavera

March and a formal Opening Night for the press on 23rd March, after 4th May the musical will move to The Old Vic theatre in London, under the artistic direction of Matthew Warchus, originally scheduled from June to August of 2020, it had to be postponed because of covid-19.

In late April 2021, The Old Vic sent a mail to all ticket purchasers to let them know 'that unfortunately the production of 'Local Hero' will no longer go ahead at The Old Vic. We have tried to make this work within the theatre's schedule once we reopen but sadly this has just not been possible'.

In October and November 2022, the musical will come back after the Old Vic cancelation at the Minerva Theatre in Chichester, South England, as part of their 2022 festival It will be directed by Daniel Evans, and with Guy Fletcher as musical director. There are no plans yet about the musical moving to any London theatre, but if that happens it won't be before 2023.

PENNAN MAPS

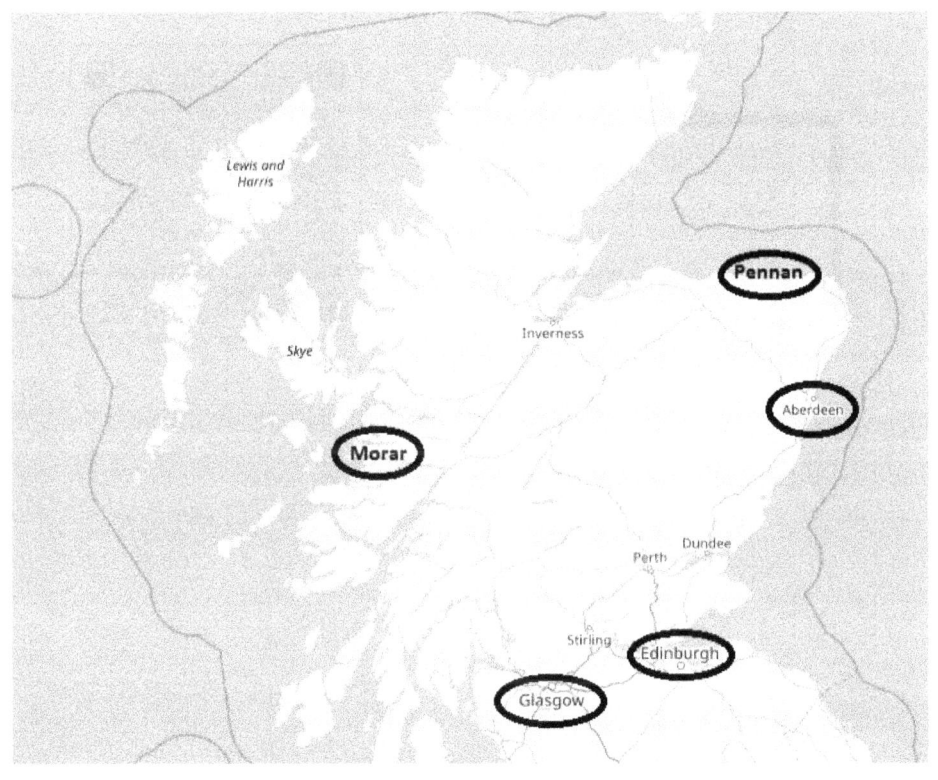

PENNAN

From **Aberdeen Union Square Bus Station** catch the **number 35** bus to **Ellon Park and Ride**. This takes forty minutes. From here catch the **68, 67 or X67 to Fraserburgh**. This journey takes about fifty minutes. From here take the line **473** to **Pennan**, a journey of some thirty minutes. Incredibly, this final journey only runs three times a week so make sure it's the day you go! The best way is probably to **hire a car,** as you can then even visit the beautiful cathedral town of Elgin and maybe even go on to Inverness. Another place to note is the nearby town of **Banff**. **The Ship Inn** was used in the film as '**The McCaskill Arms**'.

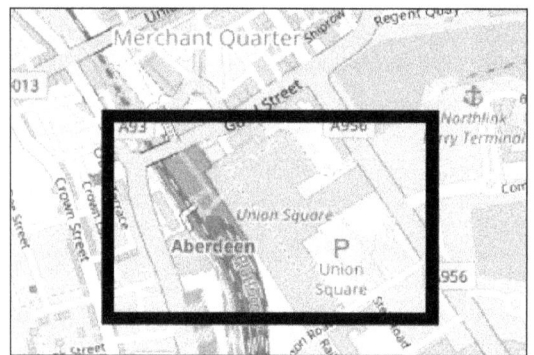

MORAR AND LOCHAILORT

Travelling the **west coast** can be done by train from **Glasgow Queen Street Low Level** on the **West Highland Line**. Catch the train to **Fort William**, then from there the **Mallaig train**, alighting at Morar. From the station at **Morar** it is less than four miles to the beaches at **Camusdarach**.

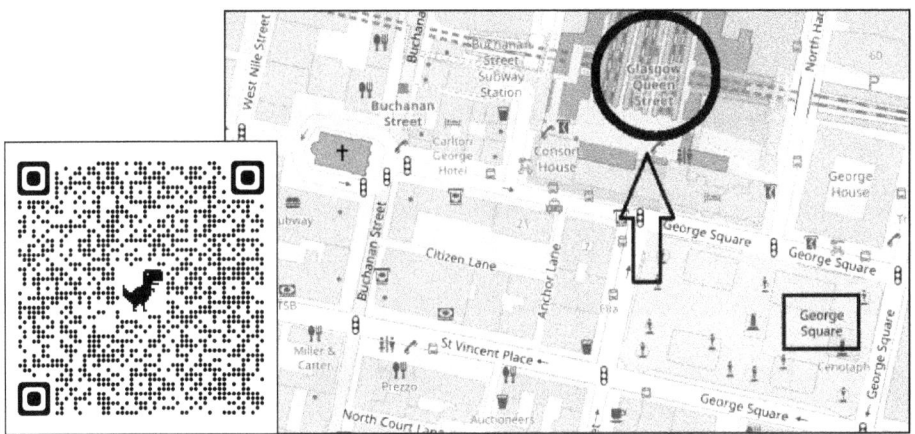

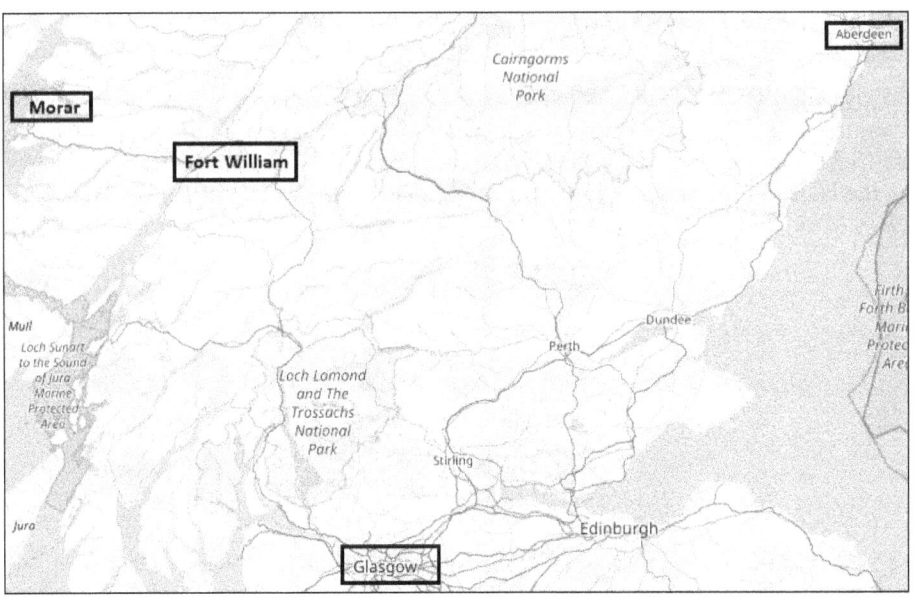

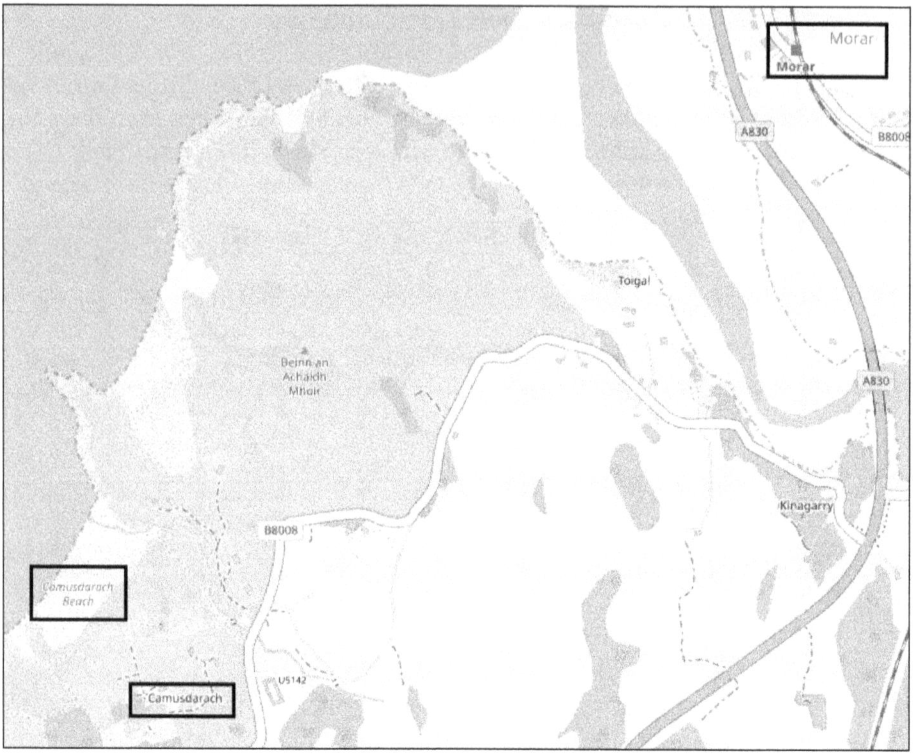

To visit the Polnish Chapel, alight from the train at Lochailort. Please note that the train stops at this station only upon request, so ask the guard before you get on the train. Also of note is that this line passes over the Glenfinnan Viaduct, made famous by the Harry Potter series of films, between Locheilside and Glenfinnan.

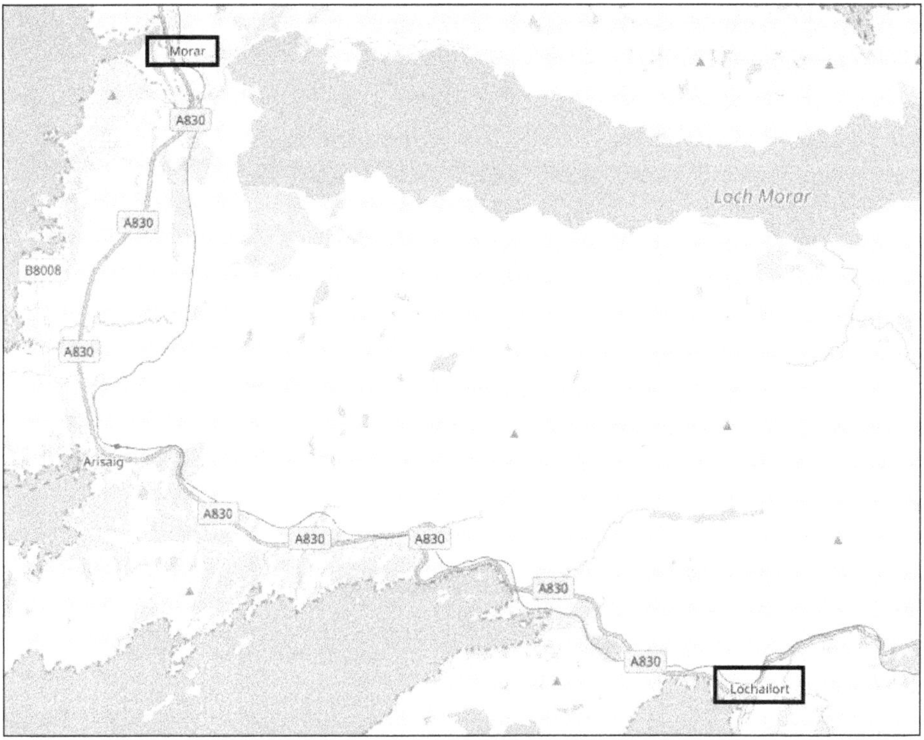
Morar
A830
Loch Morar
A830
B8008
A830
Arisaig
A830
A830
A830
A830
A830
Lochailort

12
HAMMERSMITH & SHEPHERD'S BUSH

PICTURE: JUAN PABLO BERNARDO

Again at Power Station Studios in New York, Dire Straits recorded their fourth studio album, 'Love Over Gold', the title track based on an old mural Mark used to see on a wall in Deptford during the early years of the band. The content of the album was so atmospheric that it was followed by a pure rock and roll EP called 'Extended Dance Play' with three songs on it, including 'Twisting By The Pool' that became an instant hit.

With a new studio album and an EP out, the band embarked on a tour around Europe, Australia, New Zealand and Japan, which ended with two consecutive nights at the **Hammersmith Odeon** in London. The whole tour was recorded with the idea of releasing a live album and a decision was finally taken about which songs from which dates were to be chosen - it was the last night at the Hammersmith Odeon that was selected for the live release. It was to be called 'Alchemy'. Both nights at the Odeon were filmed for a video release as well.

The Hammersmith Odeon is a Grade II listed building located in Hammersmith, a district of West London, centre of the Borough of Hammersmith and Fulham. Opened in 1932 under the name Gaumont Palace, it was designed by Robert Cromie in Art Deco style, renamed as Hammersmith Odeon in 1962, further changing its name over the years to include brand-names of different owners such as Labatt's Apollo, Carling Apollo, AEG Live, Eventim Apollo, HMV Apollo etc, often being called by the nickname of "Hammy-O". The ability to seat a large audience (up to 3,579) so close to the stage, yet with little overhang, is the key to the building's success as a concert venue. An interesting fact is that The Hammersmith starred as the Grand, Sloughborough, in the film 'The Smallest Show on Earth' (1956). It's a legendary venue where many bands have released records and videos, including the likes of *Black Sabbath, Bruce Springsteen, Whitesnake, Tears For Fears, David Bowie, Erasure, Robbie Williams, Kate Bush* and many many more.

'Alchemy: Dire Straits Live' was released in March 1984, including on the back cover some images of the inside of the Hammersmith Odeon, and the video release includes not only scenes from the interior of the venue but also exterior shots, so when fans visit the venue, memories of this video release come to mind immediately.

PICTURE: FRANCISCO JAVIER MATAS

Dire Straits played there for the first time in January 1979, where their fanbase was starting to grow, and also at the peak of their fame, during the 'Brothers In Arms" era. At that time they played six consecutive nights in December 1985 with guests including Eric Clapton, Paul Young and Hank Marvin.

It's also the venue where they played two warm-up gigs prior to the Nelson Mandela 70th Birthday Concert in Wembley Stadium in June 1988 with Eric Clapton as rhythm guitarist and where, in December 2011, Mark Knopfler played three concerts in a row closing the European Tour he played with **Bob Dylan**.

Universal Records used to be located close to Hammersmith Odeon. When a record release or tour by Mark Knopfler was imminent, posters announcing the record release or tours, such as the six nights sold out at the Royal Albert Hall in May 2010, were seen close to their building.

According to Google Maps, Universal Records has moved from this location, but maybe it's worth taking a look, as it's close by. Looking at Hammersmith Odeon, on the right walking underneath the bridge we get to Sussex Place, which where this picture was taken.

Not very far from the Hammersmith Apollo, there was a pub called **The Greyhound**, the location seen at the start of the Alchemy video recording where the band are playing pool, with a chalkboard announcing 'The Geordies Vs The Rest'. Mark Knopfler and Alan Clark, both from Newcastle Upon Tyne ('Geordie' is the nickname of inhabitants of Newcastle) were playing against John Illsley and Terry Williams. Hal Lindes is also seen playing a video game.

The place has changed since those images were shot and nowadays it's the Southern Belle. It's located at 175-177 Fulham Palace Road.

THE GREYHOUND, PICTURE MADE IN
THE 70'S, UNKNOWN PHOTOGRAPHER

THE SOUTHERN BELLE, WHERE THE GREYHOUND USED TO BE.
UNKNOWN PHOTOGRAPHER

Hammersmith is bordered by Shepherd's Bush, still in West London, where another legendary London venue is located: the Shepherd's Bush Empire, where Mark Knopfler played some very important concerts. It was here that he performed the final concerts of his two bands, Dire Straits and The Notting Hillbillies.

The Shepherd's Bush Empire was built in 1903 and the one of their first billed performers were The Fred Karno Troupe including Charlie Chaplin (1906). In 1953, the BBC bought the Empire to be used as a television studio–theatre, under the name BBC Television Theatre. The BBC left the building in 1991 and after some refurbishments by the new owner, it opened again in 1994 under its original name. It changed its name again because of brand sponsorship, becoming known lately as the O2 Shepherd's Bush Empire or O2 Empire.

Some very significant artists have recorded live albums and videos there, including *Amy Winehouse, King Crimson, Europe, The Damned, Mumford and Sons and Joe Bonamassa*.

It was there that on 23rd, 24th and 25th July 2002 Mark Knopfler played three benefit concerts under the name '**Mark Knopfler and Friends.**' These lasted two hours, playing the first half with **The Notting Hillbillies** and the second with **Dire Straits** including *John Illsley* on bass, *Guy Fletcher* on keyboards, *Chris White* on saxophone, *Danny Cummings* on drums, *Robbie McIntosh* on guitar and Geraint Watkins on keyboards. Even though it wasn't announced as a Notting Hillbillies and Dire Straits concert, but as 'Mark Knopfler and Friends', Knopfler himself introduced the concert during the first song by saying that the first half would be by The Notting Hillbillies and the second by Dire Straits. It can be said therefore that, unofficially, these were the last concerts of both bands. Some days later there was an extra concert in **Beaulieu**, Hampshire on 28th July.

The second concert was recorded on video and audio for a possible release that didn't happen. Only two songs were released in audio as extra tracks for Mark Knopfler's 2003 third solo album in the deluxe edition of 'The Ragpicker's Dream'. The songs that were debuted in the shows from that record, 'Quality Shoe', played by The Notting Hillbillies, and 'Why Aye Man' played by Dire Straits with **Jimmy Nail** were both released as bonus tracks. The videos of both songs were uploaded to the **YouTube Mark Knopfler** official site too.

Pictures taken during the "Mark Knopfler and Friends concerts by Manuel María de Miguel

HAMMERSMITH / SHEPHERD'S BUSH

Hammersmith / Shepherd's Bush

HAMMERSMITH MAPS

Shepherd's Bush Empire

Taking the **Central (red) Line** exit at **Shepherd's Bush** by the right-hand side and walk toward the park. Cross the **park** and at the end you'll get to Shepherd's Bush Empire, today known as the O2 Empire.

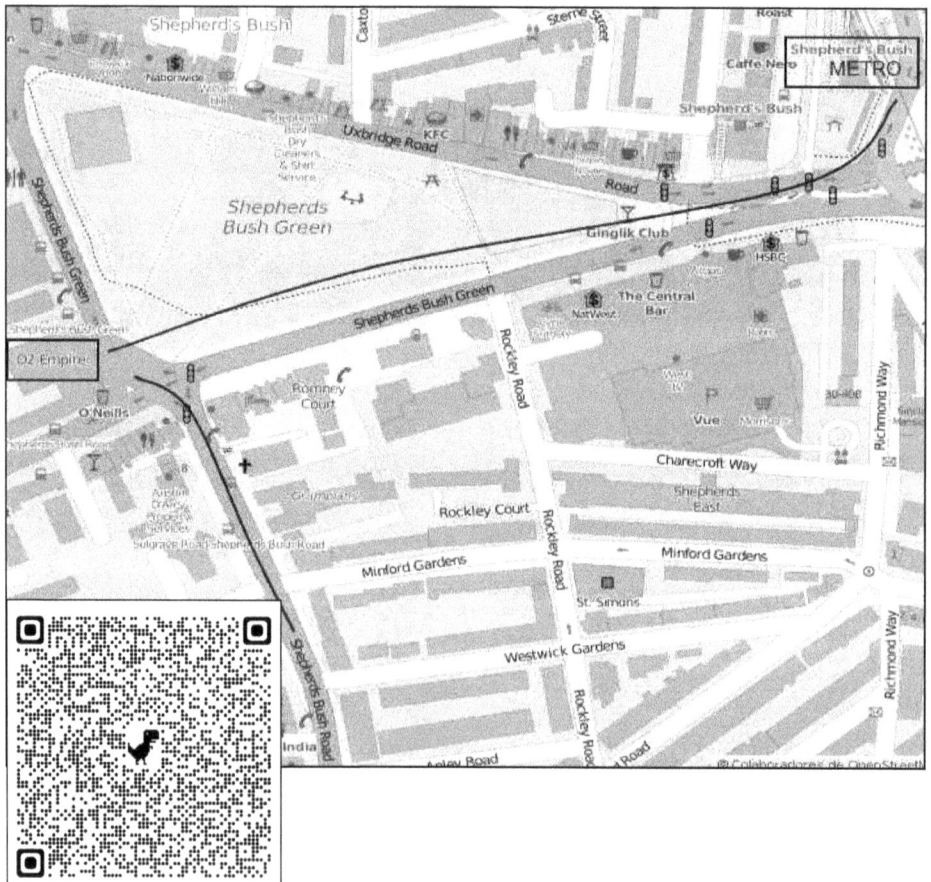

Hammersmith Apollo

Looking at **Shepherd's Bush Empire**, on your left is **Shepherd's Bush Road**. Walk past that street and in about eighteen minutes you'll get to **Hammersmith**, where you will find the legendary Hammersmith Odeon, where on 22nd and 23rd July 1983 'Alchemy' by Dire Straits was filmed.

It is, of course, possible to get to the Hammersmith Odeon directly by underground to **Hammersmith Station**, using any of these lines: **x** and do the route in the opposite way.

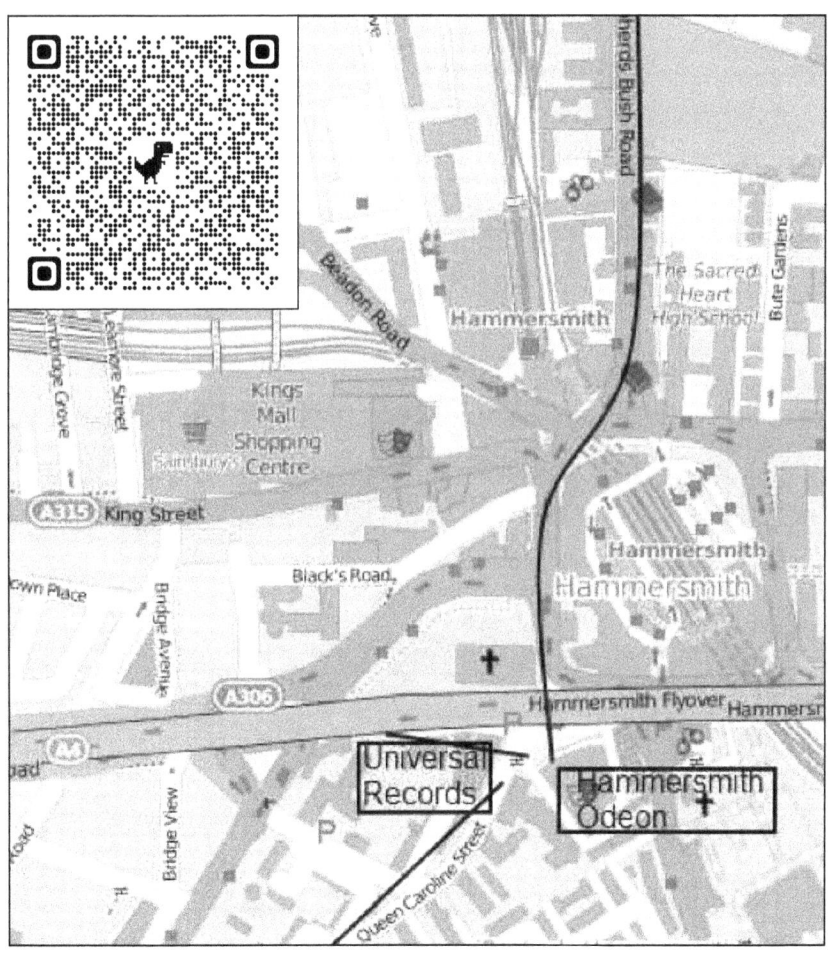

The Greyhound / Southern Belle

Looking at the **Hammersmith Apollo**, on your left, take **Fulham Road** and after **Charing Cross Hospital**, the second street on your left is **Greyhound Road**. The **Southern Bell**, formerly **The Greyhound** is in the corner between Fulham Road and Greyhound Road.

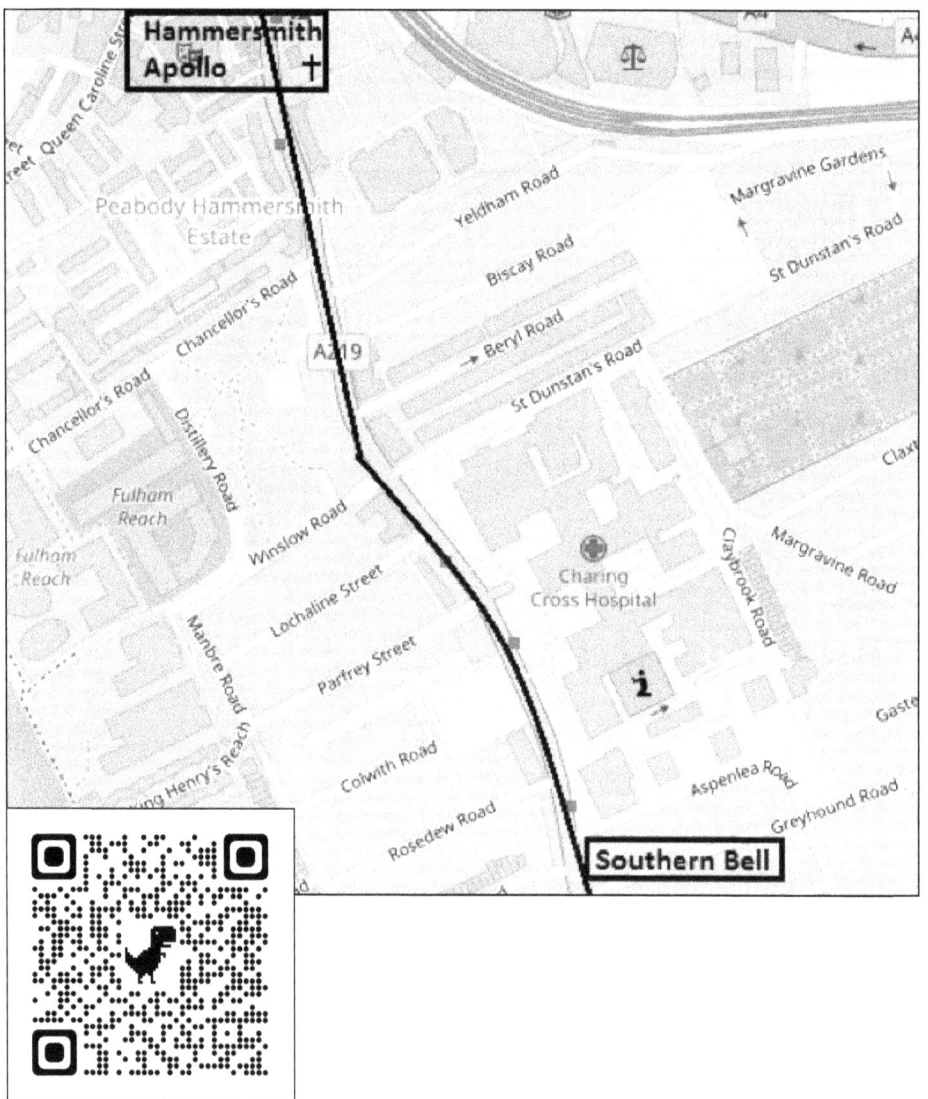

13 WEMBLEY

LIVE AID MURAL (NOW GONE). PICTURE: ÒSCAR PALLARÉS

There is a saying among musicians that you are nobody until you play Hammersmith Odeon, or Wembley, the Arena or the Stadium. Dire Straits played in both and actually even Mark Knopfler during his solo career has played the **Wembley Arena**.

The first time that Dire Straits played at the Wembley complex was at the Arena, between the 18th and 21st December 1982, during the first half of the 'Love Over Gold' tour, although the episode that will mark the band's history happened in 1985, as between the 4th and 16th July they not only played thirteen concerts in a row, but also on one of those dates they played two gigs! On 13th July, first they played two songs ('Money For Nothing' with Sting, and 'Sultans Of Swing') in **Wembley Stadium** at the **Live Aid festival**, then later at their own gig in Wembley Arena.

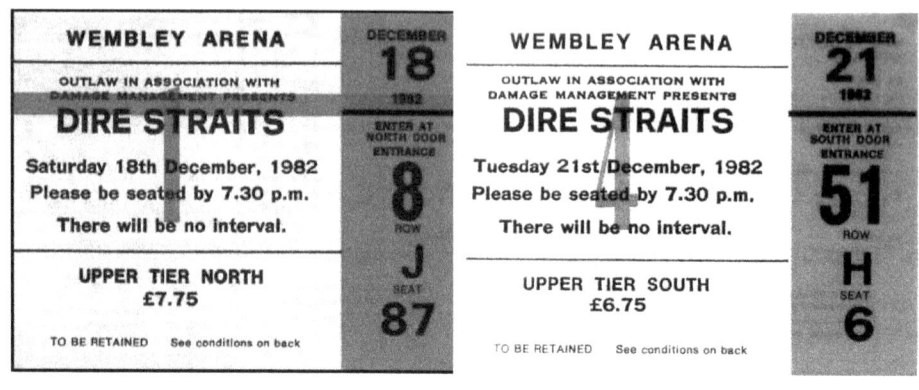

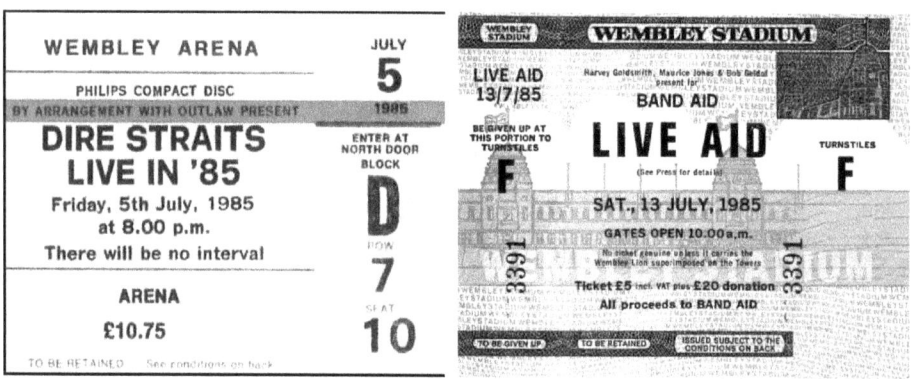

Tickets courtesy of website On Every Bootleg

During those thirteen nights in a row, Dire Straits shared the stage with a large number of guest artists such as *Pete Townshend, T-Bone Burnett, Francis Rossi, Nils Lofgren, Hank Marvin, Paul Brady, Sting and Dave Edmunds.*

After the 'Brothers in Arms' tour ended in 1986, Dire Straits started a long period of rest, only broken by Mark Knopfler and John Illsley who went back to Wembley Arena to be a part of the House Band with *Eric Clapton, Phil Collins, Elton John, Midge Ure* and many more for the **Prince's Trust Rock Gala** charity concert on 20th June 1986. After that, a disbandment of Dire Straits was rumoured, until it was announced that on 11th July 1988 Dire Straits would gather, with Eric Clapton as second guitar, for a second time at Wembley Stadium, to commemorate the **70th birthday of Nelson Mandela**, who was imprisoned at that time in South Africa.

Tickets courtesy of website On Every Bootleg

Wembley Arena. Picture: Francisco Martínez

In 1991 during the last Dire Straits tour they played again at Wembley Arena, for five consecutive nights, between 16th and 20th September, for the final time as a band. Mark Knopfler later played there as a solo artist, during his 2006 tour with Emmylou Harris.

Along **Olympic Way** there was a commemorative mural of the **Live Aid festival** with the figures of, amongst others, Mark Knopfler. The mural was modified with the stadium reconstruction, however, and the only figure that remains nowadays is the drummer.

The **Wembley Stadium** that we find now is not exactly as it was when Dire Straits played there at the two festivals, as it was demolished in 2002 and reopened after a complete reconstruction in 2007 at exactly the same place.

WEMBLEY STADIUM. PICTURE:
FRANCISCO MARTÍNEZ

WEMBLEY MAPS

WEMBLEY PARK

To travel to the Wembley complex, Wembley Park tube station is recommended, on the Jubilee (grey) Line or the Metropolitan (maroon) Line. After descending the stairs walk along Olympic Way, which will take you directly to Wembley Stadium. On its right, before you get to the stadium, is the Arena (known today as the SSE Arena, Wembley).

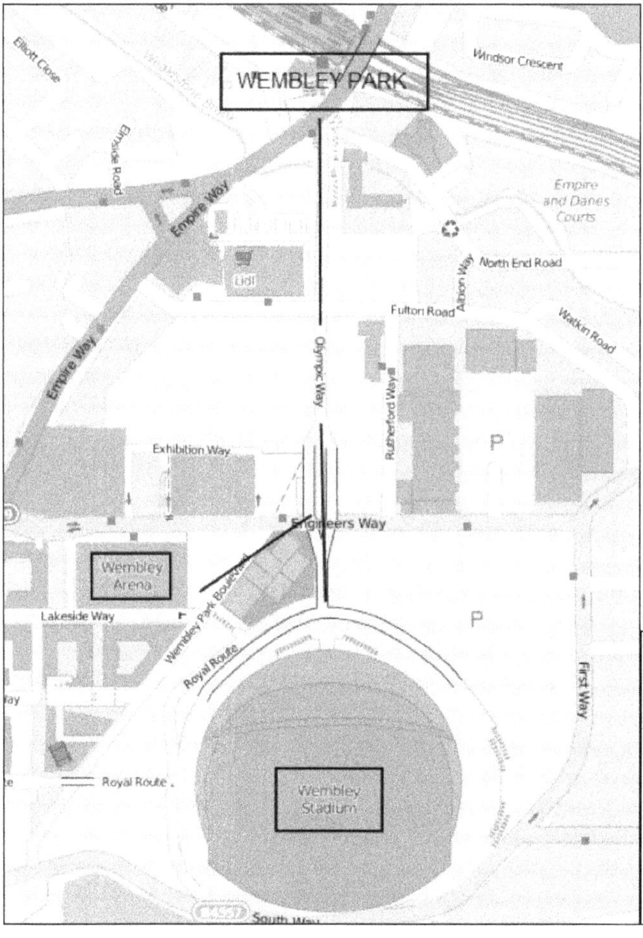

14 NEW ORLEANS

New Orleans is a city located along the **Mississippi River** in the southeastern region of the U.S. state of Louisiana. It is famous for its music, Creole cuisine and its celebrations and festivals, such as **Mardi Gras**. The historic heart of the city is the **French Quarter**, known for its French and Spanish Creole architecture and vibrant nightlife along Bourbon Street.

It's also the main subject of the song 'Planet of New Orleans', from the last studio album by **Dire Straits**, 'On Every Street'.

According to an interview **Mark Knopfler** gave to **David White**, of **4MMM FM** in **Brisbane**, Australia, broadcast on 10th November 1991[1], the song came from memories the band had of staying at a hotel in **New Orleans** during the early years

---

1. https://web.archive.org/web/20010222155639fw_/http://www.knopfler.net/interview11.html

of Dire Straits, probably around 1979, as it was the first time they visited the United States.

Mark Knopfler: *"The first time I went to New Orleans, I was hitchhiking around America. Actually I was on a Greyhound bus going around by myself with a shoulder bag, and that night I stayed a night at the Y.M.C.A. in New Orleans. That was my first time. I remember being in a little cafe and it said... there was a little sign saying "Banks serve no soup, we cash no cheques" and I realised then that in New Orleans it wasn't like America, that it was like a separate entity. Then when I went back with the band... the first tour I woke up...because the bus would pull up outside a hotel but they wouldn't wake us up if we'd been asleep all night. I woke up and looked out the window and it was on the corner of Toulouse and Dauphine. I remember writing down at the time, "I woke up on the corner of Toulouse and Dauphine" and then you know, ten, twelve, thirteen years later, it came out in 'Planet of New Orleans' as "standing on the corner of Toulouse and Dauphine".*

The first lines of the song read:

*"Standin' on the corner
Of Toulouse and Dauphine
Waitin' on Marie-Ondine"*

THE "TOULOUSE AND DAUPHINE" JUNCTION AND THE HOTEL MARIE

There is a junction between the two streets **Toulouse** and **Dauphine** in the **French quarter,** and just next to it is the **Hotel Marie**; that could be why in the next line **"Marie"** is mentioned together with **"Ondine"**, who is a fictional character relating to the history of the city.

Also other lines refer to what's mentioned in that interview about New Orleans being like a separate entity, like not being in America:

HOTEL MARIE

ENTRY TO "LOUIS ARMSTRONG PARK", LOCATED NEXT TO CONGO SQUARE

*"New Orleans
With other life upon it
And everythin' that's shakin' in between
If you should ever land upon it
Well, you better know what's on it
The planet of New Orleans"*

A bar called **Saturn** is mentioned as well, which is not far from Toulouse and Dauphine.
Not far from the junction of Toulouse and Dauphine lies **Congo Square**, which is the title of a track by **Sonny Landreth**, a singer and slide guitar player from Louisiana. Mark Knopfler plays on this song in Landreth's record "South of I-10".

The recording of the Dire Strsits song is mentioned in the autobiography by **Manu Katché**, "**Roadbook**". Katche is a renowned drummer who was called in to participate in the recording sessions of the '<u>On Every Street</u>' album and one of the songs on which he played was coincidentally '<u>Planet of New Orleans</u>', a song that, according to him, took some days until the drum parts were satisfactorily completed.

Mark Knopfler: *"My idea of heaven is a place where the Tyne meets the Delta, where folk music meets the blues"* (The river Tyne from Newcastle, and Delta meaning Mississippi)

Mississippi river in New Orleans

New Orleans

NEW ORLEANS MAPS

TOULOUSE-DAUPHINE, HOTEL MARIE, CONGO SQUARE

In the French Quarter, just at the junction of "Toulouse and Dauphine" streets, you will find the Hotel Marie. Following Toulouse Street you arrive at North Rampart Street where Congo Square is located.

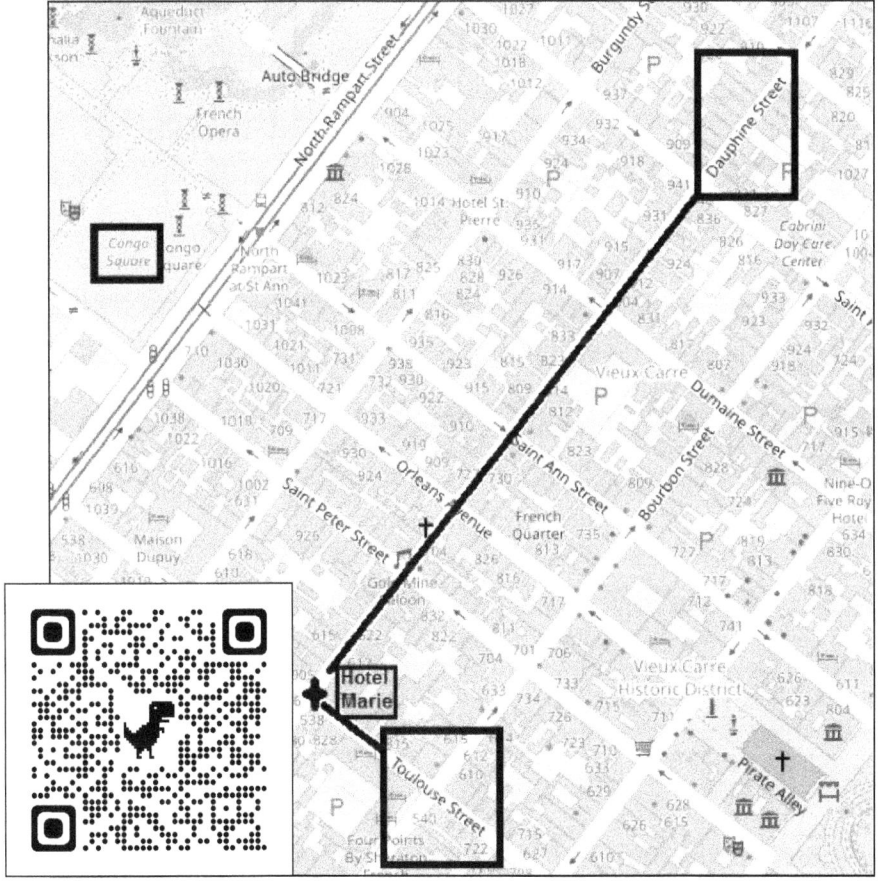

Bar Saturn

Keep walking for around forty minutes along **North Rampart street.** The street changes its name to **St Claude Avenue**, and at the corner with **Clouet street** is **Bar Saturn.**

15 EDINBURGH

ST GILES CATHEDRAL

Edinburgh is the city about which the song 'What It Is' was written. Mark Knopfler has said about it that there is "history in every stone." As the song incorporates many of the city's landmarks by name there are many places to visit. This is easy to do because Edinburgh is such a small city and it's easy to do most of this on foot with no need for public transport.

In the video for 'What It Is' you can see Mark Knopfler driving his car down the **Royal Mile**, a famous street in **Edinburgh's Old Town** where the spire of **St Giles' Cathedral** (main picture) is clearly visible. Another landmark shown is the clock on the **Balmoral Hotel** and the view along the main shopping area, **Princes Street**. This view is most certainly taken from **Calton Hill** which is an easy climb and only five minutes from **Waverley Station**. This is well worth visiting because the views are good and there are a number of fine monuments including the **City Observatory, National Monument of Scotland** and **The Nelson Monument** (which has a time ball and can be entered for a small fee).

Some scenes in the video 'What It Is', for example when the man was running for his train, were shot at **Waverley Station**. In **Princes Street** you will notice a building on your right. This is the Balmoral Hotel. The clock tower of this building was shown in the same video. It is notable that its clock runs five minutes fast to enable travellers to catch their trains! Mark Knopfler and band also used this hotel when they played at the **Edinburgh Playhouse**, as the venue isn't very far away.

Past the front door of The Balmoral is Calton Hill, where some photographs of Mark were taken for promo purposes for his second solo record 'Sailing To Philadelphia'.

BALMORAL HOTEL

NELSON'S MONUMENT AND
PLAYFAIR MONUMENT,
CALTON HILL

EDINBURGH PLAYHOUSE

The Playhouse, a venue where Dire Straits, during their 'Love Over Gold' 1982 and 'Brothers In Arms' 1985 tours, and Mark Knopfler, during his 'Shangri-La' 2005 and 'Kill To Get Crimson' 2008 tours, have played, is near to Calton Hill.

At **Princes Street Gardens**, on the way to the **Castle**, there is usually a piper playing, perhaps giving rise to the line '*high on a parapet a Scottish piper stands alone*', although the parapet mentioned may more likely point to the common sight of a lone piper playing his bagpipes high up on the ramparts of **Edinburgh Castle**, mentioned in the lyrics of 'What It Is'. The large area in front of the **Castle entrance** is where the **Military Tattoo** is held. This is the top of an extinct volcano and, owing to the way it shaped the land, there are some great views of the city from here.

The spire from **St Giles'** can be seen in the video and is only a minute downhill from the **Castle**. Going down the hill it is worthwhile having a look into some of the **closes** because some of them are real architectural gems and are a glimpse into the past. Most impressive at the **Lawnmarket** are **Lady Stair's Close** (North side, built 1622 for Sir William Gray) and **Riddell's Close** (South side) where, in 1593 James IV held a grand banquet for nobles of the Danish embassy. It was also here that teacher Baillie John McMorran was shot dead by his pupils because he refused them a holiday! This wonderful history, and more in other closes, will give you some idea as to what inspired Mark to write the song and the real meaning behind Mark's phrase "*history in every stone*" in reference to the city. Many important

PRINCES STREET GARDENS

CASTLE ESPLANADE

historical figures lived in these tenements, important discoveries were made and royalty regularly entertained here. A good website to find out the history of these closes is: http://www.royal-mile.com/royalmile-closes.html

BAKEHOUSE CLOSE, CANONGATE AND DEACON BRODIE'S TAVERN

At the traffic lights is **Deacon Brodie's Tavern** which is shown briefly in the video too. You can have a walk down to St. Giles' and have a look inside as it is open to the public. It is said to date to the early 12th century and is, in fact, not a cathedral because, post-Reformation, The Church of Scotland has had no cathedrals. It is a 'High Kirk' but is generally referred to as a cathedral.

Above **Victoria Street**, famous for its multi-coloured shopfronts, runs Victoria Terrace which contains the Quaker Meeting House and some cafés and restaurants. It is here that one of the scenes was filmed for the video of 'What It Is'. In the part where the man runs into the woman and she drops her glass to the ground, it is clear to see that it was filmed here as the loggia is visible. You can walk through the loggia and right to the end - some nice views are available across the **Grassmarket** and to **George Heriot's School**.

VICTORIA TERRACE

GEORGE HERIOT'S SCHOOL

Heading back to **George IV Bridge** you come upon the monument of **Greyfriars Bobby**, a terrier reputed to have stayed at his master's graveside for fourteen years and much loved for it by the Edinburgh people. Just behind the statue is the tavern named **Greyfriars Bobby Bar** and behind that is **Greyfriars Kirkyard** itself. This could be where the line *"there's frost on the graves and the monuments but the taverns are warm in town' came from"*.

GREYFRIARS KIRKYARD

GREYFRIARS BOBBY

GREYFRIARS BOBBY BAR

At **Chambers Street** there is another filming location. Down the street is the Victorian building which forms half of **The National Museum of Scotland**, which was designed in part by Francis Fowke, who also designed the Royal Albert Hall, one of Mark's favourite arenas. Fowke was also an engineer who pioneered the use of iron frames to create large open spaces. This can be most clearly seen inside the main hall in this museum, which is free to the public.

At the end of **Chambers Street** is located the **University of Edinburgh Old College**. Turning right onto **South Bridge** you may recognise the entry from which Mark drove his car, just as the man was running up the hill in front of him! You may enter the quad to have a look. The building was designed by the famous Robert Adam in the late 18th century and is regarded as one of the most impressive and significant academic buildings in the country. Its dome can also be seen in some of the aforementioned promo photos taken of Mark when he was standing on Calton Hill.

NATIONAL MUSEUM OF SCOTLAND

UNIVERSITY OF EDINBURGH - OLD COLLEGE

At the **Royal Mile** you will find the **Canongate Tolbooth** (**Toll Gate**, as mentioned in the 'What It Is' lyrics). Built in 1591, it is distinguished by a large clock projecting from its side. Nowadays it houses **The People's Story Museum**. It served as a **toll gate** (hence the name in the song) and later as a prison. Many of the prisoners were sent to the plantations of the Caribbean for several years' hard labour. After this period they could return to Scotland or remain in the colony. However, before their departure all the captives were marked so they could not escape their past. Women had their faces branded with an iron while men had an ear chopped off!

From the **Tolbooth** you can continue the short walk to the very end of the **Royal Mile** and find yourself at the **Scottish Parliament Building**. Directly across the road from it is the **Palace of Holyroodhouse**, the Queen's official residence in Scotland. If you walk around to the other side of the Parliament building you can see Arthur's Seat and another building shown in the video, Our Dynamic Earth. This is distinguishable as a modern, white dome. In the video the man was seen from a distance running across the front of it.

DYNAMIC EARTH

One interview quoted Mark Knopfler as saying that he wrote the song 'What It Is' after a concert in Edinburgh in 1996 on the way back to his hotel, soaking up the atmosphere in the city at night, so do visit this hotel via the **Usher Hall**. This is the venue where Mark Knopfler intended to play in 1996 but the roof was damaged by strong winds just beforehand and the venue was changed to the nearby **Meadowbank Sports Centre**, a hall inside the old **Meadowbank Stadium** (now demolished). He did, however, play at the Usher Hall when, on 27th May 1994, he guested with the Band of the Royal Scots Dragoon Guards Pipes and Drums, playing a great version of 'Going Home' from the 'Local Hero' soundtrack.

THE USHER HALL

MEADOWBANK STADIUM

In March 2019 the **musical 'Local Hero'** was premiered at the **Royal Lyceum theatre** in Edinburgh. The theatre is located on **Grindlay Street**, directly behind the **Usher Hall**. This is an historic theatre, built in 1883 by renowned architect C J Phipps and has been kept mostly original with very fine interior fittings. Unusually it was lit by electricity from the time of building and was the first theatre in Britain to be fitted with an iron safety curtain.

THE LYCEUM THEATRE IN EDINBURGH.
PICTURE BY MATT DUNCAN

Charlotte Street is clearly mentioned toward the end of the lyrics in the song "What It Is". In fact, there isn't really a Charlotte Street as such but North and South Charlotte Street with Charlotte Square between them.

According to the tour itinerary, the hotel where Mark Knopfler stayed during the 'Golden Heart' tour, when MK wrote the lyrics for 'What It Is' was **The Caledonian**, a large red sandstone building situated conveniently for the Usher Hall. Interestingly, the hotel was a former railway station up to the first floor. Only six years after opening, the other storeys were built on top, turning it into the hotel you see today. The station eventually closed in 1965.

Charlotte Square is an architectural highlight and is well worth a visit. The Square was conceived by Robert Adam as a paradigm of the Georgian ideal in the centre of Edinburgh. Over the years many important people have lived in houses here and on North and South Charlotte Street. It offered wealthy citizens in the late 18th century a means of escape from the overcrowded tenements of the Old Town. Famous residents have included Field Marshal Earl Haig at No.24 and Alexander Graham Bell at No.16.

In Rose Street, close to Charlotte Square, you would find another reference from the "What it is" lyrics, a pub named after "**the ghost of Dirty Dick**".

Edinburgh's New Town is the best preserved and most important example of urban planning in Britain and along with the Old Town is a UNESCO World Heritage Site.

As a bonus to your Edinburgh visit, take a trip by train across the famous **Forth Bridge**, another UNESCO World Heritage Site. In the video of '**What It Is**' you can see the car being driven across the Forth Road Bridge with the Forth Bridge in the background.

IT'S IN THE ROAD UNDER THIS BRIDGE WHERE THE CAR STOPS IN THE "WHAT IT IS" VIDEO. PICTURE: JULIO BRICIO

The bridge was written about in John Buchan's novel 'The 39 Steps' and it appears in Hitchcock's film of the same name. Despite being opened in 1890, it still has the second-longest single span in the world. Sadly, there are seventy-three recorded deaths of workers on the bridge. The new **Queensferry Crossing** opened in September 2017 and now rather dominates the two older bridges in terms of scale.

FORTH ROAD BRIDGE AND THE FORTH BRIDGE

Getting off at **North Queensferry** and having a walk around this little village will give you very fine views of both bridges and also the new Queensferry Crossing. You will be really close to the **Forth Bridge** as the village sits almost beneath it. There are several restaurants, cafes and pubs but don't expect too much as it is a very small place.

On the old trains across the famous Forth Bridge it was customary to throw a pre-decimal penny out of the window as one crossed the bridge for good luck but alas, with modern air conditioning the windows no longer open!

FORTH BRIDGE

South Queensferry, where this photo was taken, offers nice cafés, some small shops and a walk through the main street. It is altogether more suited to visitors and still offers great views of the bridges. It is a very popular place to visit and can get busy on sunny days during the summer months. South Queensferry is a former Royal Burgh.

EDINBURGH MAPS

Finding your way around Edinburgh is extremely simple and requires no public transport, unless one wishes to visit South Queensferry which is beyond the city limits. Edinburgh is a city of only half a million people and with a little effort it should be possible to visit everywhere in a single day. However, do allow more time if you can!

CALTON HILL

In order to reach the first destination, **Calton Hill**, start your route from outside the **Balmoral Hotel** on **Princes Street**, since this is the main thoroughfare and next to **Waverley Train Station**. If you head east, cross **North Bridge** and head toward **Waterloo Place**. The road splits here but keep walking straight ahead along Waterloo Place until Calton Hill appears on your left once you clear the buildings. This is a short walk of about two or three minutes. Calton Hill itself is an easy climb and requires no special footwear as it has a footpath. It gives commanding views of the city centre and beyond on a clear day and also contains some beautiful monuments and an old, disused observatory. At the top, there's a new al fresco cafe.

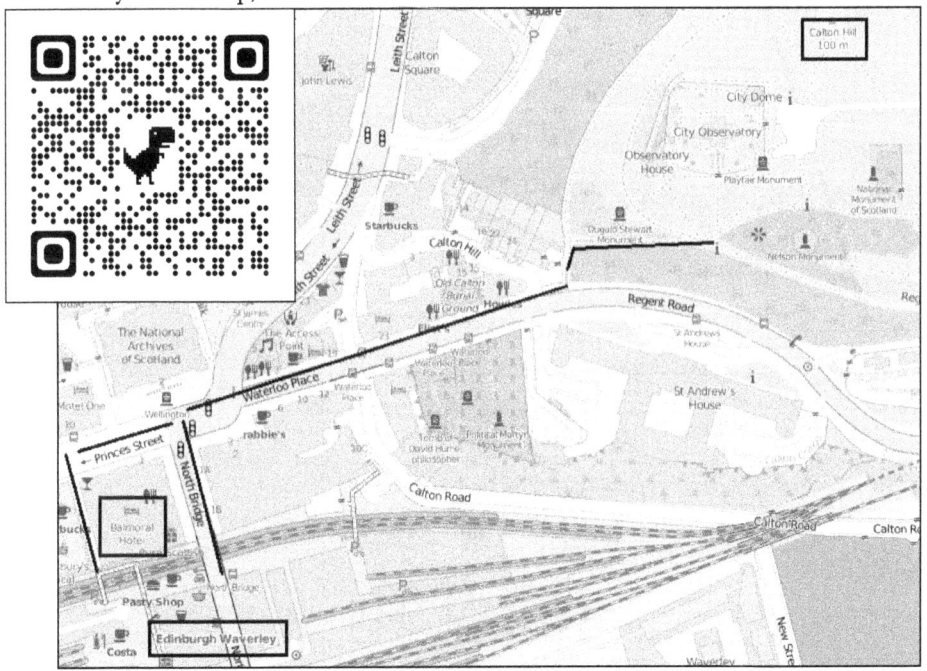

PLAYHOUSE

Descending **Calton Hill** the way you came, you can now visit the **Edinburgh Playhouse**. To do this, take the small lane immediately on the right at the bottom which is called **Calton Hill**. Follow this road to its end and turn right onto the main road, **Leith Street**. Walk down this road for a couple of minutes and just past the roundabout you will see the Playhouse on your right. As a side note, across the road is the statue of Sherlock Holmes. This is to mark the former home of author Sir Arthur Conan Doyle.

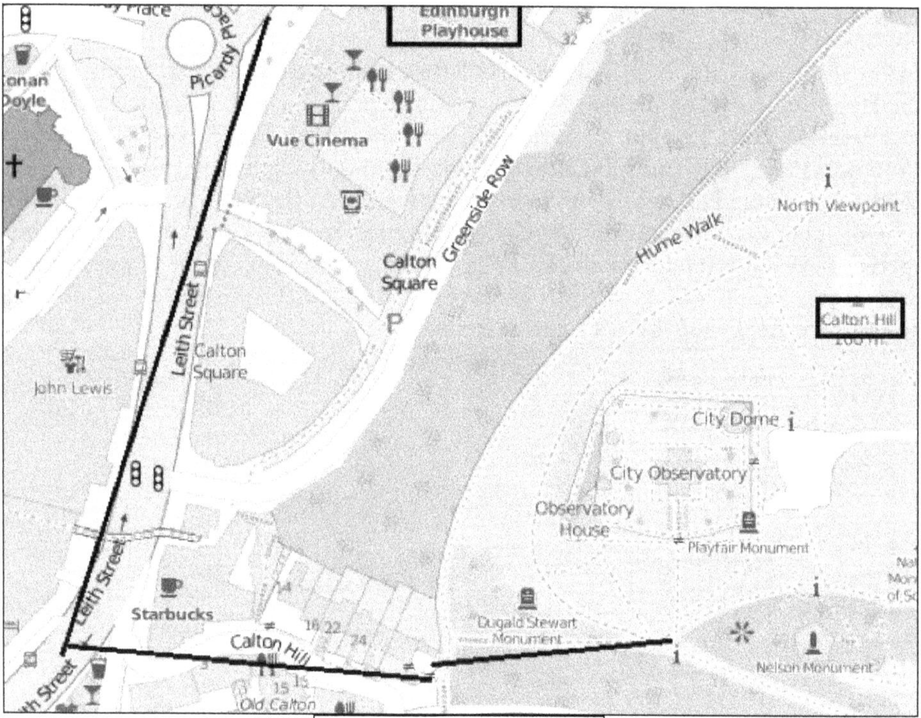

CASTLE

To visit your next destination requires about twenty-five minutes' walking across a distance of one mile. You are now going to head towards the Castle and then make your way down the Royal Mile. Start heading back up Leith Street to the very top at the traffic lights and turn right. You will soon realise that you are back onto Princes Street as you recognise the Balmoral Hotel. Walk along Princes Street until you come to The Mound where the Royal Scottish Academy and Scottish National Gallery are sited (taking a walk through Princes Street Gardens as it is more pleasant to get away from the crowds of shoppers).

Once you reach The Mound, climb Playfair Steps that run up the side of the Gallery. This will take you to a set of traffic lights. Cross the road to the right on to Mound Place, where the tall buildings are, and keep climbing. Turn the corner onto Ramsay Lane. At the very top you will find yourself on Castle Hill, the highest point of The Royal Mile. If you turn right you will soon see the Castle. Walk up to Castle Esplanade and there are great panoramic views.

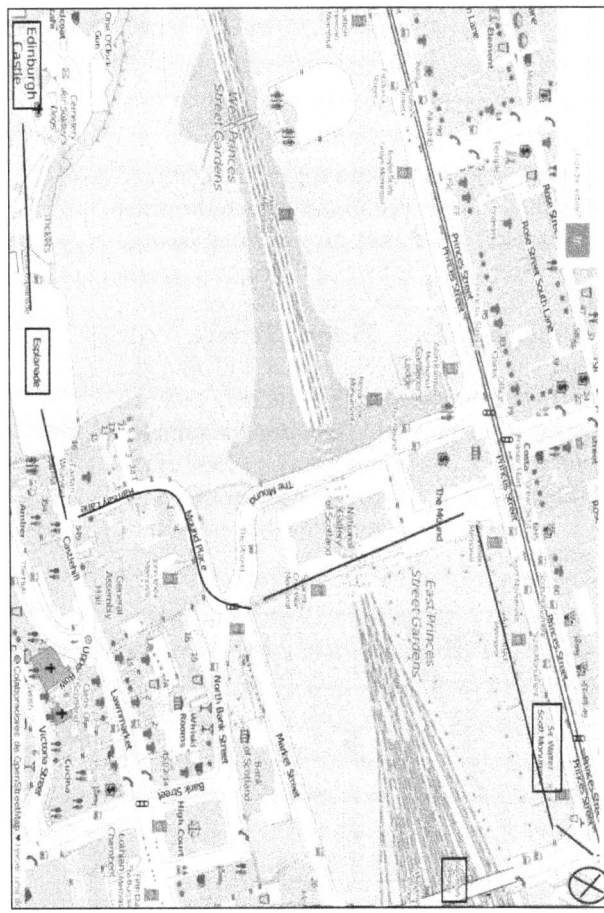

ST GILES'

Your next visit, thankfully, isn't so far away. Head down from **Castle Esplanade** toward the small roundabout at the bottom of Castle Hill, go straight on and you are now on to **Lawnmarket** (The Royal Mile is "split" into different sections by name for convenience). At the traffic lights is **Deacon Brodie's Tavern**. Cross at the lights and make your way on down to **St Giles'** on the **High Street**. Its distinctive crown spire is a major part of the city skyline and features in the video of '<u>What It Is</u>'.

VICTORIA TERRACE

Now head back up toward the traffic lights and cross the road. As soon as you reach the other side turn left and make your way along **George IV Bridge**. Take the first on the right, **Victoria Street**. This has two levels: Victoria Street and the upper level, **Victoria Terrace**. Walk along Victoria Terrace and you will find the location in the video where the man bumped into the woman, making her drop her tumbler. You can walk to the end for a nice view of the **Grassmarket** and **George Watson's College** or even have a meal at one of the restaurants, but don't drop your tumbler!

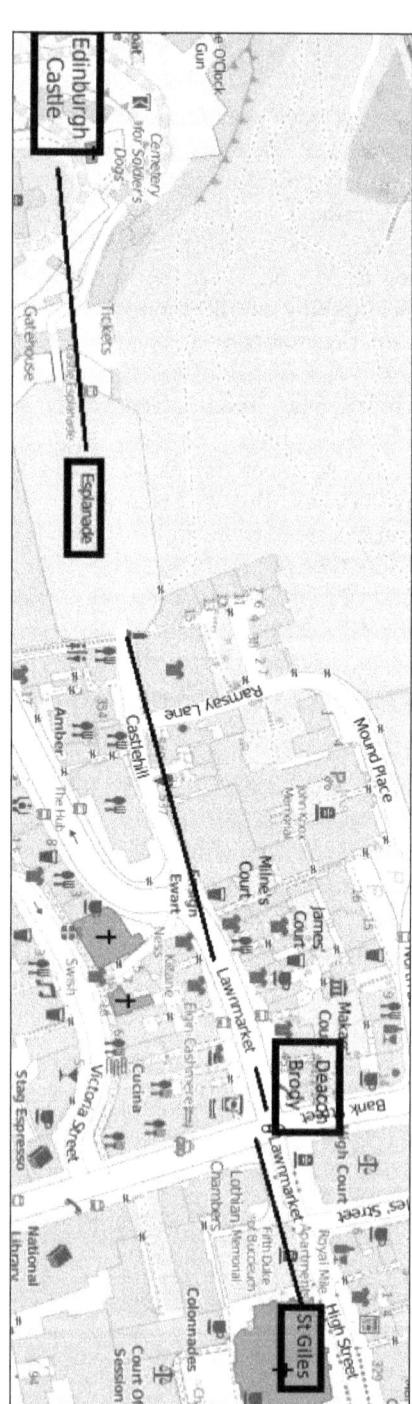

GREYFRIARS

To continue your journey head back to **George IV Bridge**, turn right and continue to make your way along past the Libraries. Keep walking and you will soon see the small statue of **Greyfriars Bobby**. Behind it is the pub and **Greyfriars Kirkyard**, where the National Covenant was signed in 1638. It is worth a look as it is historic, containing some wonderful monuments and notable burials.

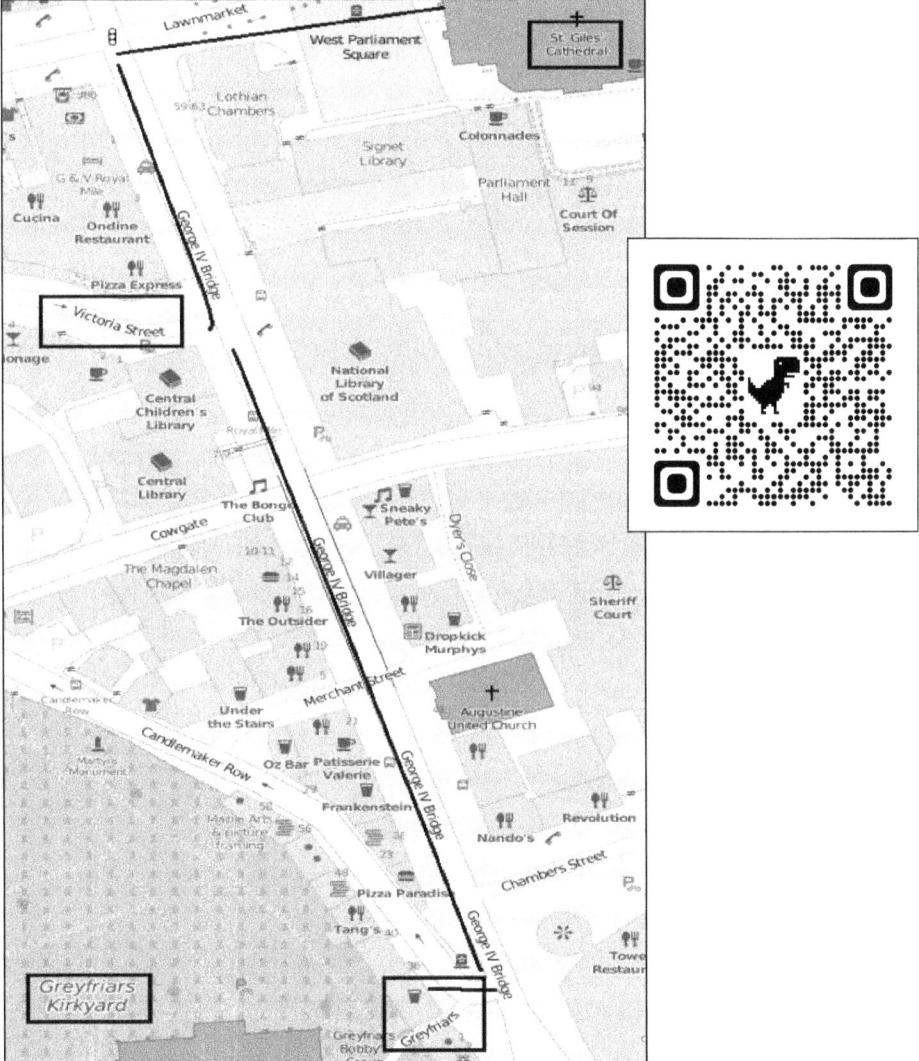

UNIVERSITY OLD COLLEGE

Next, look across the road and find **Chambers Street**. It is better to walk along the right (south) side of the street as you are going to turn right at the end. So cross the **George IV Bridge** and make your way along **Chambers Street**. On the right as you walk along is **The National Museum of Scotland**. At the end of Chambers Street, on the corner with **South Bridge** is **The University of Edinburgh Old College**. If you turn right, on to South Bridge you will see the imposing front of the building and find the entrance from which Mark drove his car.

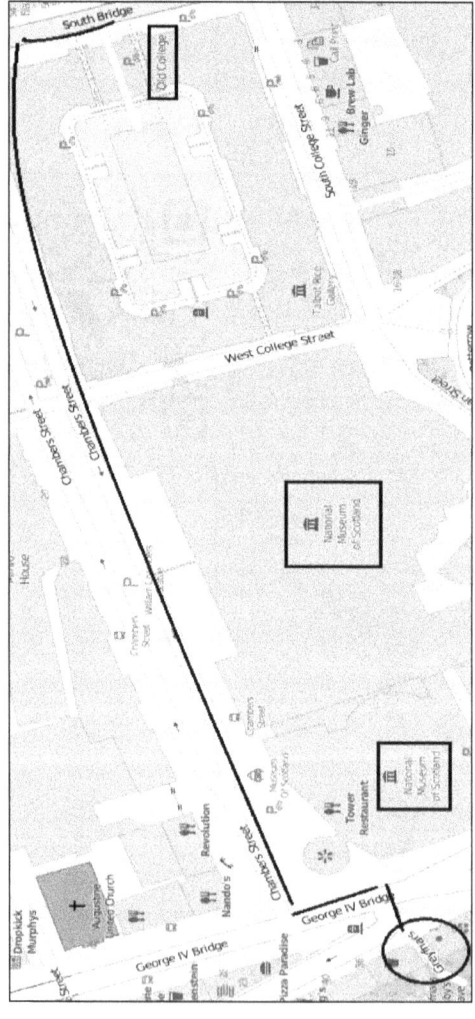

TOLLGATE

To get to your next destination, make your way back to **The Royal Mile**. This is easy as all you have to do is walk down **South Bridge** until you reach the **Tron Kirk**. Once at the Tron Kirk you are now at a crossroads with the Royal Mile running left to right. Turn right and make your way east, heading downhill toward the **Tolbooth**.

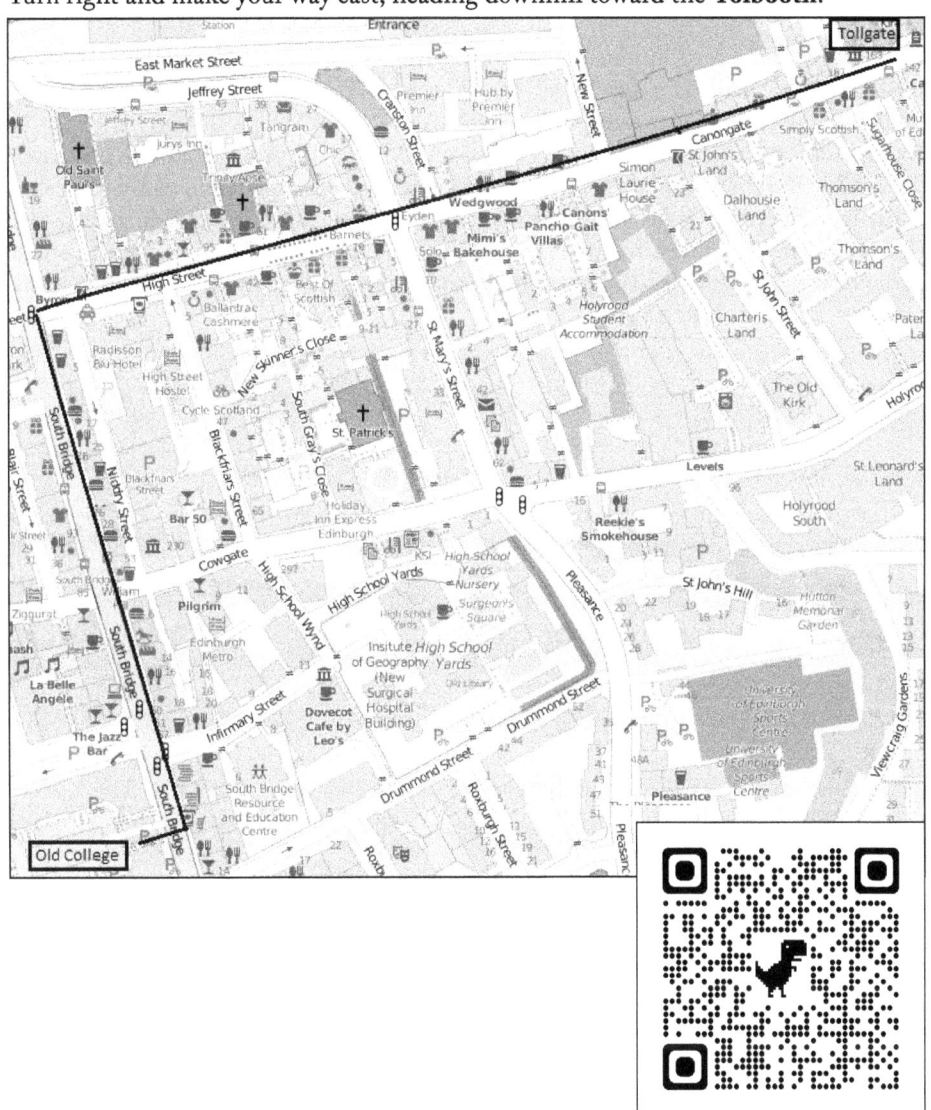

OUR DYNAMIC EARTH

Your next visit is only a few minutes away and again features in the aforementioned video. **Our Dynamic Earth** is a visitor attraction that attempts to facilitate a better understanding of earth science. It sits, appropriately, on the exact spot where James Hutton, the father of modern geology, lived and worked in the 18th century.

Simply walk to the very bottom of **The Royal Mile** where the new **Scottish Parliament Building** is located. As a side note, **The Palace of Holyroodhouse** is located across from this building if you want to have a look. As the Queen's official residence in Scotland it is a significant building. So, walk around to the other side of The Scottish Parliament Building and you will see what appears to be a large white tent with spikes - this is Our Dynamic Earth! You may recognise this distinctive building from the video as the man sprints across the front of it. There are **footpaths** around the Scottish Parliament Building to lead pedestrians around it. Directly behind this building is the extinct volcano, **Arthur's Seat**.

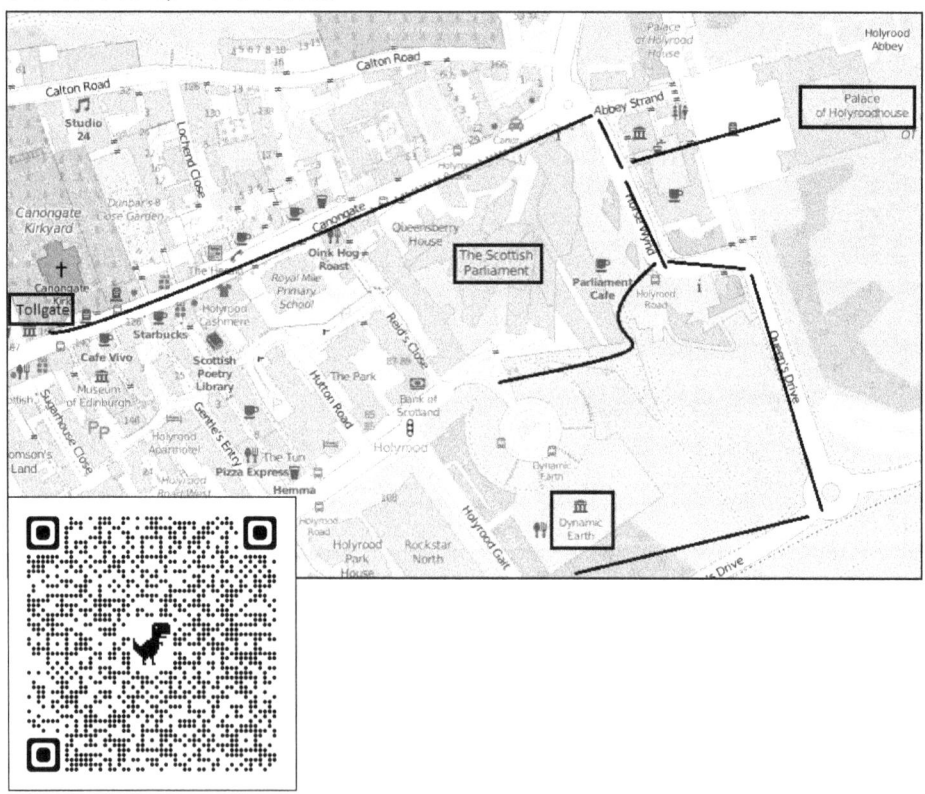

USHER HALL / LYCEUM

Your next stop is the Usher Hall, a venue Mark intended to use on his first solo tour. He had used it before with the Royal Scots Dragoon Guards when recording 'Going Home' for the 'Parallel Tracks' album. This is a walk that will take around twenty-five or thirty minutes and is 1.3 miles long so be prepared! It is however, not complicated and there are plenty of places to stop if you want a break. Simply make your way back up the Royal Mile until the small roundabout at the top of Lawnmarket, outside The Hub. Take the second left onto Johnston Terrace, a road that will take you around the Castle Rock. Take the first on the right, Castle Terrace, then walking along take Cornwall Street, the first on your left. The Lyceum is at the end of the street on the right corner. If you turn right and walk past the Lyceum you will see the Usher Hall which is just next door.

CHARLOTTE STREET

This is a mere ten-minute walk from the **Usher Hall**. Start your journey by heading downhill (north) along **Lothian Road**. Keep on the right-hand side as you will be turning right at the bottom. As you reach the end of Lothian Road there are two churches. Opposite these churches is **The Caledonian**, the hotel Mark and the band used during the Golden Heart tour. Now to **Charlotte Square** and simply walk around the church at the corner (**St. John's**) and on to **Princes Street**. Use the second set of traffic lights to cross the road so that you are walking up the right (east) side of **South Charlotte Street**. As you reach **Charlotte Square** you will find yourself outside **The Roxburghe Hotel**, which was suspect to be the hotel Mark had in mind when writing the lyrics *'on Charlotte Street I took a walking stick from my hotel'*.

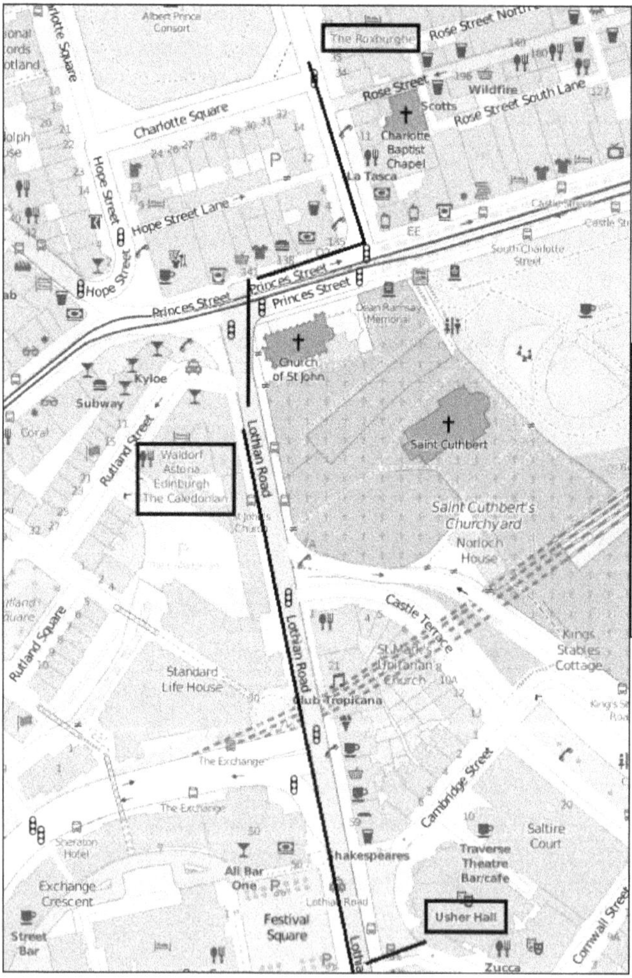

FORTH BRIDGE

To visit **North Queensferry**, use the frequent train service from **Edinburgh Waverley** to **North Queensferry Station**. The journey time is about twenty-five minutes. This is probably best enjoyed as a day trip. If you want to visit **South Queensferry** there are buses that will take you there from **Princes Street**. They are operated by **Lothian Country Buses**, a division of the local Lothian Buses. The **43** service runs every twenty minutes. Check the **Lothian Buses app** for updated information as it is very informative, including maps and fares. It will show you the bus stop number and tell you how much your journey will cost. Please note that no change is given on any Lothian Buses so have the correct fare ready.

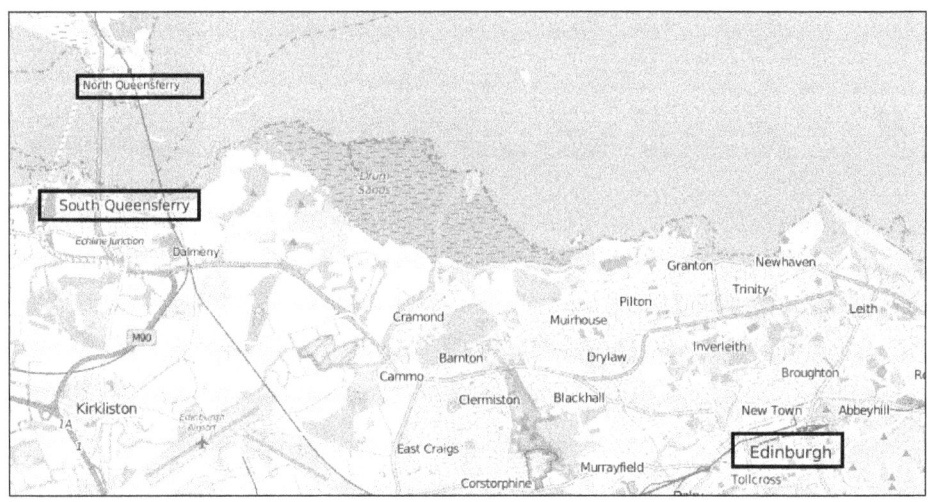

16 SILVERTOWN

THE MILLENIUM DOME (O2 ARENA)

Silvertown is a district in the West Ham area of the London Borough of Newham in East London on the north bank of the river Thames, very near to Greenwich and is the main subject of one of the Mark Knopfler songs released on his second record, 'Sailing To Philadelphia'. The song is 'Silvertown Blues', which talks about the regeneration of this area during recent years, especially in the build-up to the new millennium in 2000.

One of the main structures created for the millennium celebrations was the **Millennium Dome**, a large dome-shaped building created to host the Millennium Exhibition to celebrate the beginning of the third millennium of the Common Era. One of the main acts of the exhibition was a show called 'Ovo', written by **Peter Gabriel**. Once the exhibition was closed, the Dome was redeveloped into an entertainment complex with a big indoor auditorium, called the O2 Arena, that hosts many different types of events including musicals and sports, such as the Master Series of Tennis and basketball games during the London Olympic Games. One of the most important musical events hosted at the dome, was the last ever concert by **Led Zeppelin**, in 2007, in a tribute concert to Ahmet Ertegun, co-founder and president of Atlantic records from 1947, that helped to boost the career of many stars including Led Zeppelin, Phil Collins, Rolling Stones and many other artists in the US market.

In the lyrics of the song "Silvertown Blues" we find references to **Blackwall**, close to the large towers built in **Canary Wharf** and the docks, the Millennium Dome and the planes that land and depart from the **London City Airport**. This is close to the **Thames Barrier**, built to protect the city from floods; its construction affected the area of **Canning Town** which is also mentioned in the song and West Silvertown, another area having been redeveloped.

Glenn Tilbrook and **Chris Difford**, founding members of the band **Squeeze**, grew up in this area and their comments about how Silvertown and its surroundings had changed from their childhood days was also an inspiration to Mark Knopfler. That's the reason both of them sing in the song.

Thames Barrier, picture taken from the Pontoon Dock DLR Station

In 2015 and 2019, the Mark Knopfler "Tracker" and "Down the Road Wherever" tours made a stop at the O2 Arena. However, "Silvertown Blues" wasn't played at one of the places that inspired it. All the same, it was the closest geographically that 'Sultans Of Swing' has been played to the place where it was written, in Deptford, since the old Dire Straits days when they played at The Albany Empire and other intimate venues in the area.

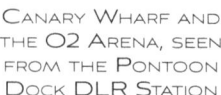

Canary Wharf and the O2 Arena, seen from the Pontoon Dock DLR Station

INSIDE THE O2 ARENA, WAITING FOR MARK KNOPFLER, MAY 22ND 2015.
PICTURE: JAVIER PELAEZ.

THE O2 ARENA, DURING MARK KNOPFLER CONCERTS IN 2015

The O2 Arena, during Mark Knopfler concert in 2019
Picture: Chris Saunders

SILVERTOWN MAPS

O2 ARENA

To visit the area where the **O2 Arena (the Millennium Dome)** is located, the underground stop is **North Greenwich**, on the **Jubilee (grey) Line**.

THAMES BARRIER

If you look around the **Silvertown** area, a visit to the **Thames Barrier** is definitely recommended. From the **North Greenwich** stop, take the **Jubilee Line** to **Canning Town**, then take the **DLR line** towards **Woolwich Arsenal** and stop at **Pontoon Dock**. From there you have great views of the **O2 Arena, Canary Wharf** and other places from Silvertown. **London City Airport** is very close as it's the next DLR line stop. Going from the **Pontoon Dock station** crossing the **Thames Barrier Park** you will get to where the Barrier is.

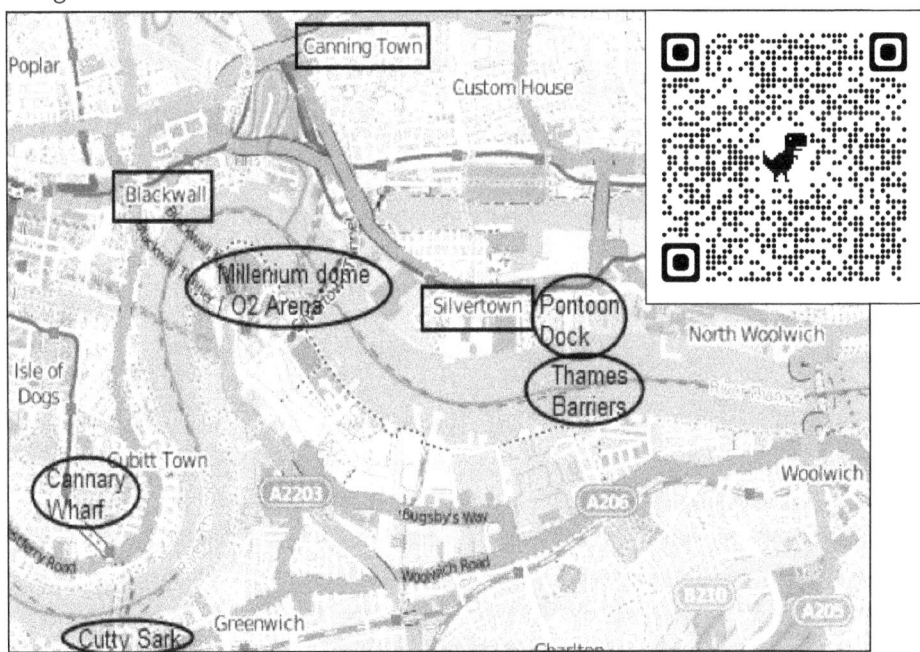

17 NEW FOREST

PICTURE BY INGRID VAN DE MAAT

In this chapter you will be travelling to the **South of England**, to an area of wide pastures and forests that is designated as a **National Park**, a status which gives the area protection under a special preservation Act of Parliament. According to some sources, Illsley and Knopfler are neighbours in this area.

In 2014, when Mark Knopfler's 'Tracker' album was released, it was accompanied by a short documentary by Danish director **Henrik Hansen**, in which Knopfler can be seen in his house in the **New Forest**, writing songs and walking with his dogs, looking at **the Solent strait** and the **Isle Of Wight**. It's not a surprise that beautiful songs emerge from such views; the New Forest and its surrounding area are worth a visit.

Picture by Ingrid Van de Maat

THE SOLENT AND THE ISLE OF WIGHT

In 1990, John Illsley bought a pub which is also a guest house, the East End Arms. It's a very popular venue in the area, with five bedrooms. When Illsley bought it he received a letter from the regulars demanding: "hands off our public bar". According to the musician, *"They wouldn't even let me repair the hole in the ceiling and when we repainted, it had to be exactly the same colour. Fine by me."*[1]

Illsley kept his word and kept the public bar intact, retaining its integrity and sense of identity.

(1) The Telegraph, by Fiona Duncan:
http://www.telegraph.co.uk/travel/destinations/europe/united-kingdom/england/hampshire/new-forest/hotels/east-end-arms-hotel/

Pictures by Ingrid Van de Maat

Pictures by Ingrid van de Maat

Picture by Olaf Bauschat

It's possible to book their rooms online at http://www.eastendarms.co.uk/

Even though John Illsley is the owner, that doesn't mean that you are going to find him there, as the pub is managed by someone else, but there's always a slim chance. Actually, there are some fans who, when there, were lucky enough to find our own Mark Knopfler, as you can see in this picture, courtesy of Andy Shipton, who told his story of this encounter in the fans' forum known as 'A Mark In Time':

BOTH PICTURES: ANDY SHIPTON

"I'm currently camping in the New Forest and thought I would go to the East End Arms for lunch. So in we go (sic) and sat by the bar having lunch was a famous musician from the 80's. My jaw hit the floor and my legs went to jelly. I didn't speak to him but he did speak to my daughter who at 3 has no idea who he is. I did get a couple of covert pics as he got into his gorgeous classic Porsche. The car got more attention than MK and it was stunning. The sound and smell when he started it up was heavenly."

In the song 'One Song At A Time' there is a mention of a place called The Pig. The song talks about Mark Knopfler leaving Deptford after achieving success in his music career, that success leading to his owning a house in the New Forest: "So if you need to reach me, you can leave word at The Pig"

There is a chance that the line above refers to a hotel restaurant called '**The Pig**' in **Brockenhurst**, which is just about seventeen minutes' driving distance from the **East End Arms**. The venue is known for having great food and atmosphere.

It's also very likely that the cover image of the 'Tracker' album, which shows Mark Knopfler posing with a guitar in a green field, was taken in the New Forest, as there are many similar places in the area.

PICTURES: JOSÉ LUIS GÓMEZ DEL POZO

THE PIG, IN BROCKENHURST.
PICTURES BY LESLIE COOKE

Beaulieu, not far from the **East End Arms**, is a village on the south eastern edge of the New Forest National Park in Hampshire; it is famous for being the home of the **British National Motor Museum** and the **Beaulieu Palace House**.

The National Motor
Museum in Beaulieu

The **Beaulieu Palace House** garden ground is where **The Notting Hillbillies** and **Dire Straits** played their last concert on 28th July 2002, under the name **Mark Knopfler and Friends**, as the culmination of the concerts at **Shepherd's Bush Empire** mentioned previously, and as such it deserves a special mention in the history of both bands. Originally part of **Beaulieu Abbey**, today it is the property of Lord Montagu, although the gardens and parts of the house can be visited. One ticket will buy entry to Palace House, the gardens and the National Motor Museum.

THE BEAULIEU PALACE, VIEW FROM WHERE THE STAGE WAS LOCATED

Not far from there, in **Buckler's Hard**, next to the **Beaulieu river**, there is a yacht harbour where a familiar vessel can occasionally be found: **The Gypsy Moth IV**, mentioned in the song "Single-Handed Sailor".

The best way to know the ship's whereabouts is by checking the following website: https://www.gipsymoth.org/

BUCKLER'S HARD

NEW FOREST MAPS

As this is a rural area, access to these places is going to be more complicated than in the cities we have already described, especially when moving from one place to the other.

The closest railway stations to the places mentioned in this chapter are **Lymington** and **Brockenhurst**. It's possible to get a travel plan from the National Rail website: http://www.nationalrail.co.uk/

If you want to visit these places by public transport, we strongly recommend carefully checking bus schedules on the Internet beforehand, as the service is very limited: buses run only on Tuesdays, Thursdays and Saturdays. In order to enjoy your visit a good travel plan is essential. We strongly recommend that you check the website timetable before you travel:
http://www.morebus.co.uk/service.shtml?serviceid=1587

The easiest way might be to rent a car or a bike, and enjoy the surroundings while travelling from one place to another.

It's possible to rent a bike here, in **Brockenhurst station**:
https://www.cyclex.co.uk/hire-new-forest

It's also possible to hire a taxi from the railway stations to get to the **East End Arms** and from there to other spots mentioned here such as **Beaulieu**. It's possible, too, to go walking if you are fit, as many of these places can be reached in a two hours' walk, according to Google.

EAST END ARMS

The closest railway station is **Lymington**. Depending on your starting point, check National Rail for train schedules. If coming from London, the starting point is **Waterloo Station**. You would then alight at **Brockenhurst** should you wish to see it.

If in Lymington, (only an eight-minute train journey from Brockenhurst) should you choose public transport to get to the **East End Arms**, leave **Lymington Town railway station** and walk along **Station Road**, turning right at **Gosport Street**; in about three minutes you will arrive at a red post, **Bridge Road bus stop**, from where the **112 Lymington bus departs - Hythe. via Lower Buckland - Boldre - Beaulieu**.

Train & Walk alternative: Train from **Brockenhurst** to B then a 45 minute walk of 2.5 Miles from the station to the **East End Arms** via **South Baddesley Road**. All week there are two trains an hour from **Brockenhurst** to **Lymington Pier** and the journey takes 11 Minutes

The **East End Arms** doesn't have a bus stop, but there is one at eight minutes' walking distance called **East End Old Post Office, South Baddesley**. This is your stop and according to Google Maps, it's the twenty-second stop from **Bridge Road** in **Lymington**, about twenty-three minutes.

The stop is on **Lymington Road**. When you get off the bus, you will have to turn back on yourself. You will see a fork on your right, with Lymington Road taking a turn left. That's the way you need to follow to get to the **East End Arms**. You'll get to the pub after an eight-minute walk.

The bus that stops at **East End Old Post Office, South Baddesley**, is the same one that goes to **Beaulieu**.

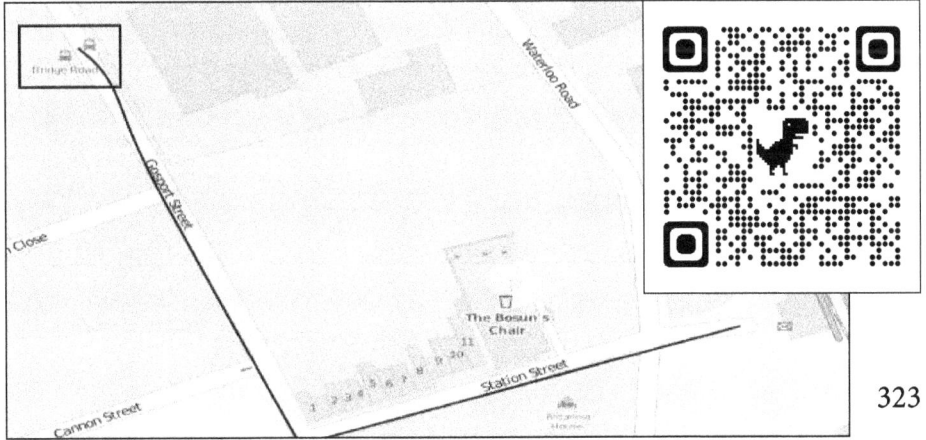

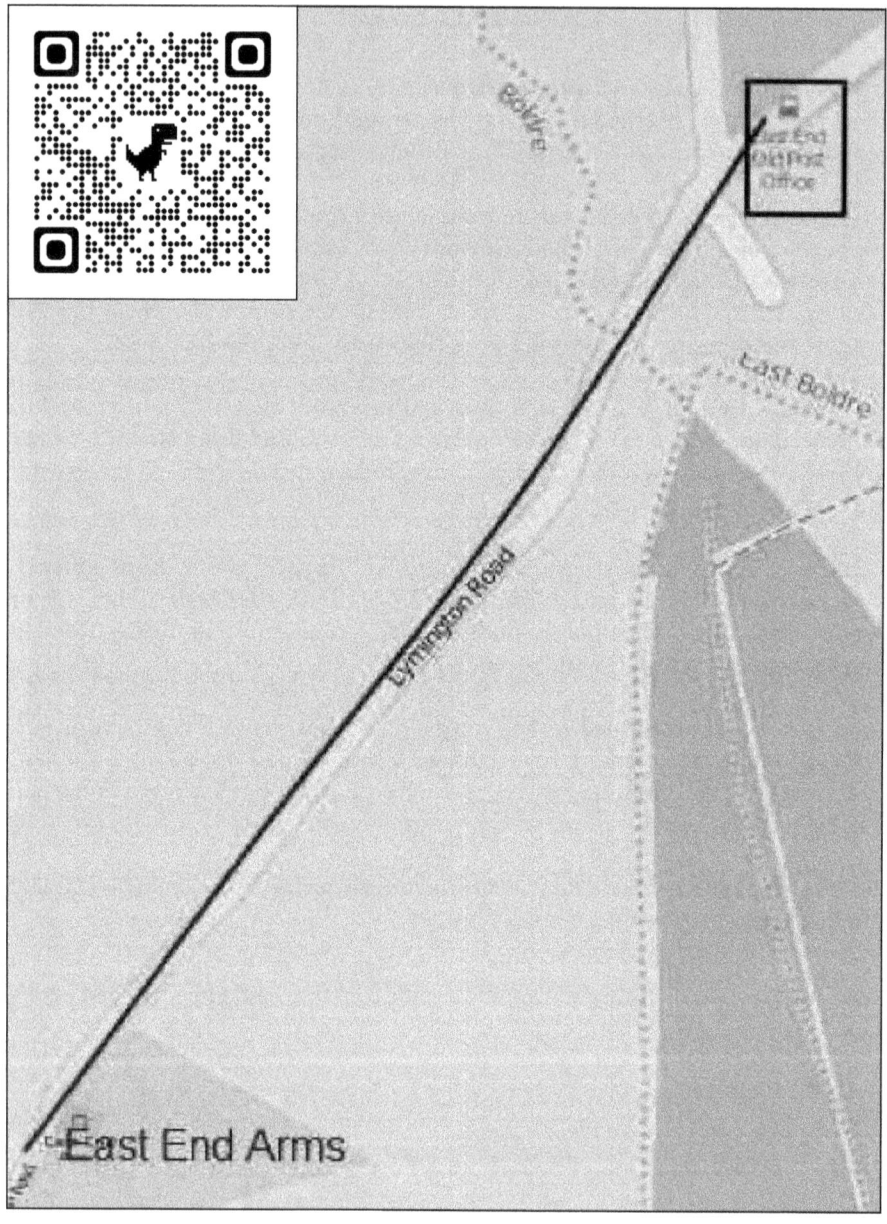

New Forest Maps

BEAULIEU PALACE

The closest railway stations would be either **Lymington** or **Brockenhurst**.

From the **East End Arms**, if using public transport, go back to the same place where the bus dropped you off at **East End Old Post Office, South Baddesley,** to **Beaulieu**, having checked the schedule earlier, (services are limited to three days a week as already mentioned). There are seventeen stops, or about sixteen minutes, until **Abbey Church** and from there walk by **Palace Lane** to get to the **Beaulieu Estate**. Optionally, you can alight at the previous stop, **Beaulieu Garage**, where you can walk across the bridge toward **Palace House at Beaulieu**.

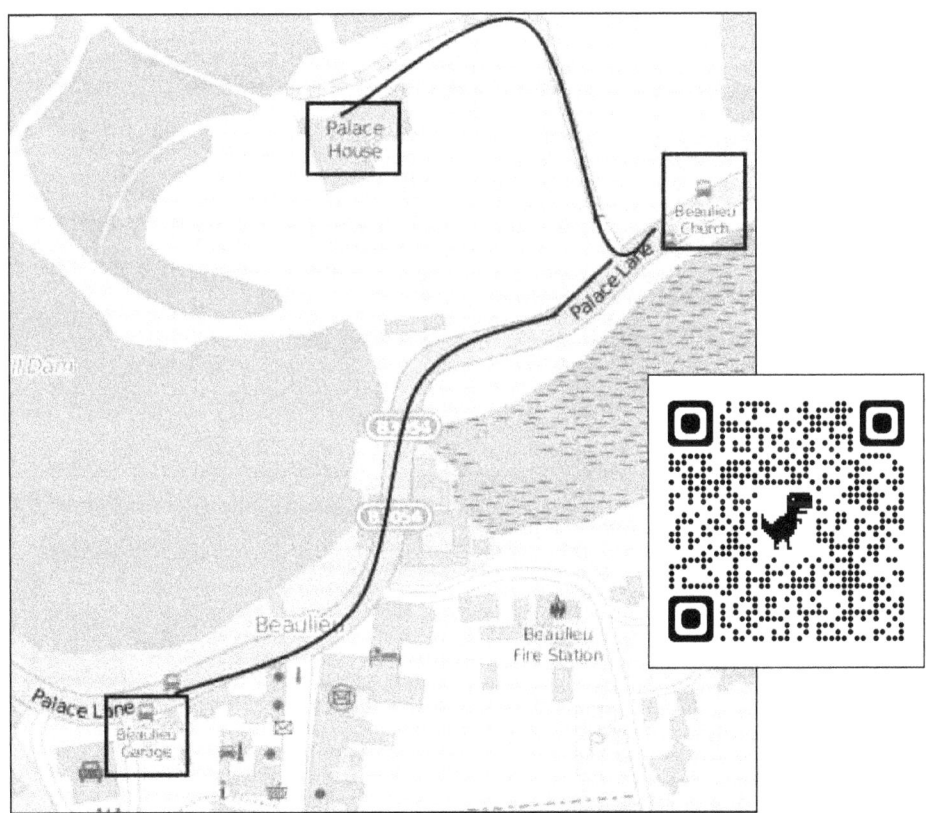

325

From **Brockenhurst**, according to Google, it takes about twenty minutes to get to **Beaulieu Palace** by bus, taking lines c1 or c3 from **Brockenhurst College station**.

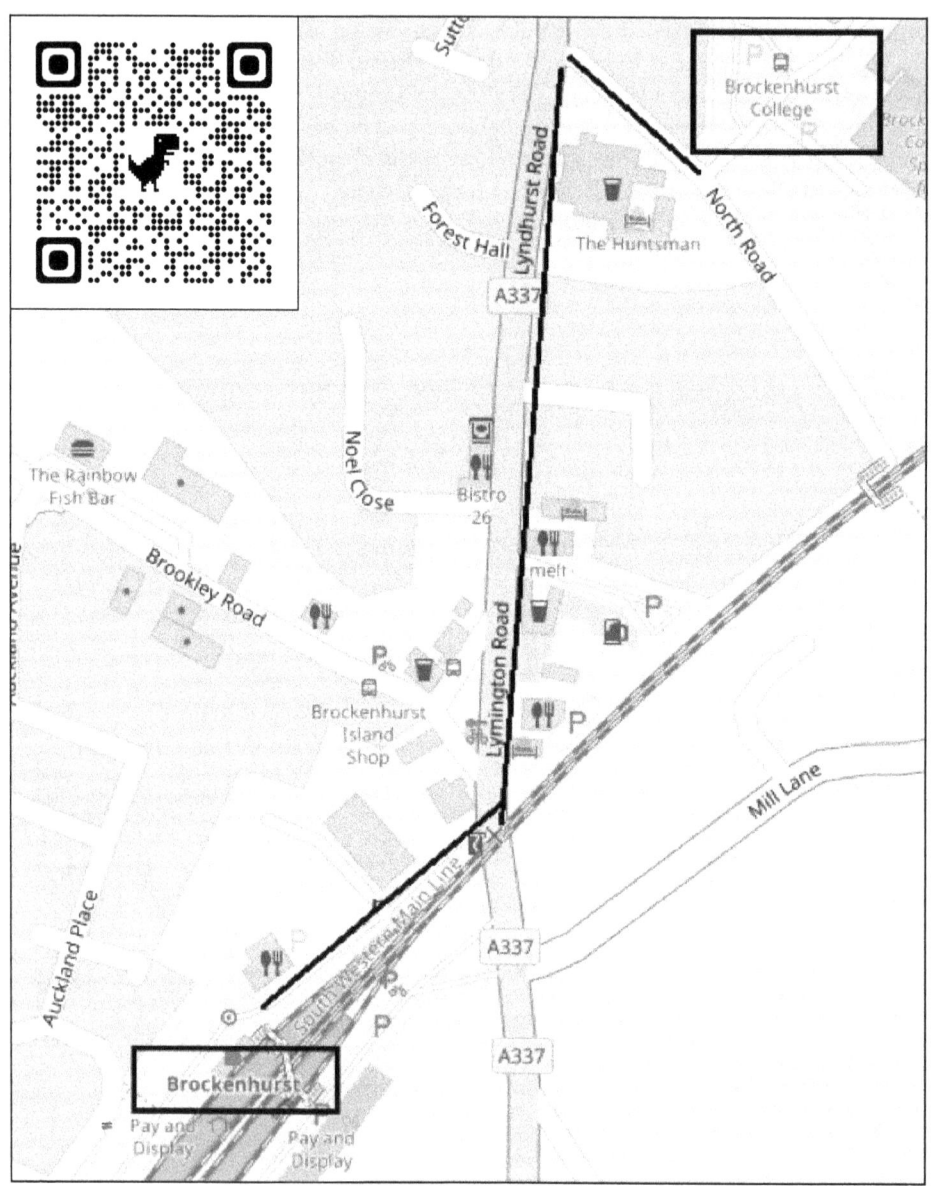

BUCKLER'S HARD

It's a seven-minute drive from Palace House, a fourteen-minute cycle or fifty-two minutes' walk to Buckler's Hard. If you decide to walk, there is a beautiful path which follows the Beaulieu River.

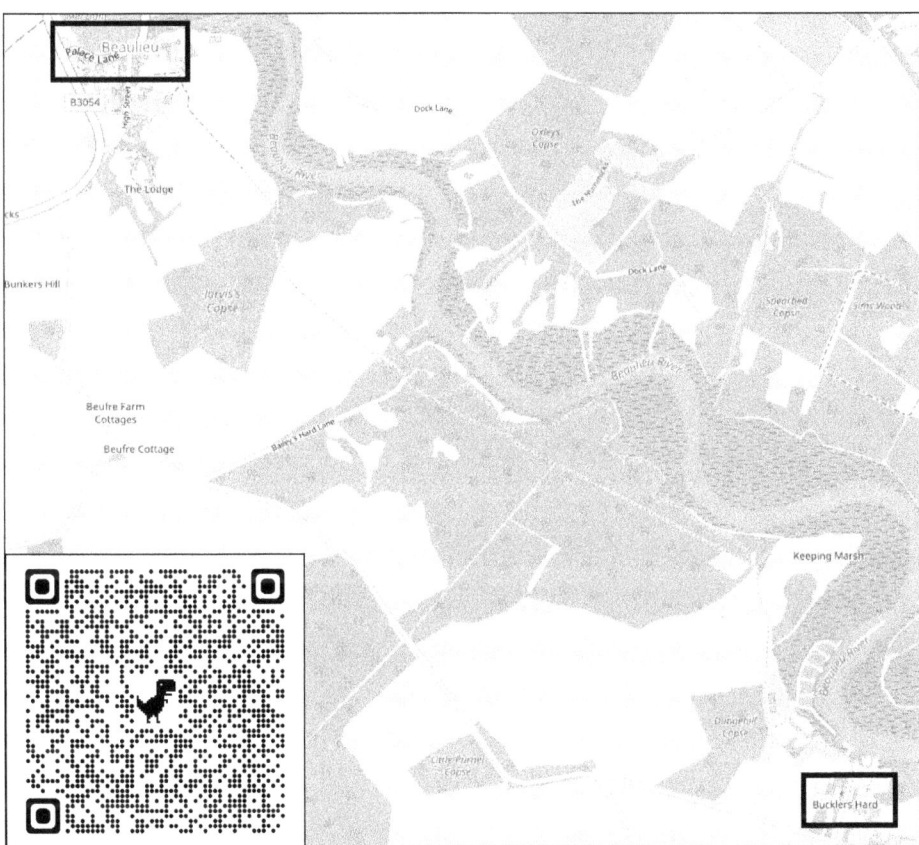

Don't forget the seasonal 'New Forest Tour' bus which offers three different tours around the New Forest. They run from July to September. The green timetable offers convenient travel to Beaulieu: http://www.thenewforesttour.info/timetable

18 SOUTHWARK

PICTURE: JAVIER PELÁEZ

Southwark is an area of South London that encompasses such attractions as **Southwark Cathedral, The Borough Market, The Tate Modern and Shakespeare's Globe Theatre**.

It's also the area of London where one can find a replica of the **Golden Hind**, the ship used by the famous privateer **Sir Francis Drake**.

Picture: Javier Peláez

'Privateering' was Mark Knopfler's seventh solo album and his first studio album to be released as a double album, containing a total of twenty tracks. Two box sets were released in addition to this standard edition: the Deluxe Edition, containing five bonus songs and the Super Deluxe Edition containing three previously unreleased tracks. Seven of the songs had already been previewed on the **Bob Dylan with Mark Knopfler** shows during the 2011 and 2012 tours.

One of these was the title track: 'Privateering'. A privateer is the name given to a sailor of a ship (or the ship itself) who embarks upon what amounts to legalised piracy. They would ride the high seas looking for enemy ships, rob them and the government would receive a cut. It was said to be backed by

The Golden Hind seen from the North bank of the Thames. Picture Javier Pelaez.

the government as a way of keeping down Navy costs. Mark has referred to feeling like a privateer on board his own ship while being on tour with his band as his crew!
Possibly the most famous of all privateers was **Sir Francis Drake**, sea captain in the Elizabethan era. Drake carried out the second circumnavigation of the world in a single expedition, the first as a single captain. The ship used was called the Golden Hind and, coincidently, after Drake's circumnavigation the ship was maintained for public exhibition at the **dockyard at Deptford**, London. The ship remained there from 1580 to circa 1650, before she eventually rotted away and was broken up. Since 1996 a replica, launched in 1973, has been berthed at **St Mary Overie's Dock in Bankside, Southwark**.

Southwark Cathedral can trace its origins back to the twelfth century, although it has been sometimes damaged badly by fire, most notably in the Great Fire of London in 1666. Since then it has gone under various stages of rebuilding including a rather unfortunate nineteenth century nave. It has a very fine interior with some notable monuments.

SOUTHWARK CATHEDRAL. PICTURE BY JAVIER PELÁEZ

SOUTHWARK CATHEDRAL. PICTURE BY JULIO BRICIO

Just south of the Cathedral is **Borough Market**. It is one of the oldest and biggest food markets in London. Originally designed in 1851 it has since been extended and now incorporates an Art Deco entrance façade to Southwark Street and a south portico Floral Hall resited from Covent Garden. Although the current buildings date back to around 1851, a market is known to have existed here as far back as 1276.

Following the south bank of the river you will arrive at **Shakespeare's Globe Theatre**. Originally built in 1599, it represented one of the earliest purpose-built commercial playhouses in England, and was one of an important cluster of four known Tudor-Jacobean theatres on the South Bank of London. Unfortunately it no longer exists, destroyed by fire in 1613; however, the current building on Bankside founded by actor and director Sam Wanamaker is a good modern recreation opened in 1997 close to the **Tate Modern**.

BOROUGH MARKET. PICTURE BY JOSÉ IGNACIO CORBALÁN

GLOBE THEATRE. PICTURE BY JULIO BRICIO

Fine views can be had across the Thames from Bankside as the famous copper dome of **St Paul's Cathedral** can clearly be seen over the river.

The **Tate Modern museum**, very near the reconstructed Shakespeare's Globe Theatre, like **Battersea** is a former power station designed by Sir Giles Gilbert Scott, although in the brutalist style. Gilbert Scott is perhaps best known for designing the iconic red telephone box. Opened in 1963, its dominant chimney stands at the southern end of the **Millennium Bridge**.

From the dome of **St Paul's Cathedral**, you can enjoy wonderful views of London and the **River Thames**, a reminder of the opening lyrics of the song 'Kingdom of Gold', also from the 'Privateering' album:

"*The high priest of money looks down on the river / The dawn coming up on his kingdom of gold*"

THE TATE MODERN AND THE MILLENNIUM BRIDGE, VIEWS FROM ST. PAUL'S CATHEDRAL DOME

VIEWS FROM THE TATE MODERN OF THE MILLENNIUM BRIDGE AND ST. PAUL'S CATHEDRAL.

SOUTHWARK MAPS

This is a tourist route so we suggest you start from **Monument Underground Station** on the **District (green) and Circle (yellow) Lines**. Take a look at the **Monument**, cross the **London Bridge**, from where you will have fine views of **Tower Bridge**, the **Tower of London**, the **City Hall of London** and even in the distance, **Canary Wharf**.

At the end of **London Bridge** turn right to find **Southwark Cathedral**, the **Borough Market** and the **Golden Hind**.

Looking at the river, continue walking on your left and you'll reach the **Globe Theatre** and the **Tate Modern**. Cross the **Millennium Bridge** to visit the nearby **St. Paul's Cathedral**.

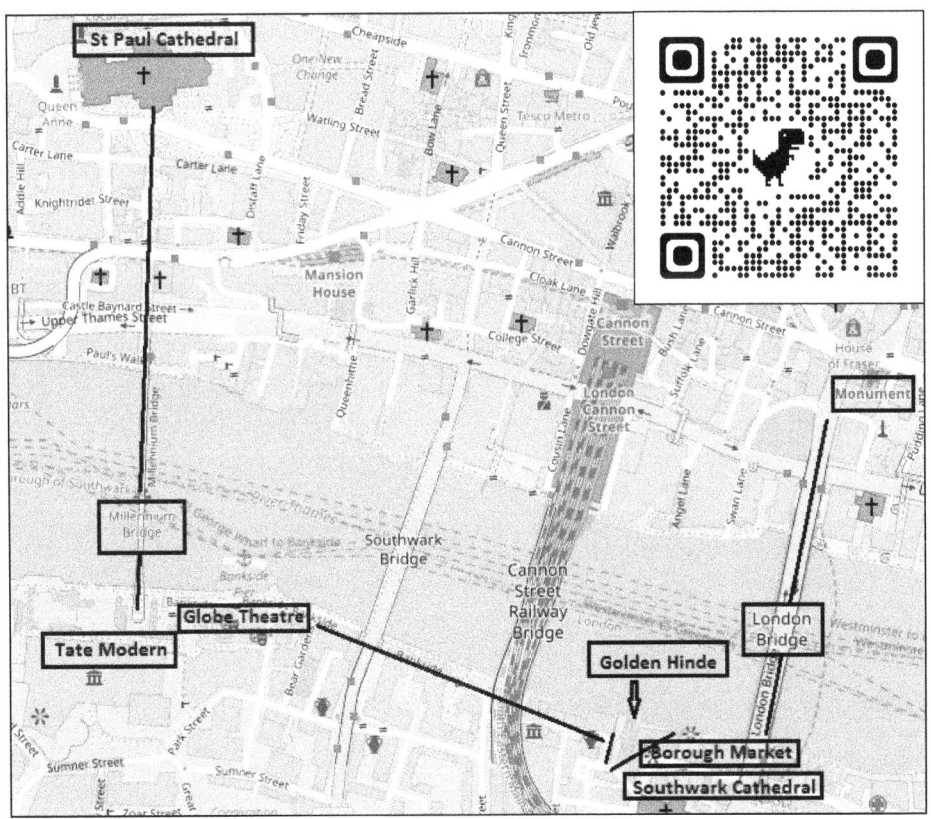

EXTRAS

19   ALABAMA

The state of **Alabama**, in the southeast of the USA, is the location of the famous **Muscle Shoals Studios**, an influence found on Dire Straits' 'Communiqué' record, but also where they recorded with **Bob Dylan** on his 'Slow Train Coming' release.

The city of Muscle Shoals has been associated with music since the 1960s and local artists began to develop what is known as the "**Muscle Shoals Sound**", with Muscle Shoals Studios opening in 1969. The original Muscle Shoals Sound Studios were located at 3614 Jackson Highway, but that site was closed in 1979 when the studio relocated to 1000 Alabama Avenue. They have since returned to their original location, however, and the building has been restored. It has been placed on the National Register of Historic Places and offers tours through the studio to visitors.

"Communiqué" was recorded at **Compass Point Studios, Nassau**, towards the end of 1978 and mixed in January 1979 in **Muscle Shoals Studios**, with some other mixing happening later in New York. The album was produced by **Barry Beckett** and **Jerry Wexler**, two veteran producers from Muscle Shoals Sound Studio.

Barry Beckett was originally a keyboardist who played in the house band called **The Muscle Shoals Rhythm Section**, one of the most distinguished American studio house bands from the 1960s to the 1980s. The band was known by the nickname 'The Swampers" and through their many recordings (thought to total around 500 individually or as a group) are recognised to have crafted the "Muscle Shoals Sound". This group left Rick Hall's FAME Studios to set up on their own and the result was Muscle Shoals Studios.

The famous record producer **Jerry Wexler** came on board owing to the strategy of **John Stainze**, the Phonogram A&R man. He wanted to get the second album, 'Communiqué', released early 1n 1979 to be able to tour the USA on the back of it. Jerry Wexler worked for Warner, was one of the most renowned producers and would bring Dire Straits to the US on the Warner record label. Mark Knopfler and his manager Ed Bicknell flew out to meet with Wexler at the legendary Muscle Shoals Studios where Barry Beckett was co-producing at the time. While there Beckett asked him to play on an old J J Cale song called "Lies" and Knopfler obliged. One wonders what happened to that recording...

One recording that did survive was made in 1979 and was made with **Bob Dylan**. It happened that Dire Straits were playing The Roxy in Los Angeles on their USA tour in March 1979 when Bob Dylan approached Mark Knopfler and said something along the lines of: "I really love what you're doing." This impromptu encounter resulted in both Knopfler and drummer Pick Withers playing on Dylan's 1979 album 'Slow Train Coming', recorded at **Muscle Shoals Studios**. **Barry Beckett** would play on keyboards and **Jerry Wexler** was producer.

According to the Dire Straits biography written by Michael Oldfield, Knopfler called Ed Bicknell, his manager, from Muscle Shoals to express his concerns about the material they were recording. "All these songs are about God", he said.

Mark Knopfler: "*Bob and I ran down a lot of those songs beforehand,*" recalls Knopfler. "*And they might be in a very different form when he's just hittin' the piano, and maybe I'd make suggestions about the tempo or whatever. Or I'd say, 'What about a twelve-string?'*"

'Slow Train Coming' was the first of what has been called, together with the 'Saved' and 'Shot of Love' albums, Dylan's Christian Trilogy and it had a good reception on release. A session outtake was the b-side of the first single from the album but in edited form. The full version, and other outtakes and alternate takes, have since appeared on two of Dylan's 'Bootleg Series' releases, namely 'Volumes 1-3 (rare and unreleased) 1961-1991' and 'Volume 13 - Trouble No More - 1979-1981'.

"The Bootleg Series Vol 1-3" also included unreleased songs from Dylan's 1983 record, "Infidels", which also featured Mark Knopfler on guitar and co-producing, and **Alan Clark** on keyboards, recorded at **Power Station Studios** in **New York**.

20 NASHVILLE

In 1985, Mark Knopfler got a call from one of his heroes to participate in his new record. **Chet Atkins** was looking for some guitar players to record duets for what would be his next project, 'Stay Tuned'. They recorded two songs together, 'Some Leather and Lace' and 'Cosmic Square Dance', in which Knopfler shares credits. In 1987 Mark Knopfler also recorded his own 'Why Worry' with Chet Atkins for his 'Sails' recording;; an instrumental version of **John Lennon's** 'Imagine' for Atkins' 1988 "Chet Atkins C.G.P", which had already been played live for the **"Secret Policeman's Third Ball"** benefit concert in London, released on CD and video, and also an instrumental rendition of the track 'I'll See You In My Dreams" in 1987.

These collaborations with Chet Atkins were recorded mostly in **Nashville**, and introduced Mark Knopfler to a new world in musical terms. He started to play as a session musician with artists such as **The Judds** and ultimately worked on, in 1990, a duet album with Atkins, recorded between Nashville and his home studio in **Notting**

Hill, London. This record would be called 'Neck and Neck". During work on this he met some of the finest musicians in the Nashville scene, one of them, **Paul Franklin**, one of the best pedal steel guitar players. Franklin was recruited by Knopfler for his next project, **The Notting Hillbillies** album, also released in 1990, and for the next (and last) **Dire Straits** record, 'On Every Street'. Franklin was also part of The Notting Hillbillies and final Dire Straits tours.

THE RYMAN AUDITORIUM, NASHVILLE

When recording 'Neck and Neck' with Chet Atkins, Knopfler met a country singer and guitar player who very much impressed him, Vince Gill, and asked him to participate in the 'On Every Street' sessions, singing backing vocals. When setting up the band for the upcoming Dire Straits tour Knopfler asked Gill to join them, an offer he declined, preferring to focus on his solo career.

MARK KNOPFLER, MARTY STUART, RICHARD BENNETT, GILLIAN WELCH AND VINCE GILL (AT THE LEFT OF THE PICTURE) NASHVILLE 24TH JUNE 1998, BY KENNETH DONALDSON.

Vince Gill: "I*t was funny because I wasn't making any money to speak of,*" Gill told **Foo Fighters** guitarist **Chris Shiflett** on the **Walking the Floor** podcast [1]. "*Session work was keeping me alive, jingles and things like that. [Joining Dire Straits] would have solved everything. It would've been a great payday. But I told Mark, I said 'Man, I can't bail. If I do this, it's gonna take a couple years out of my life. I got a new record deal; if I bail on it, it'd kind of be admitting failure.' I said, 'I can't do that; I gotta keep trying.' So I turned down the sure thing. Probably the dumbest move you could make.*"[2]

Tennesse Music Pathways / Birth of the bluegrass

During those years, and especially after the Dire Straits last tour ended, Knopfler was very active as a session player in Nashville, recording with artists such as *Ronnie Milsap, Rory Block, John Anderson, Jerry Reed, Dee Carstensen, Aaron Neville, Nancy Griffith, George Jones, Iris DeMent, Clint Black, Waylon Jennings, Kris Kristofferson, Alan Merrill* etc and of course, *Chet Atkins.*

After Dire Straits' last album and tour, Knopfler decided to disband them, and thereafter he would begin a career as a solo artist. He used his experience and contacts in Nashville at the start. His first solo album, 'Golden Heart', released in 1996, was largely recorded there with lots of different studio musicians he had met through his years of sessions in Nashville. He was so satisfied with the experience that he assembled a band for his first solo tour with some of those musicians, plus **Guy Fletcher**, who also

[1]Chris Shiflett, Walking the floor podcast: https://youtu.be/i1ZxsIV25qY
[2]iheart.com, by Andrew Magnotta. August 7, 2018:
https://www.iheart.com/content/2018-08-07-vince-gill-declined-offer-to-join-dire-straits-years-before-making-it/

participated in the sessions for the album. Producer and sound engineer **Chuck Ainlay**, who had worked on the last Dire Straits record, also formed part of the team.

That band was formed using some of the most renowned session musicians in the Nashville scene. They included **Richard Bennett**, well known as a producer and guitar player for *Neil Diamond*, **Glenn Worf** on bass, **Jim Cox** on keyboards and **Chad Cromwell** on drums, plus **Guy Fletcher**; most of them would stay in Mark's live band in the future.

One of the three film scores he recorded and released during 2000, 'Wag The Dog' and his next solo album, 'Sailing to Philadelphia', released in 2000, were also recorded in Nashville, with the same band that toured with him four years earlier, plus other musicians (for his second solo CD) such as percussionist **Danny Cummings**, who was also on the last Dire Straits' album and tour, **Paul Franklin** and many others, including special guests **James Taylor, Van Morrison, Gillian Welch and David Rawlings, Glenn Tilbrook** and **Chris Difford**, from **Squeeze**.

Emmylou Harris also participated in the sessions but the two songs they recorded for that CD ('Red Staggerwing' and 'Donkeytown') were saved as Knopfler and Harris, who met at a concert honouring Chet Atkins in 1987 called "**Chet Atkins and Friends**", for PBS, the American public television service, decided to release a duet album in the future.

During the rehearsals for the 2001 Mark Knopfler world tour, he recorded another two songs with Emmylou Harris for a tribute record to **Hank Williams** called 'Timeless'. The songs were 'Lost On The River' and Alone and Forsaken, which they would play live during the Nashville concert of that tour. **Paul Franklin** was a special guest for that night.

The third Mark Knopfler solo album, 'The Ragpickers Dream' was also recorded in Nashville in 2002 and during the same sessions, they recorded some songs with Emmylou Harris to be added to their future duet album, including 'If This Is Goodbye' as part of the sessions. Final sessions with Harris took place in 2004, again in Nashville, to complete a record that would eventually see the light of day in 2006, under the title 'All The Roadrunning'". There was a short tour in Europe and the USA, and a live CD and DVD of it released, 'Real Live Roadrunning'.

THE GRAND OLE OPRY HOUSE, NASHVILLE

During Mark Knopfler's years in Nashville there were two very important moments, the first being the already mentioned Chet Atkins special for TV, '**Chet Atkins and Friends**', recorded at the **Neely Auditorium** during the first two days of May in 1987, where Mark met **Emmylou Harris** and where he had the chance to play with musical heroes from his youth, **The Everly Brothers**. It was even more special as they sang one of his songs, 'Why Worry' live at the show, with Mark playing guitar.

That special moment ties in with a second one, a celebration concert at the **Ryman Auditorium** in Nashville on 24th June, 1998, during what was called the '**Chet Atkins Musicians Days - Witness History II**". According to a press note about the concert, it was *"Anchored by British rocker and Atkins champion Mark Knopfler"*.[3]

CHET ATKINS MUSICIANS DAYS POSTERS

[3] Jay Orr, Staff Writer, The Tennessean - Friday, June 26, 1998: http://www.martystuart.com/WitnessII-review.htm

In that concert, the Knopfler band was on the stage for the entire show, providing the backing band for many artists with whom he had worked in the past and some of his all-time heroes, such as *John Anderson, Marty Stuart, Gillian Welch* and *David Rawlings, Waylon Jennings, Johnny Cash*, who recently had covered Knopfler's song "The Next Time I'm In Town", and of course, Chet Atkins. The reason these two special moments are connected is that during the concert, Knopfler premiered a new song, titled "Two Skinny Kids", which was a tribute to **The Everly Brothers**. During the years Knopfler was in Nashville recording the songs for his "Sailing to Philadelphia" album, the song was recorded; however, it did not made the final cut and remains unreleased.

MARK KNOPFLER AND WAYLONG JENNINGS, AND WITH DAVID RAWLINGS AND GILLIEN WELCH NASHVILLE 24TH JUNE 1998, PICTURE BY KENNETH DONALDSON

MARK KNOPFLER AND CHET ATKINS, NASHVILLE 24TH JUNE 1998, PICTURE BY KENNETH DONALDSON

KRIS KRISTOFFERSON AND JOHNNY CASH. PICTURE BY RICK BELLO

The duet record with **Emmylou Harris** was the last album that Knopfler recorded in **Nashville** and the first that had parts recorded and mixed in his own recording studio in **London, British Grove Studios**. After years of recording in the best Nashville studios, Knopfler had a very clear idea of what he needed and he built his own studio based on all he had learnt from all the great places he worked there. In 2002 he found the perfect spot and started the construction of the place that would open some years later to become one of the busiest and most famous studios in London.

MARK KNOPFLER AND EMMYLOU HARRIS IN DUBLIN, DURING THEIR TOUR TOGETHER IN 2006.
PICTURE BY JULIO BRICIO.

He didn't go back to Nashville to record but he still has three of the aforementioned musicians in his band: **Richard Bennett**, **Glenn Worf** and **Jim Cox**, who now travel to London to work with him.

21 PHILADELPHIA

PHILADELPHIA AIRPORT. PICTURE BY DANIEL BETTS. UNDER CREATIVE COMMONS ATTRIBUTION-SHAREALIKE 2.0 GENERIC LICENSE.

A large Pennsylvanian city in the Northeastern/Great Lakes area of the United States of America, **Philadelphia** lends its name to Mark Knopfler's 2000 release 'Sailing to Philadelphia'. The song itself is inspired by the book '**Mason and Dixon**' by **Thomas Pynchon** that Mark was reading as he was changing planes at Philadelphia airport en route to Nashville. It tells the story of the two individuals who surveyed the **Mason-Dixon line** in the 1760s using astronomy as a guide.

The **Mason-Dixon line** was surveyed to define the long-disputed boundaries of overlapping land of the Penns, proprietors of Pennsylvania, and the Calverts, proprietors of Maryland. The dispute arose over conflicting claims to the territory from the Delaware River westward. Along the line the surveyors placed milestones brought from England, with every fifth stone in the eastern portion being a "crown stone" bearing the arms of Penn on one side and of Baltimore, Maryland on the other. **Charles Mason** (from Gloucestershire, England) and **Jeramiah Dixon** (from County Durham, England) were the surveyors.

PICTURE: JIMMY EMERSON, UNDER CREATICE COMMONS ATTRIBUTION-NONCOMMERCIAL-NODERIVS 2.0 GENERIC LICENSE

Dixon's Mother came from nearby **Newcastle** which no doubt attracted the interest of Mr Knopfler! Dixon was made a Fellow of **The Royal Society** and of **The Royal Society of Edinburgh**. He died aged 45 in the village of his birth, Cockfield. He is buried in an unmarked grave.

> *"I am Jeremiah Dixon*
> *I am a Geordie Boy*
> *A glass of wine with you, sir*
> *And the ladies I'll enjoy*
> *All Durham and Northumberland*
> *Is measured up by my own hand*
> *It was my fate from birth*
> *To make my mark upon the earth"*

Charles Mason was the son of a baker. His career began at the Royal Greenwich Observatory near London in 1756. He worked on perfecting the Lunar Tables, helping navigation at sea. Mason was a Fellow of The Royal Society. He died aged 58 in Philadelphia and is buried at Christ Church Burial Ground in the city.

"He calls me Charlie Mason
A stargazer am I
It seems that I was born
To chart the evening sky
They'd cut me out for baking bread
But I had other dreams instead
This baker's boy from the west country
Would join the Royal Society"

The burial ground is located at 5th and Arch Streets, across from the Visitors Center and National Constitutional Center.

PICTURE: JON DAWSON, UNDER CREATIVE COMMONS ATTRIBUTION-NODERIVS 2.0 GENERIC LICENSE.

PICTURES BY L.HARWELL / WWW.FINDAGRAVE.COM.

22 DETROIT

Picture by Doug Kerr, under Creative Commons Attribution-ShareAlike 2.0 Generic (CC BY-SA 2.0)

During the Making Movies tour, the band was travelling by bus to Detroit. At the time, Mark Knopfler was reading "The Growth of the Soil". The novel, written in 1917, by the Nobel Prize winning author Knut Hamsun. They were driving along a very lengthy road and Knopfler, sitting in the front of the bus, noticed that it was called "Telegraph Road". The unusual name was combined with the theme of the book to prompt the song that would become an epic on the fourth Dire Straits album, "Love Over Gold".

In 1993, while promoting the "On The Night" album on the "Rockline" radio show, in which he took questions from fans, Mark Knopfler observed: *"In fact, I was driving down that road, and I was reading a book at the time called THE GROWTH OF THE SOIL and I just put the two together. I was driving down this Telegraph Road that you're talking about, I think it's the same road, and it just went on and on and on forever. It's like what they call linear development. And I just started to think, I wondered how that road must have been when it started, what it must have first been. And then really that's how it all came about. Yeah, I just put that book together and the place where I was. I was actually sitting in the front of the tour bus at the time."*

"**The Growth of the Soil**" tells the story of a man who settles and lives in rural **Norway**. Early verses in the song follow the idea of a man who starts his life on a patch of land as a farmer. As the land slowly becomes more developed in a way that differs from what the protagonist had wanted, he comes into conflict with it. In 1921, the book was made into a Norwegian silent film.

Telegraph Road is part of **US Highway 24**. This highway runs almost 2500 kilometres from Minturn in Colorado, through the states of Kansas, Missouri, Illinois, Indiana and Ohio. At a V-junction a little north of downtown Toledo in Ohio, Highway 24 bears left and, just after this, it becomes Telegraph Road. The Telegraph Road portion of Highway 24 then runs for about 130 kilometres into Michigan, through the western edge of **Metro Detroit** and northwards, until Highway 24 itself turns left, north of Pontiac, becoming Dixie Highway and terminating near Clarkston.

Telegraph Road existed before the highway system was established and was so named because it ran parallel to a line of telegraph wires. It is a major north–south route between Toledo and Detroit. The tour bus, coming from the show in Cleveland, would have joined Highway 24 in Toledo, before turning north towards Telegraph Road and Detroit.

Knopfler started to write the song whilst still travelling on the American leg of the Making Movies tour. Initially, the song closely reflects the book's plot and Knopfler's ideas about the origins of Telegraph Road. When touring in Europe, Knopfler started to build the song with the help of his keyboard player Alan Clark, who said, in a 2014 interview for **Ultimate Classic Rock**:

"'Telegraph Road' he (Mark Knopfler) actually wrote it bit-by-bit when we were on the road. At every soundcheck for every gig afterwards, he and I would get together and we'd sort of formulate the next bit of the song. He'd written where we'd gotten up to, and we would then start making it work between us with the piano part and his part and that's how the song was

built up. I was actually present when he started writing it, which was sitting in the front of a tour bus during the 'Making Movies' tour when we were heading to Detroit -- because the Telegraph Road is actually a road that runs into Detroit.

We were driving up that road and it's a big, long, straight road and I recall it had one slight kink in it, but other than that it was perfectly straight and it went on for miles and miles and miles into the city of Detroit. The whole song was based around that journey and how somebody else might be making that journey in the early days when the road wasn't there and how the road came about. So it just fired Mark's imagination, sitting in the front of the tour bus."

There are some audience recordings from European shows in 1981 that contain these early versions of "Telegraph Road", mainly built around Clark's piano and with less guitar evident than on the final version of the song. It's very clear that the song was still growing and that these early live performances laid the foundations for what, arguably, would be the standout track on "Love Over Gold", as recorded in **Power Station**, New York, in 1982.

Bibliography

BOOKS:

Bob Dylan: Behind the Shades Revisited, Clinton Heylin. Edited by Harper Collins

Dire Straits, Álvaro Feito. Edited by Ediciones Júcar.

Dire Straits, Carlos Gámez. Edited by La Máscara.

Dire Straits, Colin Irwin. Edited by Carlton Books Ltd.

Dire Straits, Francesco Fabiano and Giancarlo Passarella. Edited by LoVeccio.

Dire Straits, Michael Oldfield. Edited by Sidgwick and Jackson.

Dire Straits, Philip Kamen. Edited by Robus Books.

Dire Straits, Silvia Grijalba. Edited by La Máscara.

Dire Straits and Mark Knopfler's London, Julio Bricio. Edited by Lulu.com.

Dire Straits: Manuali Rock 22, Giancarlo Passarella. Edited by Arcana Editrice.

Dire Straits: Solid Rock, Giancarlo Passarella. Edited by M.M.Edizioni.

Hundred Watts: A Life In Music, Ron Watts. Edited by Heroes Publishing.

Mark Knopfler - A life dedicated to music, Franck Thuillier. Edited by Lulu.com.

Mark Knopfler, An Unauthorised Biography, Myles Palmer. Edited by Sidgwick and Jackson.

Mark Knopfler Guitar Styles, Peter Evans. Edited by Wise Publications

My life in Dire Straits. John Illsley. Edited by Bantam Press

On track... Dire Straits. Andrew Wild. Edited by Sonic Bound Publishing

Roadbook, Manu Katché. Edited by Le Cherche Midi.

Surviving in a ruthless world, Bob Dylan's voyage to Infidels, Terry Gans. Edited by red planet books

ARTICLES:

- Cris Shiflett, Walking the floor podcast: https://youtu.be/i1ZxsIV25qY

- David White of 4MMM FM, Brisbane, Australia, interview by David White, broadcasted on 10th November 1991: https://web.archive.org/web/20010222155639fw_/http://www.knopfler.net/interview11.html

- BBC Leeds: Johnny L'anson interviews Dave Johnson, for BBC Leeds, February 11st 2016

- Crossfrields blog: http://crossfields.blogspot.com.es/2010/07/dire-straits-documentary-photos-and-ear.html

- Daily Mail, 1st March 1997, by Vicky Ward and Paul Bracchi: https://www.questia.com/article/1G1-110801209/a-secret-wife-and-the-love-child-that-still-haunts

- The Gearpage: https://www.thegearpage.net/board/index.php?threads/any-pensa-suhr-owners-out-there.393313/

- Grandlife blog, by Peter Foges: http://www.grandlifehotels.com/culture/the-best-little-block-in-the-world-bank-street/

- iheart.com, by Andrew Magnotta. August 7, 2018:

https://www.iheart.com/content/2018-08-07-vince-gill-declined-offer-to-join-dire-straits-years-before-making-it/

- Jack Sonni website: http://jacksonni.com/thirty-years-on/

- Jay Orr, Staff Writer, The Tennessean - Friday, June 26, 1998:

http://www.martystuart.com/WitnessII-review.htm

- Knopfler.com archive of interviews from 1979 to 2008: https://web.archive.org/web/20080603204448fw_/http://www.knopfler.net/interview_index.html

- Musician, September 1985, by Bill Flanagan: https://web.archive.org/web/20080527141355/http://www.knopfler.net/interview48.html

- Q Magazine, 1991: https://web.archive.org/web/20010222155952fw_/http://www.knopfler.net/interview10.html

- Renee Johnson writes blog. April 15, 2015, Renee Johnson: https://reneejohnsonwrites.com/2015/04/15/jack-sonni-rocker-writer-gentleman-chef/

- Rolling Stone, November 21, 1985. By Ken Tucker, David Fricke: https://www.rollingstone.com/music/music-news/dire-straits-the-rolling-stone-interview-110732/

- Rolling Stone India, September 9th 2008:

http://rollingstoneindia.com/mark-knopfler%E2%80%99s-second-act/2/

- The Telegraph, by Fiona Duncan: http://www.telegraph.co.uk/travel/destinations/europe/united-kingdom/england/hampshire/new-forest/hotels/east-end-arms-hotel/

- "What's That Song About? Blog: http://www.rockremembers.com/2009/04/single-handed-sailor-dire-straits-1979.html?m=1

GLOSSARY

(songs, records, places, people, moments) c: Chapter

5.15.a.m. - C.2
A place where we used to live - C.1
Alan Clark - C.2, C.11, C.19
Alchemy - C.4, C.12
The albany - C.4
Albion - C.1
Andra Nelki - C.6
Bank street - C.10
Basil - C.2
Basing street studios - C.9
Bearsden - C.1
Beaulieu - C.4, C.12, C.17
Bernadette - C.7
Big river - C.1
Bob Dylan - C.10, C.12, C.19
Bonnie Raitt - C.10
Border reiver - C.1
Brendan Croker - C.3
Brewers Droop - C.3
British grove studios - C.9, C.20
Brothers "in arms" BBC Documentary - C.9
Buckhurst hill - C.4
Bucklers hard - C.4, C.17
The café racers - C.4
Camden - C.7

Central Arcade - C.2
Charles Mason - C.21
Charlie Gillett - C.5, C.6
Chet Atkins: C.9, C.20
Chronicle - C.2
City varieties - C.3
Clapham - C.6
Climax blues band - C.8
Clyde auditorium - C.1
Comfort and joy - C.1, C.11
Communiqué - C.19
Congo square - C.14
Cutty shark - C.1, C.4
Damage management - C.9
Dave Johnson - C.3
Dave Pask - C.4
David Knopfler - C.4, C.5, C.7, C.9
Demos - C.5, C.6
Deptford - C.4
Dingwalls - C.7
Dinnington - C.2, C.3
Down to the waterline - C.2
Duolian string pickers - C.3
Eastbound train - C.4, C.5
East End arms - C.17
Ed Bicknell - C.7, C.9, C.11

Glossary

Edinburgh - C.11, C.15
The eldon - C.3
Elvis Costello - C.5
Emmylou Harris - C.13, C.20
Everly Brothers - C.20
Extended dance play - C.12
Fare thee well Northumberland - C.2
Farrer house - C.4
The fenton - C.3
The Fforde grene - C.3
First concert - C.4
First contract - C.7
First guitar - C.2
First record - C.9
Sir Francis Chichester - C.4
Gary Drostle - C.4
Gateshead - C.2
Gerry Rafferty - C.8, C.11
Get lucky - C.2
Gillian Welch - C.20
Glasgow - C.1
Go, love - C.2
Going home - C.2, C.11, C.15
Gosforth - C.2
Greenwich - C.4
The grove - C.3
Guitar stories - C.5, C.6
Gypsy moth - C.4, C.17
Hal Lindes - C.10
Hammersmith - C.12

Hammersmith Odeon - C.12
Harlow - C.2, C.3
Harry Phillips - C.3, C.8
Henrik Hansen - C.17
Hill farmer blues - C.2
Holland Park Mews - C.9
Hope and anchor - C.4, C.5
The Hydro - C.1
In the gallery - C.3, C.8
Industrial disease - C.9
Islington - C.5
Jack Sonni - C.10
Jeremiah Dixon - C.21
J.G.Windows - C.2
Jimmy Nail - C.2, C.12
John Illsley - C.4, C.5, C.6, C.8, C.9, C.17
John Shur - C.10
John Stainze - C.7
Just a boy away from home - C.2
Kathy White - C.2, C.3
Kingdom of gold - C18
Kitchen's music store - C.2
Last exit to Brooklyn - C.9
Last ship - C.2
Leeds - C.2, C.3
Lions - C.8
Live aid - C.13
Local hero - C.1, C.10, C.11
Loch Lommond - C.1
Loughton collegue - C.4

Glossary

Lourdes Salomone - C.10
Love over gold - C.4, C.10, C.12
Madame Geneva - C.9
Manu Katché - C.14
Mark Knopfler and friends - C.12, C.17
Matchstick man - C.3
Making movies - C.10
Metro radio arena - C.2
Metroland - C.9
Mick Dewhurst - C.3
Millennium dome - C.16
Mississippi - C.14
Money for nothing - C.10
Monteleone - C.10
Muff Winwood - C.9
Muscle shoals - C.19
My claim to fame - C.2
Nashville - C.20
Neck and neck - C.9
Nelson Mandela - C.10, C.13
New cross - C.4
New Forest - C.17
Newcastle - C.2, C.21
Newcastle United - C.2, C.11
Newcastle City Hall - C.2
New York - C.10
Notting Hill - C.9
The Notting Hillbillies - C.2, C.8, C.9, C.12
O2 Arena - C.16
One more matinee - C.3

One song at a time - C.4, C.17
On every street - C.10
The Old Vic theatre - C.11
The original oak - C.3
Oxford arms - C.6
The pack horse - C.3
Pathway studios - C.5
Paul Franklin - C.20
The Peel - C.3
Pennan - C.11
Pensa Shur - C.10
Planet of New Orleans - C.14
Plaque - C.2, C.4
Pick Withers - C.4
Polytechnic - C.3
Portobello belle - C.4, C.9
Power station studios - C.10, C.12, C.19
The Princess bride - C.9
Prince's Trust - C.9, C.10
Privateering - C.18
Quality shoe - C.12
Radio city serenade - C.10
River Clyde - C.1
River Thames - C.4, C.18
River Towns - C.3
The rock garden - C.8
Rockaway - C.10
Ron Watts - C.3
Ronnie Scotts - C.8
The roundhouse - C.7

365

Glossary

Royal Albert hall - C.9
Royal Lyceum theatre - C.11, C.15
Rudy Pensa - C.10
Sacred loving - C.4, C.5
Sailing to Philadelphia - C.21
SECC - C.1
Setting me up - C.3
Scotstoun - C.1
Shepherd's Bush Empire - C.12
A shot at glory - C.1
Silverheals - C.3
Silvertown blues - C.16
Single-handed sailor - C.1, C.4, C.17
Six blade knife - C.3
So far away - C.10
So far from the clyde - C.1
Song for swans - C.2
Sonny Landreth - C.14
Southbound again - C.2
Southside tenements - C.4, C.6
Spanish city - C.2
Squeeze - C.4, C.16
Steve Phillips - C.3, C.8
Styx - C.8
Sultans of swing - C.4, C.5
Summer's coming my way - C.3
Swan hunter - C.2
Talking heads - C.3, C.7
Thomas Pynchon - C.21
Tracker - C.17

Tunnel of love - C.2, C.7, C.10
Vince Gill: C.20
Walk of life - C.4
The water is wide - C.2
Water of love - C.3
Wembley arena - C.13
Wembley stadium - C.13 What it is - C.1, C.15
What's the matter baby - C.4
The white swan - C.4
Whitley bay - C.2
Why aye man - C.2, C.12
Wild west end - C.8
Wood wharf studios - C.4
Yon two crows - C.2
Yorkshire evening post - C.2, C.3
Your latest trick - C.10

ALSO AVAILABLE FROM LULU.COM:

Mark Knopfler - A life dedicated to music - vol 1 From Mark Knopfler to Dire Straits
Franck Thuillier

In this first volume discover the true story of Mark Knopfler, a simple man and a legendary guitarist. From his birth in Glasgow to the beginnings of Dire Straits in Deptford, from his first chords played in Newcastle to the recording of 'Communique' in the Bahamas, follow his footsteps... Proof reading by Mark Knopfler ; foreword by John Illsley.

Mark Knopfler - A life dedicated to music - vol 2 Dire Straits, glorybound train
Franck Thuillier

Second volume of Mark knopfler's biography in the form of a graphic novel. From December 1978 to the end of the summer of 1981, follow the successes and disappointments with the man himself, Mark Knopfler. Witness the first rebuilding of Dire Straits and the recognition of Mark by such great artists as Bob Dylan, Steely Dan and Eric Clapton.

Isaac's "Privateering" Tour Blog
Isaac Shabtay

During the spring-summer of 2013, I was following Mark Knopfler's "Privateering" concert tour in Europe, attending all 70 concerts in 23 countries. This book is a printed edition of an online diary I was keeping throughout the entire journey, containing an honest, open, and unedited account of what has been going through the mind of an individual crossing the Old Continent following his favourite musical group.

Isaac's "Get Lucky" Tour Blog
Isaac Shabtay

During the spring-summer of 2010, I was following Mark Knopfler's

Lightning Source UK Ltd.
Milton Keynes UK
UKHW020804230123
415815UK00016B/622